WITHDRA~~WN FROM~~
THE ~~LIBRARY~~

UNIVE~~RSITY~~
~~OF WINCHESTER~~

KA 0160721

D1610439

Images of Youth

IMAGES OF YOUTH

Age, Class, and the
Male Youth Problem,
1880–1920.

Harry Hendrick

CLARENDON PRESS · OXFORD
1990

Oxford University Press, Walton Street, Oxford OX2 6DP
Oxford New York Toronto
Delhi Bombay Calcutta Madras Karachi
Petaling Jaya Singapore Hong Kong Tokyo
Nairobi Dar es Salaam Cape Town
Melbourne Auckland
and associated companies in
Berlin Ibadan

Oxford is a trade mark of Oxford University Press

Published in the United States
by Oxford University Press, New York

© Harry Hendrick 1990

All rights reserved. No part of this publication may be reproduced,
stored in a retrieval system, or transmitted, in any form or by any means,
electronic, mechanical, photocopying, recording, or otherwise, without
the prior permission of Oxford University Press

British Library Cataloguing in Publication Data

ISBN 0–19–821782–X
(data available)

Library of Congress Cataloging in Publication Data

(data available)

KING ALFRED'S COLLEGE
WINCHESTER

305.23
HEN | 0160729

Typeset by Pentacor Ltd, High Wycombe, Bucks

Printed and bound in
Great Britain by Bookcraft Ltd,
Midsomer Norton, Bath

To
Josie and Eve

Acknowledgements

I would like to start by thanking Dr David Martin of the University of Sheffield, who supervised the doctoral research on which this book is based and provided helpful advice on matters of presentation. I was very pleased to have the comments of those colleagues who read draft chapters, and I am especially obliged to Professor Eric Evans; Dr Harold Silver; Mr Eric Tartakover; and, by no means least, the anonymous readers of OUP, most of whose observations I have done my best to heed.

I am also indebted to the following individuals and institutions: Paul Thompson and Thea Vigne for permission to quote from the 'Family and Work Experience Archive' at the University of Essex; Stephen Humphries and Geoffrey Langley for permission to quote from the 'Bristol People's Oral History Project', stored at the Central Library, Bristol; Liverpool University for permission to use the British Psychological Society Child Study Papers; the Controller of HMSO for the use of Crown Copyright material in the Public Record Office; the Keeper of Western Manuscripts at the Bodleian Library; Mrs Christina Colvin, Mr Richard Sadler and Dr P. M. Cowburn for permission to quote from private papers; and the staff at the Local History Libraries of Oxford and Birmingham. Material from Chapters 3 and 6 appeared in *Youth and Policy* and *History of Education* respectively. John Stewart assisted with the tables and Roger Griffin gave me repeated tutorials on the mysteries of the Amstrad.

It is a pleasure to extend my special thanks to the staffs of the Bodleian library and the external loans office at Oxford Polytechnic library. Equal thanks must go to the Polytechnic for granting me three terms of absence over the years, together with various sums of financial assistance.

I would also like to acknowledge my teachers at Warwick University during the period 1966–70, in particular Robin Oakey, Fred Reid, and Edward Thompson.

In addition to her own job, for the last eight years Judith Hendrick has done more than her share of the housekeeping and child-rearing, for which I am truly grateful. But it is not only spouses who may feel badly treated by aspiring authors. Children also can feel neglected as they find themselves time-tabled for the purposes of academic status. Despite the fact that my daughters have lived with 'boy labour' all their lives, I have tried very hard not to be too oppressive in this respect.

Contents

List of Tables

Abbreviations

ASEA	Apprenticeship and Skilled Employment Association
BB	Boys' Brigade
BLB	Boys' Life Brigade
Bod.	Bodleian Library
B. of E.	Board of Education
B. of T.	Board of Trade
CAB	Cabinet Papers
CCC	Central Care Committee (Birmingham)
CCC	Children's Care Committee
Chronicle	*School Government Chronicle*
CIA	Council for Industrial Advancement (Oxford)
CLB	Church Lads' Brigade
COS	Charity Organization Society
Ed.	Board of Education Papers
FBI	Federation of British Industries
HMI	Inspector of Schools
JAC	Juvenile Advisory Committee
JOC	Juvenile Organizations Committee
LCC	London County Council
LEA	Local Education Authority
PRO	Public Record Office
SCC	School Care Committee
TES	*Times Educational Supplement*
WEA	Workers' Educational Association
YMCA	Young Men's Christian Association

Introduction

> If only we can ask the right questions we shall have done
> something for a good end.
>
> F. W. Maitland, *Doomsday Book and Beyond*

Whatever our public protestations, in practice we do not
normally think of adolescents as having very much of a
meaningful historical presence. We tend to see them as the
objects of our condescension. Indeed, until relatively recently
they were altogether excluded from the larger narratives and
analyses involving national questions. And when they did
receive attention, not only were their appearances rigidly
compartmentalized, but also their treatment was narrowly
conceived as in, for example, those rather unimaginative
histories of education, labour, welfare, and, to a lesser extent,
the family, where the perspective was usually that of adults,
which left little or no room for empathy with young people.
The dominant view seemed to be that while they were
occasionally interesting in particular circumstances, generally
speaking, their historical role was peripheral.

During the last fifteen years or so, however, the pioneering
work of several scholars has done much to remedy that
neglect, and between them they have given us a number of
important interpretations.[1] But the relationship of youth to the

---

[1] C. Dyhouse, *Girls Growing Up in Late Victorian and Edwardian England*
(1981); J. R. Gillis, *Youth and History: Tradition and Change in European Age
Relations, 1770–Present* (1974); S. Humphries, *Hooligans or Rebels? An Oral
History of Working Class Childhood and Youth, 1889–1939* (1981);
F. Musgrove, *Youth and the Social Order* (1964); G. Pearson, *Hooligan: A
History of Respectable Fears* (1983); J. Springhall, *Youth, Empire and Society.
British Youth Movements, 1883–1940* (1977), and his *Coming of Age:
Adolescence in Britain, 1860–1960* (1986). On children see J. Walvin, *A Child's
World. A Social History of English Childhood, 1800–1914* (1982); I. Pinchbeck
and M. Hewitt, *Children in English Society*, 2 vols (1969, 1973) and
M. Cruickshank, *Children and Industry. Child Health and Welfare in North-
West Textile Towns during the Nineteenth Century* (1981). Important studies
of young people in North America include J. F. Kett, *Rites of Passage:
Adolescence in America, 1790 to the Present* (1977); D. I. Macleod, *Building*

fundamental problems of the years between 1880 and 1920 has barely been investigated, and the configurations of 'age' and 'class' remain equally unexplored. The purpose of this study is to begin to fill in those absences by incorporating male adolescent workers (and much will be made of their wage-earning status) into the familiar social and political histories of the period.[2] In other words, rather than being left in some suitably 'social' vestibule, young workers will be shown to have been inextricably involved in many of the arguments and processes which preoccupied influential sections of the late ninteenth- and early twentieth-century middle class.[3] This involvement, it is claimed, led to the emergence of new images of youth, and of a new set of age relations. Consequently, the account given here examines the historical truth of the sociological assertion that as age relations are part of the fabric of society, so they do not in themselves explain either change or stability. Instead it is changes in society which explain age

Character in the American Boy: The Boy Scouts, YMCA and Their Fore-runners, 1870–1920 (1983); N. Sutherland, *Children in English Canadian Society: Framing the Twentieth Century Consensus* (1976); and J. Parr, *Labouring Children: British Immigrant Apprentices to Canada, 1869–1924* (1980).

[2] The adolescent period for males has been sociologically defined throughout this study as being between the ages of 13/14 and 18/19. Definitions of adolescence are notoriously difficult to establish with any precision, and no scientific status is claimed for the one selected here. Instead, the ages chosen are those which reformers had in mind when they used the term. Social concern centred around two groups of boys: the school-leavers who had either entered, or were about to enter the pubescent stage, and who had left the discipline and control of the school for full-time employment, and the 18- or 19-year-olds who were about to negotiate what was known as the economic and occupational 'transition to manhood', with all the social consequences this involved. For useful essays on 'the stages of life' and adolescence in historical perspective see Kett, *Rites of Passage*, pp.11–37; and Springhall, *Coming of Age*, pp. 13–37. On the important themes and debates see G. Stedman Jones, *Outcast London* (1971); J. Harris, *Unemployment and Politics: A Study in English Social Policy, 1886–1914* (1971); H. V. Emy, *Liberals, Radicals, and Social Politics 1892–1914* (1973); M. Freeden, *The New Liberalism: An Ideology of Social Reform* (1978); J. H. Treble, *Urban Poverty in Britain 1830–1914* (1979); and B. B. Gilbert, *The Evolution of National Insurance in Great Britain: The Origins of the Welfare State* (1966).

[3] For example, the debates on racial efficiency, unemployment and casual labour, poverty; trade and educational efficiency, social organization, industrial relations, the emerging democracy, philanthropy and collectivism, and the manners and morals of the working class.

relations.[4] This is not to say that the latter were passively reflective, for the experiences of those concerned always conditioned them to a greater or lesser extent. Moreover, in understanding developments in age relations, what Michael Anderson has called 'attitudinal changes' are of fundamental importance. As he says, 'ideas like parenthood and childhood are socially constructed and thus can be put together in [a] diverse . . . set of ways.'[5] The following pages seek to describe and explain how and why these 'ways' were put together with reference to male working-class youth.

In general there were several reasons which explain why contemporaries saw adolescents as participants in the scheme of things. Social investigation had shown beyond any doubt that in addition to the varied occupational roles of young workers in the labour-market, the effects of their employment were felt far beyond themselves. This meant that besides their very often indispensable contributions to the family economy, as potential voters and fathers it was crucial to train them in the duties of responsibility and respectabilty in order to ensure the social cohesiveness of the home. Reformers also believed that in the interests of political and industrial harmony it was necessary to 'educate' working-class youth to see 'labour' as a moral good, irrespective of any financial reward; 'labour' was for the community; it was an obligation of citizenship. Finally, the 'revolution' in the social sciences was leading to a new understanding of the social organism as infinitely more complex in terms of causes and consequences than had previously been imagined. One aspect of this acute consciousness was a heightened and qualitatively different awareness of childhood and adolescence as distinct age stages in individual life-cycles.[6]

Between, say, 1880 and 1920 the age relationship changed in certain fundamental respects as working-class youth, redefined as 'adolescents' under pressure of events—intellectual, economic, social, and political—were perceived as important

[4] S. Allen, 'Some Theoretical Problems in the Study of Youth', *Sociological Review* 16 (1968), 319–31.

[5] M. Anderson, *Approaches to the History of the Western Family 1500–1914* (1980), 60.

[6] See below, ch. 4, s. i.

and on occasion even significant members of society. They
were no longer regarded as simply troublesome or delinquent.
From a variety of viewpoints they were seen to be deeply
involved in many of the seminal analyses which preoccupied
informed contemporary opinion. Not only were they the 'raw
material' of the future, but also it was believed that these
children of the working class, in a democratic, imperial, and
technological age, held within their grasp a potentially awe-
some power. By the end of the First World War, one gallery of
tattered Victorian images had been replaced by another, built
mainly during the Edwardian years. The new images, which
were part and parcel of the making of male youth as a
'problem', were more complex and varied, but equally well
lodged and just as oppressive.

It may well be objected, however, that such a focus
unreasonably ignores girls. In some respects this book is
intended to complement Carol Dyhouse's *Girls Growing Up*.
Like the growing girl, the growing boy was regarded with
suspicion the moment he showed signs of autonomy.[7]
Dyhouse, however, seems to ignore ageism, as she confines
herself, within the context of social class, to the feminist
interest in the construction of femininity. John R. Gillis,
whose influential study concentrates on boys, clearly
subsumes class under the weight of age. On the other hand,
Stephen Humphries, despite being conscious of age, and
writing about both girls and boys, exaggerates the importance
of class. Only Springhall, who has little to say about girls,
makes clear that adolescence 'endures the consequences of a
class society . . . simultaneously with those of age or generation'.[8]

We are still left with the question, why are female adolescents
so conspicuously neglected here? Surely working-class youth was
the problem, irrespective of gender. No one can deny that, in
certain respects, the discovery of adolescence, the economic and
social critiques to which young people were subjected, and the
proposed remedies involved both sexes. For the most part,

[7] Dyhouse, *Girls Growing Up*, p. 138.
[8] Springhall, *Coming of Age*, p. 6. See also Kett, *Rites of Passage*, p. 6 for his
hypothesis that 'moral values' were at the 'root' of the concept of adolescence.
For a brief critique of this apparent neglect of 'politics', see my review in *Social
History* (Oct. 1980), 476–7.

however, the way in which middle-class observers understood this involvement differed enormously depending on whether males or females were under discussion. Anxieties relating to boys tended to range across a number of concerns, including indiscipline, precocity, and undesirable occupational status. Of particular importance were the consequences for their future functions in the family, and for the development of physical and moral 'character' suitable for defenders of the empire, 'adaptable' wage-earners, and democratic citizens. The critique of girls was far less comprehensive.[9] It is true that they were accused of indiscipline and precocious behaviour, and complaints were made about the 'unelevating' nature of their recreations.[10] But the criticial difference between the perceptions of boys and girls was that in the case of the latter, the dominant and organizing concept around which apprehension revolved was the notion of domesticity, as exemplified by marriage and motherhood.[11] Perhaps this explains why the 'girl problem', such as it was, appears to have primarily preoccupied two groups: club managers, who sought to 'refine' and otherwise prepare their members to be 'guides' for husbands and children, and psycho-medics, including eugenists, who were fearful of maternal and racial deterioration.[12] Although the concept of 'fatherhood' should not be underestimated, (it would be a mistake to imagine that 'parenthood' always referred to motherhood), clearly boys had far more options open to them and, therefore, in many important respects, images of adolescence were structured according to gender.[13]

[9] Dyhouse, *Girls Growing Up*, p. 116, and A. McRobbie and J. Garber, 'Girls and Subcultures: An Exploration', in S. Hall and T. Jefferson (eds), *Resistance through Rituals: Youth Subcultures in Post-War Britain* (1976), 209–22.
[10] E. Cadbury, M. C. Matheson and G. Swann, *Women's Work and Wages* (1906), 268–75; M. Stanley, *Clubs for Working Girls* (1904), *passim*; F. L. Freeman, *Religious and Social Work Among Girls* (1901), 45–93.
[11] Dyhouse, *Girls Growing Up*, pp. 79–114.
[12] See Freeman, *Religious and Social Work*, *passim*; Stanley, *Clubs for Working Girls*, *passim*; C. W. Saleeby, *Woman and Womanhood* (1912), *passim*, and his *The Progress of Eugenics* (1914), *passim*; L. Montagu, 'The Girl in the Background', in E. J. Urwick (ed), *Studies of Boy Life in Our Cities* (1904); and the following articles by M. Scharlieb: 'Adolescent Girlhood under Modern Conditions with Special Reference to Motherhood', *Eugenics Review* 1/3 (Oct. 1909); 'Recreational Activities of Girls during Adolescence', *Child*1/7, (Apr. 1911), 571–86; and 'Adolescent Girls from the View-Point of the Physician', *Child*1/12 (Sept. 1911), 1013–31.
[13] See, for example, Saleeby, *Progress of Eugenics*, pp. 67–8 and 97–8.

6 *Introduction*

To treat boys and girls together, then, would run the risk of oversimplification. There would be too many generalized statements which, though vaguely true of all age relationships involving adults and adolescents, would break up into confusing parts on closer inspection of distinctive gender responsibilities. For example, the economic critique known as the 'boy labour problem' occasionally referred specifically to girl labour; at other times it was assumed to include both sexes, but usually the emphasis was on boys. In the introduction to his *Boy Labour and Apprenticeship*, R. A. Bray wrote: 'As "she" is mentioned nowhere else in this volume, it seems desirable to say a word about the girl. This book is, indeed, concerned with boys alone, but, with a few changes in details, all that is written about conditions, and all that is recommended in the way of reforms, is equally applicable in her case also.'[14] Likewise, Sidney Webb in his evidence before the Poor Law Commission, confessed: 'I have so far said nothing about the girls. But their problem is an analogous one.'[15] Both these statements indicate the common attitude among reformers, though they exaggerate the extent of the similarities between the sexes. In the case of adolescent labour, the so-called 'decline' of apprenticeship and the creation of a casual labour class were always seen as a male rather than a female problem, as was 'blind-alley' employment. Moreover, although the conditions of unskilled and 'dead-end' labour were often similar for boys and girls, the long-term social and economic effects, with respect to skill, wages, and headship of the family, were usually viewed from the male perspective. The fact that Bray, Webb, and many others could so casually include the girl in their essentially male-focused accounts, points to the patriarchal basis of their assumptions.

These assumptions can be found at all levels of the debate. Bray claimed that his recommended reforms were also applicable to girls, but this ignored the fact that his proposals and those of other reformers implicitly segregated the sexes; indeed, three of the major areas of reform: juvenile labour

[14] R. A. Bray, *Boy Labour and Apprenticeship* (1911), Preface.
[15] *Royal Commission on the Poor Laws and Relief of Distress, Report*, Appendix vol. ix, Cd. 5068 (1910), evidence (S. Webb), 184; see also that of R. H. Tawney), p. 343, Q. 86758.

exchanges, compulsory part-time day continuation classes, and the club movement, were each premissed on some form of gender distinction. Bray should have said that whereas the reforms ought to include girls, the purposes, practices, and expected outcomes would not be the same as those for boys. We can understand Bray's confusion, without agreeing with it, given that the sexist attitudes of commentators received scientific support from medicine and psychology, notably in the writings of the eugenists and, as Carol Dyhouse has shown, in those of G. S. Hall and his followers. One of Hall's leading disciples in England, J. W. Slaughter, felt that the problem of the education of girls was complicated and difficult in part because of the 'inadequate knowledge of the feminine nature', but he was in no doubt that whatever developments might occur, they were to be adjusted to 'the central fact of a woman's life, that of motherhood'.[16] The majority of writers looked on the girl as possessed not only of a particular kind of 'nature', which distinguished her from male adolescents, but also of a different destiny.

Male adolescents were the focal point of concern because they were potentially dangerous in all sorts of ways and, therefore, under the reformers' gaze, needed to be disciplined, controlled, educated, and managed. It was true that girls could also be dangerous in all sorts of ways, but in essence, middle-class opinion (and, no doubt, respectable working-class opinion) held that, in addition to being made refined, they required protection for their own sake, and for that of the nation. Despite the widespread use of their labour in the economy, they had only two (publicly) significant identities allotted to them, namely, those of wife and mother. Of course, the national importance of these was always appreciated by reformers, and certainly by various groups of women campaigners. But as they confined girls, these two spheres served to reinforce the sexism of the male–female relationship, and so reduced the wider relevance of female adolescents. Boys, on the other hand, were important for what they might do as adolescents, and because of what was seen to be their far greater potential.

[16] J. G. Slaughter, *The Adolescent* (1911), 91, 100.

My suspicion is that girls never constituted a youth problem to anything like the same degree as boys, partly because they were not perceived in the same kind of problematic contexts, and partly because in general they were not deemed to be capable of male forms of behaviour and thought. The issue was fundamentally one of social and economic power and political influence: once girls married they might come to possess a sort of power over husbands and children, and this was never underestimated, but, whatever its importance, it would be limited to the home. The power and influence which boys would come to exercise, however restricted by virtue of their class position, was far more potent, more extensive, more influential, and more 'real' in a number of different arenas.

One other note of explanation. No attempt is made here to write the history of youth 'from below'. There are a few oral testimonies, together with other illustrations of daily experiences, but in general it has not been my purpose to enquire as to how young people reacted to the processes by which they were perceived and defined. There are no deferential passages extolling the virtue of 'experience' even though I recognize that such an approach will be necessary if there is to be a total history of age relations.[17] These omissions are not the result of blind prejudice on my part, but reflect the belief that in any period, the history of young people, especially as it relates to the making of the youth problem, must be written from several different perspectives, each of which has its own priorities. Assuming that no single account can be truly comprehensive, I have chosen to focus on young male workers within the framework of certain dominant contemporary economic, social, political and intellectual issues, while simultaneously identifying and examining the attitudes and concerns of youth workers as well as those of observers and commentators who sought to influence both philanthropic and state social policies. I have no intention of devaluing the young person's experience, but I do suggest that at this historiographical stage, a 'sensitive' and 'informed' examination 'from above' will yield

---

[17] On 'experience' and the need for a sensitive and attentive aproach to the writing of the young people's history, see my 'The History of Childhood and Youth. A Guide to the Literature', *Oxford Polytechnic, Faculty of Modern Studies, Occasional Papers*, No. 1 (1981), 1–11.

valuable insights into the structuring and workings of age
relations, and of the relationship between age and class.
Accordingly my primary interest is with the exercise of power
and influence by the professional middle class and its circle, as
they came into contact with working-class adolescents.

With these thoughts in mind, I have four principal intentions. First, to argue for the significance of the wage-earning
status of working-class youth in relation to the 'boy labour
problem' (as described by contemporaries), a phrase used as a
synonym for the allegedly chaotic state of the juvenile labour-
market and for its social and economic consequences.
Definitions of the problem centred around the 'haphazard'
transition from school to work, 'excessive' occupational
mobility, the 'decline' of old-style apprenticeship, and 'blind-
alley' employment. As a result, claimed reformers, industrial
training was woefully inadequate, and the boys' 'character'
deteriorated so rapidly after they left the elementary school,
that soon they were fit for nothing more than low-grade
unskilled work. But, even more important, reformers feared
that as the boys grew into adulthood, they would perpetuate
the cycle of poverty, which in turn would continue to
demoralize the working-class family. These were important
considerations given that this was a time of developing mass
democracy and of critical adjustments between capital and
labour. However, the significance of youth as a fairly distinct
category of labour was not recognized until 'boy labour' was
established as a 'problem'. In other words, the concern of social
investigators with regard to the welfare and prospects of young
workers played a part in the development of a particular image
for them.

Secondly, a strong claim is made for the role of the social
sciences, especially child psychology, in forging the concept of
'adolescence'; in transforming it from an 'idea' into a 'social
fact' of far-reaching influence.[18] The well-known 'discovery' of
adolescence is reworked here with an emphasis on the
Edwardian rather than the late Victorian years. This is not
meant to be a straining for originality, rather it is an attempt to

[18] David Bakan, 'Adolescence in America: From Idea to Social Fact',
Daedalus (Fall, 1971), 979–95.

10   Introduction

be precise about the timing of certain crucial developments in age relations and in social policy. In contrast to the widely accepted interpretation provided by John R. Gillis, which maintains that adolescence was discovered in public schools between 1870 and 1900, this study shows that the concept only became popular among social investigators and youth workers after *circa* 1904 with the publication of Stanley Hall's two-volume psychological treatise.[19] Prior to this date, the phrase 'Boys will be Boys' merely referred, to quote Gillis, to what *'we now call "adolescence"'*.[20] Or, put another way, the term 'adolescence' had little or no linguistic value in the Victorian description of youth. It was not until the early 1900s that contemporaries were fully conscious of the concept and, more significantly, of its psycho-medical implications in terms of social analysis. The work of Hall, his British associates, and other medical figures, was of crucial importance in this context, and though reference to Hall in connection with the 'discovery' is commonplace, the images he used are rarely examined in any detail, and the extent of his influence on reformers has been virtually ignored.[21] However, the psychology of adolescence never superseded all other influences, far from it. Indeed, it is essential to recognize that social class continued to inform and condition the reformers' interpretation of the concept and, therefore, to say that 'A stage of life, adolescence, had replaced station in life, class, as the perceived cause of misbehaviour' is both exaggerated and a little misleading.[22]

Thirdly, although the economic critique of juvenile labour was fundamental to the reinterpretation of the 'youth question'

---

[19] Gillis, *Youth and History*, chs. 3, 4. Frank Musgrove, however, suggests that the nineteenth-century public school 'redefined, and, indeed, re-made the adolescent'. See his *Youth and the Social Order*, p. 55; G. Stanley Hall, *Adolescence* (1904).

[20] Gillis, *Youth and History*, p. 102. My emphasis.

[21] But see his biographer D. Ross, *G.Stanley Hall: The Psychologist as Prophet* (1972); R. E. Grinder and C. E. Strickland, 'G. Stanley Hall and the Social Significance of Adolescence', *Teachers' College Record* 64 (Feb. 1963), 390–9; S. L. Schlossman, 'G. Stanley Hall and the Boys' Club: Conservative Applications of Recapitulation Theory', *Journal of the History of the Behavioural Sciences* 9 (Apr. 1973), 140–7; and Dyhouse, *Girls Growing Up*, ch. 4.

[22] J. R. Gillis, 'The Evolution of Juvenile Delinquency in England, 1890–1914', *Past and Present* 67 (May 1975), 97.

at the turn of the century, it proved to be inseparable from a much older critical social commentary on young males which also focused on attitudes, values, and leisure pursuits. The suggestion made here, however, is that the late Victorian and Edwardian critique can best be understood as an assault on the personality of working-class adolescents. It was one which in some respects can be compared to popular middle-class criticisms of working-class life in general, certainly of the habits and attitudes of those who were deemed to be 'non-respectable': for example, the lack of forethought and self-control, the absence of principle, and the tendency toward momentariness and thriftlessness. And yet, Edwardian reformers' comments on young workers represented more than merely the fusion of age and class prejudices, for social psychology (of the crowd and the city) and child psychology (of the adolescent) gave these observations both a more profound substance and a new legitimacy. The aim, then, is to show how anxieties arising out of 'the economics of boy labour' merged with those whose origins lay in the traditions of late nineteenth-century social observation, and which focused on the 'character' of youth, to produce a comprehensive critique informed by psycho-medical writings to whom it looked for intellectual respectability and coherence.

The fourth intention is to describe and examine the use of collectivist scientific social policies which were meant to solve 'the problem', or at least to ameliorate it. Throughout the late Victorian years various youth groups had been founded, primarily aimed at organizing recreation; but by the early 1900s many reformers were coming to believe that something more was needed to deal with those 'adolescents' who were also wage-earners. Not that the youth movement was thought to have little value, rather it was to be merely one feature of the new approach, while its expertise and personnel were to be gradually incorporated into a more systematized service under the direction of local and national government. The main aspirations of the policy-makers were to organize the juvenile labour-market by means of juvenile labour exchanges with additional facilities for vocational guidance and after-care provision (all of which were established, though with varying degrees of success); and to introduce compulsory part-time day continuation schools for those employed juveniles aged between 14 and 17 who were to be turned into efficient workers and good citizens. The 1918 Education Act included 'continuation clauses', but within a few years the scheme had collapsed and the handful of schools which had been opened were forced to close. Nevertheless, the debates on the desirability and nature of the continuation principle, and on the contents of the proposed curriculum, were formative factors in institutionalizing new images of youth.

Part I

THE BROAD CONTEXT

1.   Efficiency, Labour, and Politics

1.   SETTING THE SCENE

It would be wrong to imagine that little or nothing was heard
of the youth problem prior to the 1880s. The behaviour of
young workers, and of young people in general, had long been a
cause of friction and anxiety to public commentators. Aristotle
had bemoaned the moral weakness of juveniles, accusing them
of constantly giving way to sexual desire because they could
'exercise no self-restraint'; they were 'changeful ... and
fickle'; 'passionate, irascible', liable to be 'carried away by their
impulses', and their faults were always 'on the side of excess
and exaggeration'. The Old Testament provided the animal
similes which proved so popular throughout the ages: the
young were like 'wild asses and wild heifers'; each youth was
like 'a young colt, wanton, and foolish, till he be broken by
education and correction'. In the early modern period, moralists and theologians denounced youth as the 'dangerous period
when restraint was most needed'; it was 'a slippery age, full of
passion, rashnesss and wilfulness'. And the Statute of Artifi-
cers, the first determined attempt to control the juvenile
labour market, based its regulations on the belief that 'until a
man grow to the age of twenty-four years he for the most part,
though not always, is wild, without judgment, and not of
sufficient experience to govern himself'. Thomas Shadwell
appeared to confirm this view in his comedy concerning a
youthful gang known as the Scowrers: 'I am one of the maddest
fellows about the Town, I sing, roar, serenade, bluster, break
Windows, demolish Bawdy-houses, beat Bawds, scower the
Streets . . .' Indeed, throughout the seventeenth and eighteenth
centuries apprentices were almost universally condemned for
their insolence and riotous and licentious behaviour. 'An
apprentice', said Adam Smith, 'is likely to be idle, and almost
always is so.' He regarded their degenerate life-styles as a
consequence of the decline of the 'indoor' apprenticeship
system which allowed for supervision with the master acting

in loco parentis. Similarly, Defoe lamented how in the past, servants and apprentices were 'infinitely more under subjection than they are now'. Nothing, it seemed, could be done to prevent their bawdy, drunken and often violent behaviour at feasts and carnivals, in taverns and on the streets.[1] The moralists and philanthropists continued their criticisms throughout the nineteenth century. In 1835, for instance, members of the Youth Guardian Society could be found agonizing over the juvenile immorality of 'midnight orgies, beastly and barbarous' and the effects of drink which 'wither away the last vestige of moral restraint and virtuous control'.[2] And, as Springhall and Bailey have shown, race meetings, whit-walks and street culture were all regarded as exercising undesirable influences over the young.[3] Unsurprisingly, from the 1840s attempts were made to provide alternative leisure activities, which included tea meetings, railway excursions field sports, choir outings, and penny readings, though all failed to reach the intended audience: the habitués of the penny-gaffs, cheap theatres offering entertainment to children and adolescents.[4] This reforming zeal was motivated by a desire on the part of a religious-minded middle class to organize 'rational' recreation and to promote temperance, but increasingly the source of the unease was a fear of the precocious juvenile delinquent, who in some senses proved to be the representative motif in age relations up to the 1870s.

Apprehension about the independent child was exacerbated by the spectre of youthful criminality, as it became a matter of

---

[1] K. Thomas, 'Age and Authority in Early Modern England', *Proceedings of the British Academy* 62 (1976), 16; L. Stone, *The Family, Sex and Marriage in England, 1500–1800* (1979), p. 318; S. Brigden, 'Youth and the English Reformation', *Past and Present* 95 (1982), 37–9; V. Butler, *Social Conditions in Oxford* (1912), 18; A. Yarborough, 'Apprentices as Adolescents in Sixteenth Century Bristol', *Journal of Social History* (Fall, 1979), 67–81; R. Johnson, 'Educational Policy and Social Control in early Victorian England', *Past and Present* 49 (Nov. 1970), 108; W. Besant, 'From Thirteen to Seventeen', *Contemporary Review* (Mar. 1886), 413–25; and G. Pearson, *Hooligan: A History of Respectable Fears* (1983), ch. 8.
[2] J. Springhall, *Coming of Age: Adolescence in Britain, 1860–1960* (1986), 110.
[3] Ibid. 109–13, and P. Bailey, *Leisure and Class in Victorian England: Rational Recreation and the Contest for Control, 1830–1885* (1978), ch. 2.
[4] Springhall, *Coming of Age*, p. 111.

widespread debate with the publication of studies such as *Juvenile Depravity* and *Inquiry into the Extent and Causes of Juvenile Delinquency*.[5] Youth, it was claimed, while only one-tenth of the population represented one quarter of its criminals.[6] Among the more popular explanations as to why this should be so were the allegedly malevolent effects of leisure activities, the consequences of the industrial revolution on family life, drunkenness, and independence derived from wage-earning.[7] This helps to account for the emphasis throughout the mid-Victorian years on reclaiming and reforming children and young adolescents. Reformation was of special interest to the influential reformer, Mary Carpenter, who stressed that the 'nature of a child' should indeed be seen as that of 'a *child*'. We must not, she wrote, ' treat him as a man'.[8] This plea was central to the reformers' campaign to end what they considered to be public resignation before precocity.

In the minds of some observers there was a noticeable link between Chartism and delinquency, and this may well have been responsible for the public interest in crime. Geoffrey Pearson has suggested that worries about precocious behaviour reflected 'a larger fear of the growing independence of the working-class' which provided 'the focal point for the mid-century preoccupation with mounting lawlessness'.[9] The question remained, however, as to what course of remedial action should be adopted. The answer was encapsulated in Mary Carpenter's approach, combining reclamation and reformation, as a separate system of juvenile justice began to take shape with special 'reformatory' schools for offenders and 'industrial' schools for those deemed to be 'beyond control'. The ensuing legislation, like most of the other Parliamentary Acts concerning 'juveniles', related to children and young adolescents, that is, those under 16. This means that while age

---

[5] See M. May, 'Innocence and Experience: The Evolution of the Concept of Juvenile Delinquency in the Mid-Nineteenth Century', *Victorian Studies*, 18/1 (Sept. 1973), 7–29; Springhall, *Coming of Age*, pp. 157–66; Pearson, *Hooligan*, pp. 175–81.

[6] Ibid. 164.

[7] Ibid., ch. 7.

[8] May, 'Innocence and Experience', p. 7. See also J. Heywood, *Children in Care: The Development of the Service for the Deprived Child* (1959, 1965 edn.), 42–7.

[9] Pearson, *Hooligan*, p. 167.

specification occurred, the focus of attention was on 'saving' children, rather than on adolescents as a *separate* age-group.[10]

If, then, we are looking for a public debate on the problem of youth, we shall not find it in this period. It seems likely that concern for the teenager arose primarily from the work of evangelical reformers and philanthropists who were responsible for the establishment of various homes, refuges, institutes, brigades, and clubs.[11] This development occurred partly under the influence of the American evangelist D. L. Moody, who led several campaigns in Britain between the 1860s and 1890s and whose disciples prepared to convert young people for a community-wide religious awakening.[12] The initial impetus, however, probably came from the Ragged School Union (1844), which began to open refuges for boys who were either unemployed or had some form of casual employment; from the Bands of Hope which by the 1850s had extended their meetings to adolescents; and from the YMCA (1844), at least for the respectable apprentice. By the 1860s, perhaps earlier, a number of hostels were opening in order to cater for boys who had either come from rural areas to find work in towns and were without proper accommodation, or had spent their lives in institutions and were without any sort of home. In London alone there were about 200,000 such boys, and by 1870 an organization called Homes for Working Boys had been founded in an attempt to tackle the problem. Working with adolescents was rapidly becoming a distinct form of philanthropic activity, quite separate from child rescue. So much so that within the next decade 'youth work' spread well beyond the evangelical

[10] The Factory Act 1831 had extended limitation of hours to all cotton mill employees under 18 and distinguished between 'child' (9–13) and 'young person' (13–18). But the emphasis continued to be on children. See, e.g. H. Mayhew, *London Labour and the London Poor* (1861), *passim*; and P.P. *Children's Employment Commission* (1863–7), Cd. 3170, 3414–I, 3548, 3678, 3796, xv, xxii, xx, xxiv, xvi.

[11] See K. Heasman, *Evangelicals in Action: An Appraisal of the Social Work in the Victorian Era* (1962), ch. 7, especially pp. 124–5; and W. McG. Eagar, *Making Men: The History of Boys' Clubs and Related Movements in Great Britain* (1953), ch. 2–4.

[12] C. Binfield, *George Williams and the YMCA: A Study in Victorian Social Attitudes* (1973), *passim*, and Heasman, *Evangelicals in Action*, pp. 27, 107–8, *and passim*. Heasman notes that Moody viewed 'the period of adolescence' as being 'of supreme importance in the later development of men and women': p. 107.

impulse as numerous agencies and individuals representing both Church and secular interests came forward to counter the crisis of the 1880s.[13]

But religiously inspired philanthropy was only one aspect of the changing image of young people, which in turn was gradually affecting age relations. In his *The Seven Curses of London* (1869), the investigative journalist James Greenwood wrote about 'working boys' and made a prophetic reference to what would come to be known as 'adolescence': 'The law takes account of but two phases of human existence—the child irresponsible, and the adult responsible, and overlooks as beneath its dignity the important and well-marked steps that lead from the former state to the latter,' and he added, 'how critical and all important a period in the career of the male human creature, is "boyhood" '.[14] Greenwood's interest in the adolescent was also evident in a later work published in 1883, by which time he was focusing on the 'blind alley' as a feature of the juvenile labour-market:

In the life of the London labourer there is usually one period that of all others is fraught with peril . . . It is at the time when he becomes a 'hobbledehoy' . . . neither a man nor a boy . . . There is always a demand in London for boys between fourteen and seventeen, and the wages paid them are not illiberal . . . But, unfortunately, this satisfactory condition of affairs does not last very long. In the great majority of cases employers of boys do not need anyone older . . . It is a melancholy fact that . . . young fellows of from seventeen to nineteen are a drug in the unskilled labour market. They are too big to be classed with boys, and not old enough or sufficiently able-bodied to elbow their way in the already crowded ranks of the lower order of adult labourers.[15]

Although this description underwent considerable revision by social scientists over the next thirty years, it never lost its relevance for the 'boy labour problem'.

While Greenwood was conscious of the social, and no doubt the economic significance of adolescent workers, there was

---

[13] On the youth organizations see John Springhall, *Youth, Empire and Society: British Youth Movements, 1883 to 1940* (1977), *passim*; Eagar, *Making Men, passim*, and Heasman, *Evangelicals in Action*, ch. 7.

[14] J. Greenwood, *The Seven Curses of London* (1869; 1981 edn.), 39.

[15] Greenwood, *Odd People in Odd Places* (1883), 114–16.

little serious study of either the supply of, and the demand for their labour, or of the consequences for the adolescents themselves. The perception of teenage wage-earners constituting an economic problem (with widespread social repercussions) was relatively slow to evolve. The first serious consideration given to 'boy labour' appeared in the Royal Commissions on Technical Instruction and on the Depression of Trade and Industry held in 1884 and 1886 respectively. The complaints, especially from trade-union witnesses, though familiar throughout the century, took on a new significance in the late Victorian period as it became clear that economic, social, and political life had entered a new, uncertain, and, in some respects, ominous phase.

2. YOUTH INVOLVEMENT IN THE ISSUES

The 1880s has proved to be a very attractive starting-point for a number of historical studies and it is not hard to see why this should be so: one has only to mention the 'Great Depression', the 'rediscovery' of poverty, the 'Labour Problem', the progression of class politics with the 'new' unionism and the revival of socialism, the beginnings of New Liberalism, and the origins of collectivist welfare policies. It is rare, however, to find youth mentioned in any of these areas as a subject worthy of examination. This omission seems strange given that in their analysis of family poverty and in their studies of unemployment, unskilled labour, and low incomes, investigators were certainly aware of the importance of adolescent wage-earners. Similarly, 'class politics' also embraced adolescents in so far as reformers and educationalists viewed young workers, in particular boys, as emerging participants in the politics of industrial relations and in the democratic process. This view then led them, as part of their attempt to combat what one historian has called the 'erosion of the liberal consensus', to insist that the proposed part-time day continuation schools should instruct their pupils in the principles of 'citizenship'.[16]

Greenwood's account of 'working boys' coincided with a

[16] The phrase is taken from R. K. Webb, *Modern England* (1969), title to ch. 9.

rash of revelatory publications, each of which cast doubt on the ability of capitalism to maintain the momentum of 'Progress' by either abolishing or controlling levels of poverty.[17] The process may be said to have begun with Henry George's *Progress and Poverty* (1881), and continued with Andrew Mearns's *The Bitter Cry of Outcast London* (1883), the *Royal Commission on Housing* (1884–5), articles in the *Pall Mall Gazette*, Arnold White's *The Problems of a Great City* (1886), George Sims's *How the Poor Live* (1889), the first volume of Charles Booth's *Life and Labour of the People* (1889), and *In Darkest England and the Way Out* (1890), written by William Booth, the Salvationist. These writings are too familiar to require detailed discussion, except to reiterate that they all contributed to a new awareness of, and a new interest in, the causes and consequences of poverty. An awareness of poverty was by no means novel in itself. Among others, Dickens, Disraeli, and Mayhew had each exposed it at various times. But by the 1880s the cumulative effect of exposés, social surveys, and the evidence of Royal Commissions served to spread alarm through informed middle-class circles. Unemployment had reached a crisis point as the growing 'Labour Problem' began to merge with that of poverty to constitute the major social issue. Furthermore, incipient industrial unrest coupled with the revival of socialism posed the prospect of civil strife, hence Stedman Jones's description of the atmosphere of the period as mainly one of 'fear', rather than, as Beatrice Webb suggested, 'guilt'.[18]

As part of an explanatory procedure, social scientists increasingly turned towards unemployment, underemployment, and low wages, and this in turn led them to see the problem of labour as one which required the most urgent solution. Moreover, the labour question seemed to be central not only to

[17] On ' Progress' see discussions in, e.g. M. Freeden, *The New Liberalism: An Ideology of Social Reform* (Oxford, 1978), *passim*; G. Stedman Jones *Outcast London* (1971), 6, 7, 9, 16; and S. Collini, *Liberalism and Sociology: L. T. Hobhouse and Political Argument in England, 1880–1914* (1979), *passim*; P. Clarke, *Liberals and Social Democrats* (1978; 1981 edn.), 14–18.

[18] Stedman Jones, *Outcast London*, p. 285; see also Pt. III, *passim* for discussion of the issues; T. S. Simey and M. B. Simey, *Charles Booth. Social Scientist* (1960), especially pt. I, and Harris, *Unemployment and Politics*, ch. 1 for role of unemployment and casual labour.

economic and social distress, but also to industrial relations, foreign competition, technological change, and to the more general social and political crises. Thus it is in this context that 'boy labour' should be seen as fundamental both to the analysis and the proposed remedies. The fact was that once poverty became the issue—its nature, causes, and consequences—all parts of the social organism were open to inspection and dissection. The result, where youth was concerned, was a more developed appreciation of the significance of *age* (certainly by influential middle-class interests), in relation to the labour-market, and to young people in each of their participatory roles.

2.1. National efficiency

One of the most important 'contexts' in which these roles were examined was that of 'national efficiency'; and despite the fact that reference to the campaign is commonplace among historians, before moving on it is appropriate to make some mention of its influence on the maturing youth problem. There is no doubt that increasing anxiety about 'efficiency' in the early 1900s, more or less coincided with the public debate on 'boy labour' and with the popularization of the concept of 'adolescence'. So it would be surprising if middle-class perceptions of, and attitudes towards, working-class youth were not conditioned to a certain degree by the ideas and arguments of the movement. Participants in the discussion on the 'boy labour' problem, for example, often spoke in terms of 'human material' and the 'waste' of resources.[19]

The campaign for national efficiency, which developed at the end of the nineteenth century, was a 'reaction against Gladstonianism'. It took as its dominant themes the decline of Britain as a great military and economic power in the face of competition from Germany in particular, and the loss of confidence in traditional liberalism.[20] The movement as a

[19] One of the best-known studies was A. Freeman, *Boy Labour: The Manufacture of Inefficiency* (1914). See also A. Paterson, *Across the Bridges* (1911), pp. 10, 256–7; R. H. Tawney, 'The Economics of Boy Labour', *Economic Journal* 19 (Dec. 1909) 536; M. E. Sadler (ed.), *Continuation Schools in England and Elsewhere* (1907), pp. xii–xiii.

[20] G. R. Searle, *The Quest for National Efficiency* (1971), ch. 1.

whole was an attempt to provide an alternative theory of government which would promote efficiency in all areas of public and private life. The cathartic moment came with the experiences of the Boer War in which the British Army performed so miserably.[21] Such was the extent of the criticism, that the government appointed three separate inquiries into various aspects of the conduct of the war. But the lessons to be learned went beyond the military to include political and administrative factors and the liberal values underpinning them. Although the movement did not possess 'a homogeneous political ideology', it had a recognizable core in its attempt 'to discredit the habits, beliefs and institutions that put the British at a handicap in their competition with foreigners and to commend instead a social organization that more closely followed the *German* model'.[22] Apart from admiration for the German Army and Bismarckian social insurance, it was the 'highly organized educational system' which attracted reformers' attention, and of particular interest, at least to educationalists and boy labour critics, was the feature of compulsory part-time day continuation schools for adolescents.[23]

Broadly speaking, the controversy served to provide youth reformers with a framework within which much of their economic and social criticism could find a convenient and significant centre, more so than in the 1880s and 1890s, since it gave their critiques a new urgency and a political relevance. However, to understand the connection between the youth problem and the quest for greater efficiency in all areas of the nation's affairs, it is essential to recognize that the focal point of this concern was 'the condition of the people' or, as Gilbert writes, 'the matter of physical efficiency'.[24] This in turn linked up with the broader interest in Social-Darwinism, with its

---

[21] Ibid., ch. 2.

[22] Ibid., p. 54.

[23] M. E. Sadler, 'Compulsory Attendance at Continuation Schools in Germany' and C.E.Stockton, 'The Continuation Schools of Munich' in M. E. Sadler (ed), op. cit., pp. 513–34 and 535–47; R. H. Best and C. K. Ogden, *The Problem of the Day Continuation School and Its Successful Solution in Germany: A Consecutive Policy* (1914).

[24] Bentley B. Gilbert, *The Evolution of National Insurance in Great Britain* (1966), p.60 and chapter 2; and Searle, op. cit., pp. 60–67.

ambition to promote a fit people in order to achieve internal racial effectiveness and to compete internationally for survival and supremacy. The most popular expression of this desire was the science of eugenics, whose spokespersons represented Britain as wasting its human resources, and pointed to the declining birth-rate and the apparent physical deterioration of the population, in particular 'incapacitated manhood'.[25] 'Womanhood' was certainly not ignored, as anxieties about the living and occupational conditions of working-class girls and women were widespread, especially their child-bearing, child-rearing, and domestic abilities. Nevertheless, the dominant theme remained the prospects of British manhood in various spheres: military, economic, imperial, and, by no means least, parental.

Such an atmosphere easily explains why 'boy labour', and all that the term involved, came to be seen as part of the social problem. And as the movement for greater efficiency 'gave social reform what it had not had before—the status of a respectable political question',[26] so the difficulties associated with youth were felt to require urgent solution. There is no doubt that working-class adolescents were involved in several of the most significant and controversial issues of the period. But if we are to understand why 'boy labour' caused such alarm, and the way in which it affected the image of youth as well as the developing age relationship, it will be helpful by way of an introduction to describe the nature of this involvement in two fundamentally important contexts: labour and politics.

2.2 *The 'Labour Problem'*

The 'Labour Problem', as Roger Davidson has written, had diverse consequences in that it related to 'three main areas of dysfunction within the labour-market': industrial unrest, unemployment and irregular work, and economic and social distress arising from insufficient income.[27] Each one involved young workers. Industrial relations, for example, were

---

[25] Gilbert, op. cit., p. 60; Dyhouse, op. cit., pp. 91–5.
[26] Gilbert, op. cit., p. 60.
[27] Roger Davidson, *Whitehall and the Labour Problem in Late Victorian and Edwardian Britain*, (1985), pp. 35.

important because the focus of attention after 1880, in addition to being on 'manning requirements' and 'demarcation' was also on apprenticeship ratios.[28] The 'Great Depression' together with foreign and domestic competition had to a certain extent undermined business confidence and reduced profit margins, thereby forcing employers to seek ways of lowering costs. Nor was it simply a question of numbers of apprentices, for in the minds of tradesmen all types of juvenile (and female) labour were thought to threaten the status of skilled workers and the wage-rates of adult males. The references to apprenticed and other forms of juvenile labour in evidence given before the Royal Commissions on Technical Instruction and the Depression of Trade and Industry, merely mirrored the growing apprehension among trade unionists (and increasingly among social scientists and administrators) about the role of the young worker. It was undoubtedly a matter of considerable concern in the boot and shoe and engineering industries, and it grew in significance during the hearings of the Royal Commission on Labour (1891–4).[29] The trade-union witnesses made three claims: apprenticeship, they said, was either in decline or being disregarded by employers; secondly, under the impact of new machinery, there was an increasing tendency to substitute juveniles for adults; and thirdly, half-trained apprentices were being exploited as semi-skilled workers. Of course, the Labour Commission discussed many other issues besides juvenile labour, but the recurring complaints served to push young workers into a new prominence vis-à-vis manning levels in particular and changes in general in the 'structure and social relationships of production'.[30]

The subject was sufficiently important for the Webbs to devote nearly fifty pages to it in their Industrial Democracy

[28] Ibid., p. 37; see also J. E. Cronin, Industrial Conflict in Modern Britain, (1979) p. 93.
[29] For evidence from Royal Commissions, see below chapter 3. See also, Alan Fox, A History of the National Union of Boot and Shoe Workers, 1874–1957 (1958), passim, J. B. Jeffrys, The Story of the Engineers, 1800–1945 (1946), passim, Charles More, Skill and the English Working Class, 1870–1914 (1980), passim, and W. Knox, ' British Apprenticeship, 1800–1914', Ph. D. thesis (Edinburgh, 1980) and his 'Apprenticeship and De-Skilling in Britain, 1850-1914', International Review of Social History, pt. 2 (1986), pp. 166–84.
[30] Quoted in Davidson, op.cit., p.35.

(1897); in a later edition (1902), they returned to the problem, commenting that 'the serious evil of "boy labour" has still not been grappled with' and went on to warn:

Perhaps the gravest social symptom at the opening of the twentieth century is the lack of physical vigor [sic], moral self-control, and technical skill of the town-bred, manual-working boy. In the industrial organisation of today there are hundreds of thousands of youths, between fourteen and twenty-one, who are taken on by employers to do unskilled and undisciplined work, at comparatively high wages for mere boys, who are taught no trade, who are kept working long hours at mere routine, and who are habitually turned adrift, to recruit the ranks of unskilled labour, as soon as they require a man's subsistence.[31]

Alfred Marshall, the economist, also drew attention to the 'growing demand for boys to run errands and do other work that has no educational value'.[32] But it was Charles Booth, rather than either Marshall or the Webbs, who popularized both the extent of juvenile labour and the different ways in which it was used. He reminded his readers that the 'recurring note throughout the whole of the industrial volumes of the present inquiry is that the whole system of apprenticeship is either dead or dying', and he focused on the ease with which parents could

get a boy on leaving school into a place where his earnings will enable him at once to add a few shillings a week to the family exchequer, but in which he learns nothing that will help him to a maintenance in after life. At sixteen such a lad . . . is too big for boys' work, and is not content with a boy's wage. He tries for a rise, and tries in vain; drifts into casual employment . . . trusts to chance for a living, marries at twenty, and is presently adding his weight to the mass of 'unemployed' for whose labour no market can be found.[33]

By the 1890s it was clear that not only did young workers figure in the organization of the labour-market, but also they had come to be regarded as an economic and social problem in themselves. Obviously they were of more than peripheral

[31] S & B. Webb, *Industrial Democracy* (1897, 1902 ed.), pp. 454–89, 704–15, liv–v.
[32] A. Marshall, *Principles of Economics* (1890; 1961 edn.), 182.
[33] C. Booth, *Life and Labour of the People of London* (1902 edn.), iii. 227–8. The reference to apprenticeship is quoted in Springhall, *Coming of Age*, p. 82.

interest. The Webbs, Booth, the Labour Commission, and the growth and radicalization of trades unionism turned the employment of adolescent labourers and apprentices into an issue that could not be ignored, which explains why it was raised time and time again in discussions on the mounting industrial and political unrest. As this 'unrest' was part of the emergence of class politics, it deserves further consideration, but for the moment we need to look at 'boy labour' in relation to the second and third areas of the 'Labour Problem' which formed the core of the poverty question, namely, unemployment and low wages.

Informed observers knew that the nature of poverty could not be scientifically analysed without a prior examination of unemployment and casual labour, so it is not surprising to find the OED first recording the terms 'unemployed' in 1882 and 'unemployment' in 1888, though the concept itself did not begin to be generally used until the mid-1890s. Moreover, according to José Harris, 'The debate that grew up around the subject called in question many of the prevailing orthodoxies in political economy, political theory, and social administration; and by the end of the decade unemployment was seen by many writers on social problems as the root of crime, vagrancy, and prostitution, and as the "sphinx of the age".'[34] At first little or no mention was made of juveniles, though as awareness of poverty became more widespread, and social scientists began to examine the mechanisms of the labour-market, in particular the apparently perpetual over-supply of unskilled labour, together with the level and composition of family incomes, so it became obvious that the young worker had to figure in any overall analysis. Similarly, once the market began to be extensively investigated by Llewellyn Smith, Booth, Rowntree and Beveridge, it was evident that all its features were interwoven, though the exact relation of juvenile to adult labour remained rather vague.[35] It is also well known that the new understanding of poverty and unemployment brought calls for a 'scientific' social policy for dealing with the problems, and in response both Beveridge and

[34] J. Harris, Unemployment and Politics: A Study in English Social Policy 1886–1914 (1971), 4.
[35] Ibid., ch. 1.

Churchill, two of the most influential figures, made special provisions for young people in terms of vocational guidance and juvenile labour exchanges.[36] In addition, educationalists, youth workers, and politicians were calling for a programme of compulsory part-time day continuation schools.[37]

From all sides, then, the adolescent wage-earner was the subject of concern, investigation, and recommendation. The problem was threefold: first, by and large the nature of adolescent occupations was said to be such that they contributed in one way or another to adult unemployment. This might be caused by the use of half-trained apprentices in place of either skilled or semi-skilled men, or by virtue of the 'blind alley' which was held to be responsible for thousands of boys being turned adrift some time prior to manhood, without any of the skills necessary to secure them a place in an already overcrowded labour-market. Secondly, regardless of the effect of unemployment, unskilled and casual workers were usually low-income earners; so much so, as all the social surveys showed, that the health, efficiency, and stability of the family were felt to be endangered. Thirdly, besides the alleged 'decline' of apprenticeship, there was the widespread fear that adolescent labourers represented a perpetual supply of un-skilled and often merely casual labour with all its attendant economic and social distress.[38]

Thus we have the principal reasons why 'boy labour' became a major 'problem' in the late nineteenth and early twentieth centuries: it seemed to be symptomatic of the chaotic condition of the labour-market; it contributed towards the creation of adult unemployment; and, in the long term, it was partly responsible for the demoralization of the working-class family. One other factor is worth mentioning here. It is now fairly well recognized that during the period there was no simple substitution of an objective socio-economic analysis in place of the older and subjective moral categories which had emphasized what contemporaries regularly referred to as 'character'. In fact punitive notions and 'character' scrutiny continued to be important features of the Liberal welfare

[36] See below, Ch. 7.
[37] See below, Ch. 8.
[38] See below, Ch. 3.

reforms. And nowhere was this more so than in relation to young people.[39] Far from abandoning their interest in moral rectitude, reformers interpreted the 'discovery' of poverty as meaning that 'character' was even more crucial in securing permanent employment with proper wages, and this led them to intensify their ambition to promote the appropriate training schemes, though their essentially political crusade was often masked by scientific investigative procedures.[40]

2.3 Class politics

The connection between images of youth and the development of 'class politics' is probably not immediately apparent, but it is hard to deny that by the early 1900s, if not before, social theorists and other commentators perceived adolescents to have a political role in the evolving industrial democracy.[41] Moreover, they recognized that this new political order would require a different kind of age relationship from that which had existed in the past. But first we need to have a clear understanding as to what occurred in the world of labour and trades unionism. The 'onset of democracy', which may be taken as beginning in 1867, developed apace with the 1884 Reform Act and the redistribution of seats in 1885 and coincided with the socialist revival, the growth of trade union membership and the 'new' unions, and the beginning of the movement for independent labour representation.[42] While the economy boomed, as it did during the mid-Victorian period, it was possible to construct a consensus of sorts between capital and sections of labour. However, once the decline in prices and profit margins set in, employers were forced to cut costs in order to make themselves more competitive. This resulted in a combination of strategies, including mechanization, specialization, payment by results, and more intensive managerial supervision, all of which bit deeply into 'traditional' agreements and practices. Not unnaturally, as we have seen, skilled

[39] Stedman Jones, *Outcast London*, pp. 313–14.
[40] See below, Chs. 3, 7 and 8.
[41] Webb, *Modern England*, Pt. III; H. V. Emy, *Liberals, Radicals and Social Politics, 1892–1914* (1973), *passim*; Davidson, *Whitehall and the Labour Problem*, and K. Burgess, *The Challenge of Labour* (1980), ch. 3, 4.
[42] See, e.g. Webb, *Modern England*, pt. III Burgess, *Challenge of Labour*, chs. 2–4.

men resented what they saw as the dilution of their skill, the loss of control over details of the job, and the consequent decline in status; they were also alarmed over the rapid growth of the semi-skilled work-force, whose own members were full of apprehension about job security, wage-levels, and conditions of employment.[43] This helps to explain why the 'decay' of apprenticeship and the use of juveniles and female labour on specialist machinery raised such emotional questions. Although the wave of strikes and the expansion of 'new' unionism between 1889 and 1891 soon evaporated, there was continuing unrest in several industries as groups of employers sought to introduce new management styles and more efficient production processes. Even after the victory of the employers' counter-attack in the 1890s, the mood on the shop-floor remained confrontational.[44] H. V. Emy tells us that the unions were no longer willing to accept 'the orthodox theory of production which stressed saving and the sanctity of capital, managerial freedom of production, labour as cost and flexible wage-rates', instead, they sought a 'minima of wages, hours and conditions to be imposed by legislation upon the market'.[45]

We see, then, a situation in which legislative and political enactments were assisting in the evolution of a liberal democratic state, while simultaneously industrial relations and labour politics were being radicalized. When this is considered alongside the recognition of poverty and unemployment as fundamental social problems, the inherent tensions and contradictions make plain the degree to which the mid-Victorian consensus had been eroded. More precisely, the many values, attitudes, and political allegiances forged in the mid-century were either under siege or had collapsed by 1900. What happened subsequently was the emergence of a different set of alliances, economic principles, and political priorities. Emy's summary is apposite:

---

[43] See e.g. Davidson, *Whitehall and the Labour Problem, passim;* Burgess, *Challenge of Labour, passim;* Cronin, *Industrial Conflict, passim.*

[44] Burgess, *Challenge of Labour* chs. 2–4, and his *The Origins of British Industrial Relations* (1975); E. Phelps Brown, *The Growth of British Industrial Relations* (1959).

[45] Quoted in Davidson, *Whitehall and the Labour Problem,* p. 39.

The substance of political debate was altering, the rules of the game were being redrawn to take account of new contestants and vastly different interests and perspectives, and in consequence political activity, the behaviour of the players, the conduct of elections, the content of legislation, was responding to a new set of stimuli whereby the programmes, commitments and policies denoted a direct and continuous link between values, expectations and goals upon a national scale.[46]

Of all the 'boy labour' reformers, it was perhaps the educationalists and philosophical idealists, several of whom were one and the same, who were most acutely aware of adolescents in relation to class politics.[47] Writing in 1903, Michael Sadler, the doyen of the educationalists, claimed that 'all the great questions of our time seem to have opened up roads which converge in the question of education' and this in turn was a matter of 'order'.[48] The threat of disorder—economic, social, and political—gave many observers the 'sense of an impending clash', especially during the period of the 'Great Unrest' just prior to 1914.[49] 'Order' seemed to be an essential prerequisite for the future of liberal democracy, and it continued to be seen as such during the war and in the period of post-war reconstruction. The immediate concern was the possibility that political power might come to rest in uneducated hands, which explains why the inculcation of citizenship was regarded as so important by those who campaigned for the compulsory part-time day continuation school. Consequently, nowhere was the notion of 'the community' (a fundamental element of citizenship) felt to be more necessary than in the struggle to reconcile the conflicting interests of capital and labour. To this end, education had its part to play in the process of building what was in effect intended to be a redesigned consensus with 'new contestants' and revised 'rules of the game' in accordance

[46] Emy, *Liberals, Radicals and Social Politics* p. viii.
[47] See below, ch. 8, s. 3.2.
[48] Sadler, 'National Ideals in Education', An Inaugural lecture at University College of Wales, Aberystwyth (1903) and 'The Ferment in Education on the Continent and in America', *Proceedings of the British Academy*, 1903.
[49] See S. Meacham, 'The Sense of an Impending Clash: English Working-Class Unrest before the First World War', *American Historical Review* 77/5 (1972). But see also M. Bentley, *Politics without Democracy* (1985 edn.), 326–45.

with the changed 'substance of the political debate'. So the adolescent, as both potential voter and trade unionist, entered directly into the political arena.

From the perspective of 'boy labour' reformers, and other interested figures, the involvement of working-class youth in class politics was a multi-faceted affair, usually conceived in terms of the 'character' young workers brought into adulthood. The principal objectives of political practice (in all its forms, including the social, the economic, and the educational) were to produce a system of industrial relations in which the employees were contented and co-operative (but also occupationally intelligent and 'adaptable'), and a participatory democracy staffed by responsible 'citizens' who were not only self-realizing and conscious of duties as well as of rights, but also willing to manifest these obligations in the service of employers, family, government, and country. The necessary educational course, in the broadest sense, required instruction in what the middle class regarded as its standards: self-control, stamina, sobriety, thrift, 'gamesmanship', and, perhaps most important, definite and conscious moral principles. In the absence of these virtues and without an appreciation of either duty, self-realization, or citizenship, 'Progess' itself might be in jeopardy.[50]

[50] For a flavour of the contemporary debate about the meaning of Progress see Freeden, *New Liberalism*, pp. 81–2, 91–2; see also debates on 'Character' as an essential feature of 'Progress', ibid., *passim*; Collini, *Liberalism and Sociology,passim* and his 'The Idea of "Character" in Victorian Political Thought', *Transactions of the Royal Historical Society* (1986), 29–50.

2. Aspects of the Juvenile Labour Market, 1900–1914

1. NUMBERS AND OCCUPATIONS

One of the outstanding demographic facts of the period is the decline in the proportion of adolescents (and of young people in general) in the total population in favour of middle-aged persons. The adolescent group, defined here as those aged between 14 and 19, declined from 15.4% to approximately 14%. In other words, in England and Wales, about 1 in 7 of the population aged 10 and upwards was an 'adolescent'.[1] For our purposes, however, the significant percentages are those involving occupied persons. These show that throughout the period, while the number of adolescent workers increased by 4%, (as opposed to 14% for the *total* occupied population), as a proportion of the total labour force, they declined by 1.7% — from 20.3% to 18.6% — and that as a proportion of the total male labour force, male adolescents fell from 16.8% to 15.2%.[2] Clearly, while accounting for between 1 in 5 and 1 in 6 of all those employed, young workers were not swamping the labour market; in fact, the Edwardian decline was the continuation of a trend which began in the late Victorian era.[3]

The details of the distribution of young workers among the census orders make it immediately obvious that half their number was employed in the four largest orders: domestic services, textile fabrics, dress, and conveyance of men, goods, and messages, and when metals, machines, and implements, and agriculture are added, then the figure is nearly two-thirds.[4] In some respects this suggests a somewhat concentrated

---

[1] Table 1.

[2] Tables 2a and 2b.

[3] The percentage for the 10–19 age-group between 1881 and 1891 was approximately 22%. For changing age constitution see *Census, Occupations and Industries*, Cd. 7019 (1913), lxxviii, pt. 1, p. xii; *General Report, 1911*, Cd. 8491, xxxv p. 62 and D. Read, *England, 1868–1914* (1979), 382–4.

[4] Table 3.

demand for juvenile labour, but the heavy concentration of girls in the three largest orders gives a distorted impression as regards males. Unlike girls, boys tended to be more evenly spread throughout the orders, with the main employer being conveyance, followed by metals, mining, food, and textiles.

A far more precise location of adolescents, however, can be found by looking at the principal occupations.[5] Several of these more or less depended upon young workers for either the majority or at least a substantial part of their labour force: vanguards and boys (96.2%), day-girls and day servants (71.5%), post-office messengers (75.8%), messengers, porters, watchmen (74%), newsboys and newsvendors (82%), wool and worsted spinning processes (56%), milliners (43%), and cotton workers, undefined (41.1%). Moreover, in 14 other occupations the proportion of juveniles was between 30% and 40%, and in a further 30 it was between 20% and 30%. Bearing in mind that adolescent workers were approximately 2O% of the total occupied population, it seemed that in many trades there was an 'excessive' amount of youthful employment. This subject, referred to by Booth as 'exaggerated proportions' of boys and young men, was crucial for the Edwardian reformers who regarded it as one of the causes of 'blind-alley' labour.

The degree to which different occupations and orders called upon adolescent labour altered throughout the period.[6] In several orders both the proportions and the numbers declined—in the building trades, for example, juveniles declined by nearly 50% as against 10% for all those occupied.[7] Those orders in which the number and proportion of adolescents decreased included wood, furniture, fittings and decoration, brick, cement, pottery and glass, and precious metals. In the

[5] Table 4. The totals concerned involve the 10–19 age-group, but since the official total number of 10–13-year-olds was so small (falling from 208,392 to 146,417), this is effectively an adolescent age-group (14–19). The 106 occupations have been arbitrarily described as 'principal'—those employing 5,000 or more young persons—as a means of reducing the total of 472 census headings. Even so, those listed here account for 2,500,000 of the 3,200,000 young workers.

[6] Tables 3 and 5. The problems involved in making accurate comparisons between the two censuses are explained in *Guide to the Census Reports, 1801–1966* (1977), pp. 53–4; and *General Report, 1911*, pp. 12, 97, 100, 627, 639, 653–4, 688.

[7] *General Report, 1911*, pp. 123–4. See also Table 3.

majority of orders, however, the numbers of young workers increased, sometimes by in excess of 30,000, as in textiles, metals, food, mining, and commerce.

When occupations only are considered, then in addition to the dramatic reduction in the number in building, adolescent labour became less important in several other employments, such as carmen, carriers, carters and waggoners, and black-smiths and strikers.[8] Among railway workers and erectors, fitters and turners, the decline was of lesser proportions. The principal numerical increases occurred in clerking, mining and quarrying, and among messengers, porters, and watchmen. (The latter group was viewed by 'boy labour' reformers as 'uneducative' in the extreme.) It is perhaps worth emphasizing that in those occupations which witnessed a fall in the size of the juvenile work-force, the decline was absolute; the increases, on the other hand, were relative, with the important exception of messengers, porters and watchmen, among whom increases were also absolute. This made the messenger group especially prone to 'blind-alley' conditions, or so it was claimed. Employment in commerce and food and drink was also felt to offer little chance of secure adult livelihood. The *General Report* of the Census in 1911 drew attention to butchers, meat salesmen, grocers, and greengrocers, where the problem lay in the more rapid increase in the age group 15–20 than in the 20–25-year-olds, which led the *Report* to conclude that these were likely to be 'blind-alley' occupations.[9] In addition to messengers, and food and drink, clerical work was also thought to have blind-alley characteristics, and given that these occupations together employed approximately 450,000 adolescents, this view was obviously fundamental to the critique. However, those industries which were large employers of adolescents tended to be expanding rapidly and, therefore, all things being equal, in normal circumstances, the young people would be absorbed into the adult labour-force without too much difficulty.[10]

---

[8] Table 4. For a discussion of the detailed changes in various industries, see the *General Report, 1911*, pp. 108–39.
[9] Ibid. 139.
[10] Table 6.

2. CHOOSING AND FINDING EMPLOYMENT

Becoming a full-time wage-earner was both more complex and yet more straightforward than many middle-class observers were prepared to admit. Complexity was present in the sense that there were a number of channels through which the young person sought, obtained, and evaluated all kinds of information affecting employment opportunities. This meant that the filtering processes were culturally distilled, so much so as to make the transition from school to work bear little resemblance to the 'haphazard process' described by reformers.[11] This was especially true in those regions which were dominated by particular industries: textiles, steel-making, mining, and engineering. Irrespective of their region, however, individual youths experienced little or no difficulty in understanding the practices since community network systems provided trusted forms of assistance in choosing and finding work. The transition was also straightforward in that it was not necessarily traumatic for school-leavers, the majority of whom had probably been part of the world of work, through part-time jobs, for at least a year or two prior to their thirteenth or fourteenth birthdays and, therefore, possessed a knowledge of what work involved and the experience of wage labour.[12]

Of course the overriding factor in choosing and finding work

[11] J. O. Dunlop and R. D. Denman, *English Apprenticeship and Child Labour* (1012), 342; S. J. Gibb, 'The Choice of Employment for Boys', *Economic Review* (Oct. 1904), 436; C. Booth, *Life and Labour of the People of London*, 2nd ser., *Industry* (1903 edn.), v. 289.

[12] On the lack of trauma, see J. Springhall, *Coming of Age* (1986), 55–6; E. Roberts, 'Learning and Living: Socialization Outside School', *Oral History* 3/2 (Autumn 1975), 23; D. N. Ashton and D. Field, *Young Workers* (1976), 11–16; M. P. Carter, *Home, School and Work: A Study of the Education and Employment of Young People in Britain* (1962), 195–211; P. Brannen, 'Industrial and Economic Change and the Entry into Work', in P. Brannen (ed.), *Entering into the World of Work: Some Sociological Perspectives* (1975), 116. But the process may not have been without its problems as some modern studies have shown that a 'substantial' minority of school-leavers do suffer serious difficulties. See J. Maizels, *Adolescent Needs and the Transition from School to Work* (1970), 304, 312; Ashton and Field, *Young Workers*, pp. 94–118; D. N. Ashton, 'From School to Work: Some Problems of Adjustment Experienced by Young Male Workers', in Brannen (ed.), *Entering Into the World of Work*, pp. 54–69. On the influence of dominant industries see Carter, *Home, School and Work*, pp. 88–129, and Ashton and Field, *Young Workers*, pp. 37–8.

was the nature of the local demand for juvenile labour. In Oxford, for example, the absence of large-scale industries and the need to service a substantial middle-class population ensured that there was no shortage of 'fetching and carrying' employment. In Norwich, with its low-wage industries, women and juveniles were in demand for factories producing washing requisites, mustard, vinegar, and confectionery. The distribution of adolescent labour in Oldham, as one would expect, was very different: 56% of school-leavers went into textiles, 25% into clothing, building, metals, and woodwork, but only 1% into 'blind-alley' employment. The transport sector in the large commercial and trading centres of Liverpool, Bristol, and Newcastle provided thousands of boys with jobs, while in London different districts exerted different influences: boys in schools close to the City would become office-boys or clerks, those from the Stratford district would go to the railway, and those in Wapping and Limehouse might go to be lightermen, boilermakers, and riverside workers.[13]

Obtaining employment involved two related processes: choosing a job and finding a job. The exact nature of the relationship between the two is difficult to gauge except in the general sense where regional and local employment opportunities tended to determine both the choice and the means used to find a suitable vacancy. There were, however, numerous other influences affecting either one or both processes, and these can be divided into two broad categories: the semi-official and more formal agencies such as schools, youth organizations, private employment bureaux, and (after 1910) juvenile labour exchanges; and the other influences, informal, very often seemingly casual, involving personal application on the 'off-chance', newspaper and shop-windows advertisements, factory notice-boards, and arrangements made by parents,

[13] C. V. Butler, *Social Conditions in Oxford* (1912), 52–3; C. B. Hawkins, *Norwich: A Social Study* (1910), 42, and 212; *Royal Commission on the Poor Laws and Relief of Distress* (hereafter *Poor Law Commission*); C. Jackson, *Special Report on Boy Labour* (hereafter *Special Report*), Cd. 4632 (1909), Appendix vol. xx, xliv, p. 4. However the figure of 1% in blind-alley jobs is misleading because there was also a considerable amount of dead-end employment in textile trades. See also J. G. Cloete, 'The Boy and his Work', in E. J. Urwick (ed.), *Studies of Boy Life in Our Cities* (1904), 109, and *Education, Elementary Schools (Children Working for Wages)* pt. 2 (1899), vol. lxxv, p. viii.

relatives, friends, and neighbours.[14] The role of youth groups and private agencies, such as apprenticeship committees, was probably negligible because they dealt with relatively few applications, though the former in covering a larger geographical area, especially in the provinces, were no doubt of more importance than the latter. Of far greater significance, however, were the teachers and schools, described by one investigator as constituting an 'unofficial labour bureau', used by the children, their parents, and employers.[15] It is not easy to interpret 'calling on the off-chance'; sometimes it referred to the boy's personal initiative, on other occasions it involved a 'tip-off'. When boys were asked by investigators how they had found employment, the commonly recorded answer was either 'self' or 'self, parents, and friends'.[16]

Among the considerations many young people and their parents had in mind when looking for work, were the relative attractions of different trades, variations in conditions of entry and training facilities, the relation of boys' labour and wages to that of men, the relative number of boys and men in different trades and the chances of permanent employment in each, and

[14] See below ch. 7. For other details see H. J. Hendrick, ' "The Boy Labour Problem" in Edwardian England: A Study in the Relationship between Middle-Class Reformers and Working-Class Adolescents', Sheffield University Ph.D. thesis (1985), ch. 2.

[15] Ibid., and J. Parsons, 'The Work of an Apprenticeship and Skilled Employment Committee', *Toynbee Record* (Mar. 1907), 77; A. Greenwood, *Juvenile Labour Exchanges and After-Care* (1911), 41–2; F. G. D'Aeth, 'An Enquiry into the Methods of Obtaining Employment in Liverpool', *Transactions of Liverpool Economic and Statistical Society* (1907), 32; F. Keeling, *The Labour Exchanges in Relation to Boy and Girl Labour* (1910), 13; N. B. Dearle, *Industrial Training* (1914), 196; *School Government Chronicle*, 3 Dec. 1910, p. 469.

[16] For details see Hendrick, ' "Boy Labour Problem" ', ch. 2: e.g Birmingham Central Care Committee, 1st Report (1912), p. 29 and *3rd Report*, p. 31; Booth, *Life and Labour*, p. 289; Dearle, *Industrial Training*, pp. 198, 200; S. J. Chapman and W. Abbott, 'The Tendency of Children to Enter their Fathers' Trades', *Journal of the Royal Statistical Society* (May 1913), 599, 603; *Poor Law Commission, Report on Boy Labour*, p. 163. See also 'Family and Work Experience Archive' (Essex), Work (1–35), No. 24, pp. 48, 52. For the role of parents, neighbours, *et al.*, see Booth, *Life and Labour*, p. 293, and Dearle, *Industrial Training*, pp. 198, 200. For examples of father and brother finding employment for school-leaver, see 'Bristol People's Oral History Project', MSS., R008, pp. 30–31 and R039, p. 11, respectively; and 'Family and Work Experience Archive' (Essex), Work (1–35), No. 34. For the importance of informal networks in the 1970s, see Ashton and Field, *Young Workers*, pp. 46–7.

the industrial conditions determining the development of trades.[17] Cleanliness and respectability of occupations were also important factors, as were 'non-income attributes', including working environment, social life, and distance to and from work.[18]

3. THE SIGNIFICANCE OF 'AGE'

Reformers knew that 'age' mattered throughout the labour-market, just as they knew that within the juvenile market it determined, or could determine, both the type of employment available and, so they claimed, the effect of certain occupations on individual character. Aside from the initial point of entry from school, there were two groups of male juvenile workers, though neither was governed by a rigid age boundary: the younger were aged 14 to 16 (it could be 14 to 15 or 14 to 17 depending on the type of employment), while the older adolescents were aged between 16 and 18 or 17 and 19 years. The essential point to grasp is that there were two fairly distinct adolescent labour-forces, membership of which was primarily based on age. Furthermore, sometime between the eighteenth and twentieth birthday came the period known as the 'transition to manhood', which in certain respects was central to the debate on 'boy labour' since it was claimed that at this age youths found themselves without either the skill or aptitude necessary to equip them for adult employment.[19]

Given that the distinction between workers in early and late adolescence was often difficult to identify in occupational terms, some examples from each group might be helpful for the sake of descriptive clarity. Those aged between 14 and 16 were more likely to be found in fetching and carrying jobs: errand-boys, van-boys, warehouse-boys, messengers, porters, shop-boys, and boys in various branches of the textile trades, especially the woollen and worsted spinning processes.[20] In

[17] Anon., 'The Boy in Industry', *Toynbee Record* (June 1905), 152.
[18] Dearle, *Industrial Training*, pp. 198, 205. For 'Non-income attributes' see M. Casson, *Youth Unemployment* (1979), 49, 52. I have assumed these were also operative among Edwardian youth.
[19] A. Freeman, *Boy Life and Labour: The Manufacture of Inefficiency* (1914), 199–205.
[20] Details in *Census, Occupations and Industries*, Cd. 7019, (1913), lxxix, table 13.

addition to the numerous 'odd jobs' found in factories and workshops, many of which were regarded as preparatory for apprenticeships, there were those trades which used school-leavers for a couple of years before dismissing them, as in branches of furnishing where it was customary to employ glue-boys and shop-sweepers until they were 16 or 17.[21] The characteristic feature of the younger age-group was that it included thousands of boys waiting to begin their apprentice-ship, unlike the older youths, who were destined for unskilled and semi-skilled labour. The fact that apprenticeship usually began between the ages of 15 and 17 meant that this was the period when the most dramatic job changes occurred.[22] It is hard to come by representative examples of the occupations of these older adolescents because they were distributed through-out virtually the entire occupational structure, the few exceptions being those jobs which demanded a strong physique. By and large, however, one could expect to find them working as labourers in factories, in the building trades, and at the docks; in textiles as loom-boys, doffers, and shifters, as rivet-boys in shipyards, 'drawers-off' in sawmills, 'layers-off' in printing works, 'boy-turners' in railway workshops, machine-minders in engineering and woodworking trades, and in a host of other trades requiring either 'boy-minders' of automatic machines or cheap unskilled labour.[23]

There was a certain elusiveness about the 'transition to manhood', despite the view (probably correct) of several investigators that sometime after the eighteenth birthday 'New openings have then to be searched for, and new beginnings made.'[24] In the absence of statistical evidence, the impression was that adolescents were absorbed as men, 'and in most cases in the same general employments', although approximately half of them would have had to change their jobs.[25] Many of those emerging from their apprenticeships, and

[21] On odd jobs see, e.g. Lady F. Bell, *At the Works: A Study of a Manufacturing Town* (1907), 138; on the furnishing trades, Jackson, *Special Report*, p. 12.

[22] Jackson, *Special Report*, pp. 49–52.

[23] *Occupations and Industries*, table 13; Tawney, 'Economics of Boy Labour', pp. 517–37; A. Williams, *Life in a Railway Factory* (1915), 40–59.

[24] R. A. Bray, *Boy Labour and Apprenticeship* (1911), 160.

[25] Freeman, *Boy Life and Labour*, p. 203.

others in commerce and retailing, would no doubt have continued in the same employment, as would many in unskilled occupations, but others almost certainly were making their way out of designated unskilled labour into the growing market for semi-skilled jobs, as happened in the Leicestershire boot and shoe industry.[26] The expansion of semi-skilled employment during this period was an important development since it could not help but draw a large proportion of its labour from adolescents in the 'transition' stage.

4. APPRENTICESHIP

Of all young workers it was the apprentice who most clearly represented the distinction between juvenile and adult labour, and who figured prominently in the reformers' economic critique. Charles More has provided some useful details on the number of apprentices and the industries which made most use of them.[27] He estimates that of the total number of employed males aged between 15 and 19, which was 1,882,855 in 1906, some 395,700, or 21%, were either apprentices or 'learners', who were distributed throughout nearly thirty industries, with the two largest groups being found in building with 100,000, and in engineering with 94,100.[28] As the word 'learnership' suggests, there was more than one type of apprenticeship. Indeed, one of the difficulties in identifying this method of instruction lies in the flexibility of the term. A government enquiry, which attempted to distinguish between the different forms, concluded that 36.2% of boy trainees were 'indentured apprentices', 37.7% were 'apprentices under agreement' and 26.1% were 'learners'.[29] Precious metals, shipbuilding, and glass appear to have had a high proportion of their trainees under indenture papers, while building and electricity supply favoured the 'agreement' method, as to a lesser extent did glass, wooden-vehicle building, and baking. Learnerships

---

[26] Jackson, *Special Report* , pp. 49–52.
[27] C. More, *Skill and the English Working Class, 1870–1914* (1980), 98–103. see also *Census. General Report, 1911*, Cd. 8491 (1917–18), xxxv, p. 166, table lxi.
[28] Table 7. For a definition of 'learner', see More, *Skill and the English Working Class*, pp. 64–5.
[29] Table 8.

were more popular in pottery, sawmilling, boot and shoe, clothing, and baking. It is impossible to give an accurate figure for the number of apprentices at each age between 15 and 19, except to say that the majority began to serve their time after their sixteenth birthday. R. H. Tawney suggested this in his own small survey, and it was officially confirmed in the early 1920s in a study of the length of apprenticeships in the engineering, shipbuilding, building, furniture, and printing trades.[30] The main exception to the five-year apprenticeship beginning at 16 was the printing industry, although in the other industries between 27% and 48% of boys served six or seven years.

The questions asked by reformers, who were primarily concerned with quality rather than numbers, could not be answered by statistics of this nature, since not only did they believe formal apprenticeship to be in decline, but also the instruction given was often too narrow and specialized, and many employers were said to exploit apprentices by using them as cheap labour. On the other hand, it is reasonable to assume that during the period 1880–1914, apprenticeship remained fairly widespread throughout the main industries. It has already been shown that in 1906 just over 20% of male workers aged between 15 and 19 were apprentices of some sort, and the 1920s' enquiry concluded that it was still a necessity for 'occupations definitely accepted as skilled'. However, where 'specialization of process and of product' was possible, a new class of semi-skilled worker had arisen who received his training via either learnership or upgrading.[31] What was true of the post-war years was almost certainly true of the Edwardian era.[32] The enquiry also made a comparison between the strength of apprenticeship in 1909 and 1925 which revealed an increase in the proportion of apprentices in the building industry and a decrease in printing, while in engineering, shipbuilding, and furniture trades there were different tendencies

[30] Dearle, *Industrial Training*, p. 216 and More, *Skill and the English Working Class*, p. 70. See Tables 9 and 10.
[31] *Enquiry into Apprenticeship and Training in 1925–6*, 7 vols. (1927–8), *Report* (hereafter *1928 Report*), p. 3.
[32] J. W. F. Rowe, *Wages in Practice and Theory* (1928), 87–103 and 263–70. see also Dearle, *Industrial Training*, p. 233.

in different directions.[33] But this was only a partial answer because it took no account of the new trades and processes which were developing prior to 1914 in which there was no need for old-style time-serving, and where the nature of 'skill' was very different from, that of, say, the traditional engineer.[34]

The argument over the nature of late Victorian and Edwardian apprenticeship continues to the present time where it connects with the 'de-skilling' debate, so the confusion and apprehension among reformers is perfectly understandable.[35] Whatever criticisms might now be made of the reformers' exaggerated claims, it remains true that there was 'a slow decline in apprenticeship in many old crafts' which were subject to either intense subdivision of labour or where the trend was towards mechanized production, with the job being learned by 'following-up' and 'migration'. Furthermore, there was no training of workers as apprentices in the new industries, such as chemicals, light engineering, and floor cloth and linoleum manufacture.[36] In these and in various trades where semi-skilled processes had multiplied there was no call for 'craftsmen', but just as traditionally 'skilled' workers were being replaced or superseded by the semi-skilled, so too were many of the unskilled. As N. B. Dearle noted at the end of his study of industrial training methods in London, overall the number of skilled men in 1914 was larger than ever before, but

[33] *1928 Report*, pp. 43–4. It concluded that apprenticeship was 'still of supreme importance in the modern industrial system . . . and by far the most systematic method of entry into the ranks of skilled men in the most important industries of the country': p. 163.

[34] More, *Skill and the English Working Class*, pp. 46–50 and 70–71; W. Knox, 'British Apprenticeship, 1800–1914', Edinburgh University Ph.D. thesis (1980), pp. 36–58; H. A. Clegg, A. Fox and A. F. Thompson, *A History of British Trade Unions since 1889*, (1964), i. 26, 148; A. Fox, *A History of the National Union of Boot and Shoe Workers* (1958), *passim*; J. B. Jeffrys, *The Story of the Engineers*, (1946), 117–27; James Hinton, *The First Shop Stewards' Movement* (1973), 59; Rowe, pp. 93–103, 263–70, and A. L. Levine, 'Industrial Change and Its Effects upon Labour, 1900–1914', London University Ph.D. thesis (1954), *passim*.

[35] See Knox, 'British Apprenticeship', *passim*; and his 'Apprenticeship and De-Skilling in Britain, 1850–1914', *International Review of Social History*, pt. 2 (1986), 166–84; More, *Skill and the English Working Class, passim*; Hinton, *First Shop Stewards' Movement, passim* ; Levine, 'Industrial Change', *passim*; and S. Wood (ed.), *The Degradation of Work?* (1982), *passim*.

[36] More, *Skill and the English Working Class*, pp. 181–2.

the number of semi-skilled was very much larger and increasing more rapidly than the former.[37]

5. OCCUPATIONAL MOBILITY

Despite occupational mobility, or job-changing, or the 'quit-rate', being a crucial means whereby young workers helped to facilitate supply and demand in and around the juvenile labour-market, its structural role was largely ignored by reformers except in so far as they saw it as evidence of the 'excessive' freedom of working-class youth and as representative of the 'blind-alley' character. In reality, the influence of 'age' divisions in the market meant that some degree of job-changing was inevitable in each of the three groups: 14–16, 16–18, and the 'transition to manhood' at 18–20—though not always for the same reason.

The first group might be divided between those boys doing odd jobs prior to beginning an arranged apprenticeship; those in search of an apprenticeship, so that this was the reason for their mobility; and those who had neither expectation of, nor ambition for, finding a place and who simply moved about looking for the 'best' job. Mobility among older adolescents and those negotiating the 'transition' is more difficult to chart. The Birmingham investigator, Arnold Freeman, who reminded his readers that the majority of juveniles were absorbed into adult employment, could not show how many job changes were involved. None of the statistics, he said, gave any indication 'of the multifarious interchange of occupations that goes on all the time between boyhood and manhood; nor do they show us to what extent the *same* boys go on in the same employment as men'. [38]

[37] Dearle, *Industrial Training*, p. 234.
[38] Freeman, *Boy Life and Labour*, p. 203. It was not until the 1930s that juvenile occupational mobility began to be properly studied. Generally speaking, however, these findings confirmed the impression of Edwardian reformers, namely, that about half the youths in the samples changed jobs once or more within the first two years after leaving school, and about one-fifth changed jobs twice or more. The best known surveys are L. Lewis, *The Children of the Unskilled: An Economic and Social Study* (1924); J. Gollan, *Youth in British Industry* (1937); J. and S. Jewkes, *The Juvenile Labour Market* (1938); see also C. Cameron, A. Lush, and G. Meara, *Disinherited Youth* (1943); T. Ferguson and J. Cunnison, *The Young Wage Earner: A Study of*

6. A SEPARATE JUVENILE LABOUR MARKET?

There is little doubt that there was a separate market for
juvenile labour in late Victorian and Edwardian Britain. There
are numerous ways in which such a market may be identified,
but the common view among contempories (and historians)
was that it could be found, in some sense or other, wherever a
substantial 'excess' of juveniles existed.[39] The question of
excessive numbers of young wage-earners in particular occupations will be discussed in relation to the fears of reformers
concerning the 'blind alley', but for the moment we should
consider the extent to which certain occupations relied upon a
disproportionate number of adolescents.[40] It has already been
shown that in addition to large 'excesses' among van-guards
and boys, day-girls and day servants, post-office messengers,
messengers, porters, watchmen, newsboys and newsvendors,
wool and worsted spinning processes, milliners, and cotton
workers undefined, each of which had a juvenile labour-force of
more than 40%, there were 14 other occupations in which the
proportion was between 30% and 40%, and a further 30 in
which it was between 20% and 30%.[41] When these figures are
compared with the proportion of adolescent workers in the
total occupied population (between 20.3% and 18.6 %)
throughout the period, then the extent to which many
occupations were heavily reliant upon juvenile labour becomes

Glasgow Boys (1951); Carter, Home, School and Work, and his Into Work
(1966); Maizels, Adolescent Needs, and Ashton and Field, Young Workers. See
Table 11. In a small sample of oral history respondents (approx 12) the majority
found their work 'hard and boring': Bristol People's Oral History Project. File
'Questionnaires Followed Up'. One old man, remembering why he moved jobs
as a youth, said simply, 'More money. My mother was desperate for money':
Family and Work Experience (Essex) Work (1–35), No. 25, p. 17.

[39] Historians who support this view include G. Stedman Jones, Outcast
London (1971), 68–70, and J. H. Treble, 'The Market for Unskilled Male Labour
in Glasgow, 1891–1914', in Ian MacDougall (ed.), Essays in Scottish Labour
History (1978), 124–27. See also Bray, Boy Labour, p. 149; Dearle, Industrial
Training, p. 383, and Dunlop and Denman, English Apprenticeship, p. 318. On
economic theory see N. Bosanquet and P. B. Doeringer, 'Is there a Dual Labour
Market in Great Britain?' Economic Journal 83 (June 1973), p. 433.
[40] Table 4.
[41] See s. 1 above; and Jackson, Special Report , p. 5 for excess of boys in
clerical work, sections of metal trades, brick-making, glass trades, cotton and
wool, rope manufacture, and milk-sellers.

apparent.[42] The census-takers themselves drew attention to this phenomenon when they compiled a table showing 22 occupations in which there was a 'high proportion' of males under 20 to the total aged 20 and upwards, excluding van-guards and van-boys, newsboys, post-office messengers, and messengers, where the numbers of adolescents actually exceeded those over 20. In some cases the numbers of 10–18-year-olds even exceeded those aged between 18 and 21.[43]

This picture was implicit in Booth's London survey where he discussed the 'age distribution of the occupied classes' in order to show how 'opportunities for employment shift from trade to trade as the workers pass from boyhood to old age'.[44] In only a few trades, he said, such as cabinet-making, engineering, iron and steel, leather-dressings, bookselling, and milling, was the age distribution the same as that of the whole occupied population, so that the boy who began in any one of them could reasonably expect to end his days in it. Similarly, there was little 'deviation' of any age-group among either brass, copper, tin, or lead workers, engine-drivers and artisans, musical instrument makers, saddlers and harness-makers, general labourers, seamen, tailors, hatters, and the law.[45] There was, however, a 'strongly marked excess' of youths of 20 and under among warehousemen, messengers, and factory labour (undefined); and a 'moderate' excess among workers in soap, candle and glue manufacture, chemicals, hemp, jute and fibre, paper, and the civil and municipal service.[46] Other areas showing some degree of 'excess' included railway service, printing, tin canister, and boot-making.[47] Booth thought that as the young people were ejected from their juvenile employment they re-emerged in other unskilled and semi-skilled occupations: messengers reappeared as railway workers; young

---

[42] Table 2a.

[43] *Occupations and Industries*, Cd. 7018 (1913), xxix, pt. 1, pp. 466 and 468.

[44] Booth, *Life and Labour* v. 43.

[45] Ibid., 44.

[46] Ibid., 45. See also Bray, *Boy Labour*, p. 148 where he mentions messengers, clerks, office-boys, transport, errand-boys, and printers.

[47] Booth, *Life and Labour*, p. 46; Stedman Jones, *Outcast London*, pp. 69–70 citing Booth, ii. 189; i. 387–8; iii. 236, and P. G. Hall, 'The East London Footwear Industry, An Industrial Quarter in Decline', *East London Papers* 5/1 (Apr. 1962), 41.

domestics became either outside domestics, coffee- or lodging-house keepers or publicans, cabmen, stablemen and police-men; boys who had been factory labourers, or who were employed in the manufacture of soap, candles, and chemicals, might become dock labourers, gas workers, or coal-porters.[48]

In looking at the structure of the juvenile labour-market, the aim has been to provide the necessary basic information with which to understand and evaluate the economic critique of reformers and other commentators. Much of the critique was exaggerated, simple-minded, confused, moralistic, and mis-informed. Contemporary unease, however, was not entirely misplaced. The critics were statistically correct in identifying several occupations in which there was an 'excess' of juveniles. But irrespective of any excess, the census demonstrates the large numbers of employed adolescents in 1911: more than 200,000 in each of five groups of industries; in textiles the figure rose to over 600,000, and in domestic services it was well over 500,000.[49] The visibility of 'fetching and carrying' employment made it especially worrying for reformers, who saw it as exemplifying the general absence of supervision and instruction in young people's lives. They were also acutely conscious of what they saw as likely adverse consequences for young workers, arising from the rapidly changing industrial structure involving new machinery and subdivision of process and of labour. No less disturbing was the continued (for it was not new) and real decline of indentured and old-style apprenticeship, even though contemporaries were often muddled in their use of the language of 'skill'.

[48] Booth, *Life and Labour* v. 51. The probability of a separate youth market is partially confirmed by labour economics theory which sees two labour-markets: the primary and the secondary. See L. C. Hunter and C. Mulvery, *Economics of Wages and Labour* (1981 edn.), 145 , and P. B. Doeringer and M. J. Piore, *Internal Labour Markets and Manpower Analysis* (1971), 166. In neo-classical economic theory, both markets are determined by labour *supply*, whereas in opposition, 'dual' labour-market theory argues that the markets are determined by labour *demand*. See Hunter and Mulvery, *Economics of Wages and Labour*, pp. 269–70.
[49] Table 3.

Part II

DEFINING THE PROBLEM:
WORK, ADOLESCENCE, AND PERSONALITY

3. The Boy Labour Problem: the Economic Critique

It is not easy to find two or more reformers who shared exactly the same view of the juvenile labour-market in all its aspects. In practice various analyses were offered, representing individual and group concerns, many of which were subjective, partial, and contradictory, but all viewed young workers as a 'problem'.[1] Regardless of the writings of Charles Booth and the Webbs, and the evidence taken before Royal Commissions in the 1880s and 1890s, the reformers' perception, at least in its popular guise, belonged very much to the Edwardian years, beginning with the publication in 1904 of *Studies of Boy Life in Our Cities*, edited by E. J. Urwick, the young sociologist from Toynbee Hall, who urged his readers to acknowledge the working boy of London, 'no longer as an abstraction but as the very concrete and offensively living reality he unquestionably is'.[2] The collection was evidence of a growing national interest in urban youth, but the most prophetic essay was on 'The Boy and his Work', where the author noted that 'in spite of its importance it is a problem to which hitherto but little attention has been paid, neither the sociologist nor the economist has considered it worthy of serious study'.[3] By 1914 it would be impossible to make such a reprimand for this was the beginning of a deluge of literature on the subject. The variety of anxieties that found shelter under the umbrella of 'boy labour' was aptly described by Norman Chamberlain, the Birmingham social reformer:

One bewails the disappearance of apprenticeship and the growth of

---

[1] For an earlier debate on young people in the Tudor period, see I. Pinchbeck and M. Hewitt, *Children in English Society*, (1969), 223–75.

[2] E. J. Urwick (ed.), *Studies of Boy Life in Our Cities* (1904), x. The first pamphlet on 'boy labour' appears to have been Revd S. J. Gibb, *Boy Work and Unemployment*, (1903).

[3] J. G. Cloete, 'The Boy and his Work', in Urwick (ed.), *Boy Life*, p. 103.

unskilled or semi-skilled boy labour; another the restlessness of the modern boy with his ever changing jobs; to a third, boys' work means a reservoir of cheap labour exploited to supplant the grown man; to a fourth, the throwing up of lads of eighteen and nineteen out of regular work into the casual market; street-trading, textile half-timers, and juvenile crime are other subjects, each with their own special devotees.[4]

To this list Chamberlain added his own special interest, namely, 'the way in which the average boy obtains work'. Although the objective condition of the transition from school to wage-earning has been briefly described, it is relevant here to begin with the reformers' subjective view of the 'haphazard process', and then proceed to examine the other principal features of the problem which were, 'excessive' occupational mobility; 'blind-alley' employment; the 'decline' of old-style apprenticeship; and the economic and social consequences.

1. THE 'HAPHAZARD' TRANSITION FROM SCHOOL TO FULL-TIME EMPLOYMENT

The majority of commentators believed that the allegedly haphazard transition from school to work was one of the initial causes of the boy labour problem, especially the way in which the process was said to encourage entry into 'blind-alley' employment, with all its dire repercussions. In general there were several objections to the popular means of choosing and finding the first full-time job: ignorant and greedy parents; thoughtless youth; the inadequacy of facilities offered by schools, philanthropic agencies, youth groups, and educational labour bureaux; and the casual nature of newspaper, shop-window and factory notice-board advertisements.[5] Furthermore, given the high demand for juvenile labour and the complex modern industrial structure, contemporaries shared the view of Frederic Keeling, the Fabian labour exchange

---

[4] N. Chamberlain, 'The Labour Exchanges and Boy Labour', *Economic Journal*, 19 (Oct. 1909), 401. For the American concern about 'apprenticeship and boy labour', see J. Kett, *Rites of Passage* (1977), 144–52.

[5] This was a general criticism referring to all adolescent job choices and applications.

manager, who saw 'the task of choosing a career for a boy or girl wisely' as 'becoming more and more difficult'.[6]

While critics were sympathetic to the kind of advice offered by such bodies as schools, clubs, and private and philanthropic employment agencies, viewing them as representatives of appropriate and rational values, many were inefficient and, with the exception of teachers, could reach only a small minority of young people. Moreover, none of the personnel in these groups possessed adequate knowledge of either local or regional vacancies or of training opportunities; their organization lacked method, and they had neither the time nor the resources to offer a reliable and comprehensive service. The very informality of advertisements was sufficient to incur reformers' disapproval: it was unorganized; there was no chance of the youth receiving informed guidance, and it encouraged a carefree and irresponsible attitude towards work.

The fundamental criticism of the transition, however, referred to the influence of the community in general, and of parents in particular, on school-leavers who, it was claimed, were left to decide for themselves so that the matter became one of 'pure chance': always something to be avoided by those steeped in middle-class morals.[7] The 'complex economic society of to-day' meant that 'the facts of industry in a large town are too many to be grasped by an ordinary workman', and though artisans were sometimes given credit for taking an interest in their sons' choice of occupation, parental ignorance was seen as the major obstacle to an effective transition.[8] 'Great as are the evils of . . . choice of high wage occupations', wrote one reformer, 'the evils of total absence of choice are

---

[6] F. Keeling, *The Labour Exchange in Relation to Boy and Girl Labour* (1910), 9.

[7] See, e.g. R. A. Bray, 'The Apprenticeship Question', *Economic Journal* 19 (Sept. 1909), 407; Chamberlain, *Labour Exchanges*, p. 401; *Report of the Consultative Committee on Attendance, Compulsory or Otherwise, at Continuation Schools*, (hereafter *Consultative Committee on Continuation Schools*) Cd. 4758 (1909), xvii, pp. 62, 90; C. Booth, *Life and Labour of the People of London*, 2nd ser., *Industry* (1903 edn.), v. 289.

[8] Keeling, *Labour Exchange*, pp. 9–10; *Consultative Committee on Continuation Schools*, p. 62; Frederic G. D'Aeth, quoted in C. Jackson, *Report on Boy Labour in London and Certain other Towns*, (hereafter, Jackson, *Special Report*) Cd. 4632 (1909), xliv, p. 183.

probably as great'. In a large number of cases, he continued, 'there is an aimless drifting into any kind of job that comes along', and even where 'some sort of deliberate selection is made it has . . . very little relation to the probable future conditions of the labour-market'.[9] School-leavers, according to N. B. Dearle, were never made to 'think' about what 'work' involved; too often the boy was compelled to 'take his chance like his father did'.[10] Equally popular was the charge that poor parents were more interested in their children's wages than in their future, though it was appreciated that family circumstances often made any other course unrealistic.[11] On the other hand, some parents, it seemed, were simply 'lamentably feckless'. [12] The thought of young people themselves making a choice without adult assistance was cause for alarm since working-class youth was deemed to be by nature irresponsible, thoughtless, unreasonable, and irrational. The boy, whose own idea of occupational preference could be dismissed as 'hazy', was said to look for work with 'no fixed idea in his head', and to 'simply drift into the first opening he comes across without the slightest effort at discrimination'.[13] In the words of the Revd Spencer Gibb: 'the entry into work is taken without care or plan, thought or question'.[14]

Reformers viewed the transition process with some anxiety because they looked on it as being largely responsible not only for the growth of 'blind-alley' employment, but also for subsequent 'excessive' occupational mobility, both of which, they argued, were disastrous for the economic and social security of the adult labourer and his family, besides encouraging youths in indiscipline, laziness, absence of forethought and self-control, and other bad habits. There was, however, another but related objection to the practices involved in the move-

[9] A. Greenwood, *Juvenile Labour Exchanges and After-Care*, (1911), 6; Cloete, 'Boy and his Work', pp. 105–6.
[10] N. B. Dearle, *Industrial Training* (1914), 199, 202–3; see also C. E. B. Russell and L. M. Rigby, *Working Lads' Clubs*, (1908), 198, 207, 212.
[11] Urwick (ed.), *Boy Life*, p. 89; Cloete, 'Boy and his Work', p. 105.
[12] Russell and Rigby, *Working Lads' Clubs*, p .288.
[13] Cloete, *Boy and his Work*, pp. 108–110; see also A. Freeman, *Boy Life and Labour: The Manufacture of Inefficiency* (1914), 174 and Chamberlain, *Labour Exchanges*, p. 40l.
[14] S. J. Gibb, *The Boy and his Work* (1911), p. 6.

ment from school to wage-earning which arose not so much from middle-class ignorance as to their meaning, as from a deep-rooted hostility to them. The casual and unprofessional nature of the means of choosing and finding jobs was regarded by observers as exemplifying the waste, the inefficiency, and the instability so commonly associated with the working-class 'character', or at least that exhibited by the unskilled and the poor. There was nothing unusual about this attitude, for as this study proceeds, time and time again the tensions and contradictions inherent in an analysis of 'boy labour' which could not (or would not) divorce issues of class morality from those of economics, will become evident.

2. 'EXCESSIVE' OCCUPATIONAL MOBILITY

The apparent ease with which young workers were able to move from job to job was widely commented on, being regarded as symptomatic of the disorganized condition of the juvenile labour-market, and as having a corrupting and demoralizing effect upon the boys. Such 'excessive' mobility seemed to illustrate their premature freedom, their reluctance to persevere, their indifference to the work ethic, and their failure to learn.[15] R. A. Bray, one of the most respected of the 'boy labour' group, remarked on how all those who have 'any intimate knowledge of the subject agree that boys repeatedly move in an almost aimless fashion from one situation to another'; it was a period which made training and 'even ordinary discipline ... impossible'. Nor was he willing to allow any rational motive for the change of job: it was made 'for the mere sake of change to see what happens'.[16] Cyril Jackson, author of the special report prepared by the Poor Law

[15] For examples of adverse comments on juvenile occupational mobility see evidence of various witnesses before the *Royal Commission on the Poor Laws and Relief of Distress* (hereafter, *Poor Law Commission*), vol. ix, *Unemployment*, Cd. 5068 (1910), xlix, especially Webb, Tawney, Bray, Urwick, and Sadler; Appendix VI of Jackson, *Special Report*, p. 177; Freeman, *Boy Life and Labour*, pp. 188–94; S. Rowntree and B. Lasker, *Unemployment: A Social Study* (1911), 8–10; Greenwood, *Juvenile Labour Exchanges*, pp. 6–8; R. A. Bray, *Boy Labour and Apprenticeship* (1911), 142; C. Jackson, *Unemployment and Trade Unions*, ch. 6; and Cloete, 'Boy and his Work', p. 111.

[16] Bray, *Boy Labour*, p. 126 and his 'The Apprenticeship Question', pp. 406–7.

Commission, was especially worried about the 'instability' of those who 'light-heartedly throw up job after job', although he admitted that the average youth made only three changes between the ages of 14 and 19. This did not, however, prevent him from arguing that mobility among the classic blind-alley occupations, such as errand, shop, van, and messenger work, damaged any prospect of the youth becoming a skilled worker: 'very few boys can pick up skill after a year or two of merely errand-boy work'. Boys who had left school, he wrote, 'alert and full of hope' became after a period of excessive mobility, 'dry, dull, stupid, irregular and hopeless men'.[17] Dearle saw juvenile mobility as a deplorable characteristic of the 'blind-alley character', which included a 'roving and unsettled' disposition, 'a dislike of steady and regular industry', the loss of 'all sense of responsibility', and in extreme cases, the youth developed 'into a casual, not only by habit but by preference'.[18] At worst, when 'the stimulus and restraint given by the desire to learn' was absent, boys were easily led into a criminal life-style.[19]

The accusations made against young workers can be divided into several categories, notably: selfishness, irresponsi-

[17] Jackson, *Special Report*, pp. 20–3 and his *Unemployment and Trade Unions* (1910), 59–61, and 'Apprenticeship and the Training of the Workman', *Edinburgh Review* (October 1912), 417. See also Freeman, *Boy Life and Labour*, pp. 188–94, although he admitted that sometimes youths were laid off. A. P. was just the sort of youth reformers had in mind. He began at 14 as an errand boy but left after five weeks because of 'differences with employer' and went into an oil-refining factory where he remained for a year on piece-work. He was then unemployed for several months until he became a bottle-washer at a chemical works for a twelve months, but the steam and dampness forced him to quit. There followed another period of unemployment before he found a temporary job for three and a half months as an attendant at a skating rink. However by his eighteenth birthday, he was once again unemployed. Examples of the typical pattern of mobility among unskilled juvenile males were: bottle-washer—errand-boy—waiter; errand-boy—groom—newspaper-seller—machin-ist at oil mill; printers' machine attendant—errand-boy—pottery labourer; junior clerk—telegraph messenger—printer's feeder; beer-bottler—butcher's errand-boy—van-boy. See Rowntree and Lasker, *Unemployment* pp. 10–14. A more detailed account of mobility of boys in different social groups is given in Freeman, *Boy Life and Labour*, pp. 13–76. See also, e.g. 'Family and Work Experience Archive', 'Work' (1–35), no. 8.

[18] Dearle, *Industrial Training*, pp. 384–5.

[19] *Poor Law Commission*, evidence (Tawney), p. 335 (paras. 17–19). See also the Webbs in *National Conference on the Prevention of Destitution; Report and Proceedings* (1911), 81.

bility, lack of self-control (including a reluctance to persevere), and a certain irrationalism. These were, it hardly needs to be said, moral definitions of adolescent behaviour. Critics apparently had no conception of a strategic purpose for occupational mobility and paid little or no attention either to the influence of blind-alley-type employment in necessitating some degree of movement, or to the age-structure of the juvenile labour-market which also dictated a certain amount of job-changing. And they hardly considered the possibility that young workers might be genuinely seeking to improve their prospects.[21]

But why did reformers respond in this way? In an interesting and revealing comment, Arnold Freeman suggested that 'the more fundamental cause' of mobility was a 'matter of psychology', and he referred readers to his chapter on 'Adolescence', which clearly implied that he was interpreting the boys' economic behaviour from a psychological perspective. In effect Freeman drew upon the psycho-social 'discovery' of adolescence to stress the necessity for guidance, supervision, and control because the 'critical years' (of adolescence) were, he felt, delicately balanced between good and evil.[20] Another factor, the significance of which is perhaps less obvious, was the movement involved in occupational mobility, which made adolescents very difficult to see—it created a sense of invisibility at a time when social science was seeking to make all features of the social problem at least figuratively visible and, therefore, it was hoped, knowable. In this respect, mobility could be seen by observers as representing, both literally and figuratively, the failure of the philanthropic middle class to make influential contact with urban youth. It was not without reason that Freeman asked: how could the boy be brought 'under efficient control if he is drifting from one occupation to another?'.[21]

Secondly, the close relationship between the economic and the social features of the critique, meant that assessments of 'character' were always integral to the debate. Reformers constantly stressed that, besides the loss of good habits of

[20] Freeman, *Boy Life and Labour*, p. 192. For the importance of this, see Ch. 2.
[21] Freeman, *Boy Life and Labour*, p. 194.

discipline and regular work, and the liking for a roving and unsettled life, mobility also undermined 'stamina, conscientiousness, as well as perseverance', together with other virtues. Of course this was not an accusation levelled solely at young people, nor was it confined to the Edwardian period, for 'character' in all its forms was a pervasive feature of Edwardian social observation, and beyond. Nevertheless, the single most important reason for deploring 'excessive' occupational mobility concerned its adverse effect on the development of those attributes which would enhance the individual's ability to obtain permanent and respectable adult employment. For those who failed to 'work steadily', warned Dearle, giving 'character' an economic quality, 'little or nothing is possible':

The lad who sticks to his job fits himself for another that is allied to it, whilst the one who is always moving will not fit himself for anything; and if his employment should give him merely discipline, steadiness and application, these will stand him in good stead. Restless habits deprive him even of these qualities, and so increase still further the separation between his occupation in youth and manhood.[22]

3. BLIND-ALLEY LABOUR

The most evocative and frequently-expressed criticism of the juvenile labour-market referred to the prevalence of 'blind-alley' employment. The term itself, as the economist and lecturer, Arthur Greenwood noted, was 'a phrase of the market-place', used 'as a means of characterizing the chief evil' of boy and girl labour, and one that was 'loosely interpreted to convey a multitude of sins'.[23] Bray offered a comprehensive definition when he described this type of occupation as having five features: 'they lead nowhere'—boys only were engaged, and when they reached manhood, they were dismissed; the employing trades were mainly concerned with 'fetching or carrying something—messages, letters, parcels'; the working conditions were poor, with long hours and periods of idleness which meant that in neither case was 'there the possibility of

[22] Dearle, *Industrial Training*, pp. 385, 388. On the very important question of 'habits' and their role in the formation of 'character' see below, ch. 3, s. 3.
[23] A. Greenwood, 'Blind Alley Labour', *Economic Journal*, 22 (June 1912), 309.

much supervision', and often the tasks were arduous, with the boys having to carry heavy goods over long distances; the occupations called for alert, obedient, and intelligent boys— 'the qualities which are in peculiar degree the product of the elementary schools'—but they were 'squandered' by employers; and finally, not only did the 'blind alley' lead nowhere, but in the majority of cases, at the end of his time, the youth was 'distinctly inferior' to what he had been on leaving school.[24]

R. H. Tawney, author of an influential and widely quoted investigation, offered a more subtle definition when he described the 'blind alley' in relation to 'labouring' in order to make a distinction between this type of employment and the 'training' of apprentices or learners. Labouring involved youths who were 'employed solely with a view to the present utility of their labour' and, as they were not given any kind of training, their work was something of a dead end.[25] Tawney, however, was sensitive to the effect of 'age' among 'blind-alley' employees. Thus he made a further distinction between the younger adolescents, 14- to 16-year-olds, often waiting to begin an apprenticeship, who might be employed as van-boys, milk-boys, or as messengers for wages which did 'not compete in attractiveness with apprenticeship' and, who would therefore leave before their sixteenth birthday, and those who remained in other kinds of 'uneducative' jobs until they were 18 or 19, kept there by relatively high wages, ranging from nine to sixteen shillings a week. These were the 'general labourers' in foundries and sawmills, the builders' labourers, the loom-boys, doffers, or sifters in weaving, the oven-boys, rivet-boys, packers in soap works, machine-minders in furniture factories and 'in numberless other such occupations in which they are

[24] Bray, *Boy Labour*, pp. 123–30. On the 'blind alley' in transport see *Report of the Departmental Committee on Hours and Conditions of Employment of Van Boys and Warehouse Boys*, Cd. 6886 (1913), xxxiii, and *First Report of the Standing Committee on Boy Labour in the Post Office*, Cd. 5504, (1911), xxxix. On physical, mental, and moral deterioration see also C. E. B. Russell, *Social Problems of the North*, (1913), 128; Jackson, *Special Report*, p. 27; Minutes of LCC Education Committee, 24 Feb. 1909, p. 204, quoted in Bray, *Boy Labour*, p. 128; and his evidence before *Poor Law Commission*, Cd. 5068, xlix, p. 326, Q. 96504 and p. 328, Qs. 96573–7.

[25] R. H. Tawney, 'Memorandum' submitted to *Consultative Committee on Continuation Schools*, pp. 308–9; and his 'The Economics of Boy Labour', 19 *Economic Journal* (December 1909), 533.

performing some simple operation, often as an assistant to a man'. In trades or industries where there was no need to recruit trained workers, or where cheap juveniles could do just as well as expensive men, there was, he said, 'always a force at work tending to increase the employment of boys without any reference to the openings in the industry' for them when they reached manhood. Consequently, at the age of 18 or 19 the youths found themselves ill-fitted to compete for adult jobs, being without any marketable skill, and so were exposed to either 'unemployment or casual employment'.[26] This idea of mental, moral, and physical deterioration, with its antecedents in middle-class fears for social stabilty, was a continuing thread throughout the critique.

But the 'blind alley' was not so easily defined as first impressions suggested and several reformers, while condemning the conditions of such employment, stressed the complexity of the term. Greenwood was emphatic in warning of the difficulty in categorizing any job as being a 'blind alley' because 'there is probably no industrial occupation which does not provide relatively permanent openings for a number of workers in it.' He cited van-boys, not all of whom were dismissed since a proportion became carmen, just as a proportion of errand-boys found adult employment in the same trade, and a number of young textile workers found work as weavers. Sometimes, he said, it was not the excessive proportion of juveniles to adults that gave a job its blind-alley character, but rather a set of particular circumstances: an office-boy in a large firm would have a good chance of being made permanent, while in a small firm the same boy was likely to be dismissed when he asked for an increase in wages. In fact, very often taking the blind-alley vacancy was the only

---

[26] Tawney, 'Memorandum', p. 313; *Poor Law Commission*, his evidence, pp. 331–2. The textile industry provided examples of young 'piecers' who left at 20 without training and went to work in either the foundry, tannery, railway goods yards, or as unskilled labourers. They were also said to be in poor health after having worked since they were 16 in 'the stuffy vitiated atmosphere'. Another problem arose with the 'Little piecers' who left at 17—too old for apprenticeships. Jackson, *Special Report*, p. 137. For the critical views of the supervisor of Stockport Juvenile Employment Bureau, see Russell, *Social Problems of the North*, pp. 58–9. See also Russell for general description of blind-alley occupations in the North, pp. 54–64.

way into skilled, semi-skilled, or more highly paid employment, as in many of the textile processes. For Greenwood, the essence of the 'blind alley' lay in its age specificity, but there was nothing necessarily 'evil' about it. Industrial regulation, he argued, would 'raise the conditions of work', without 'affecting the central fact of the "blind-alley"—insecurity of employment on the attainment of a certain age'.[27]

In his seminal study of unemployment, William Beveridge examined the role of the 'blind alley' within the context of the 'loss and lack of industrial quality', thereby associating it with industrial training. In many respects his analysis was similar to that of Tawney: he, too, emphasized the absence of 'learning' and the tendency for the older adolescent to remain in unskilled labour and, therefore, 'to overcrowd that already crowded market'. He also agreed that young workers lost the good habits of their school days and that many were tempted into the life of the casual. Furthermore, he acknowledged that 'the great bulk' of applicants to Distress Committees were men who had been juvenile blind-alley employees. However, he saw no inevitable connection between such unskilled labour and unemployment because there were other causes of overcrowding besides the dead-end job, while the casual labour-market was liable to be recruited from 'all who at any time are in difficulties'. In Beveridge's view, then, the significance of the blind alley lay in the lack of 'training' or 'learning' which, 'though it does not create employment', undoubtedly facilitated it by helping to swell the ranks of unskilled labour.[28]

For Freeman, 'blind alley' was much too vague a term to be of any real value, nor could it be used as a synonym for 'unskilled' because juvenile labour in general made little or no demands on 'skill', and the same was true of most adult occupations. Were the classical blind-alley situations, he asked, any more so than the majority of juvenile jobs, few of which offered the certainty of adult employment? Freeman echoed Greenwood in suggesting that, the term should be confined to differentiating between the employment opportunities offered by individual firms—that is, where one firm

[27] Greenwood, 'Blind Alley Labour', pp. 309–11.
[28] W. H. Beveridge, *Unemployment: A Problem of Industry* (1909), 125–31.

promoted, say, its errand-boys, while another always dismissed them. Only in the latter case was the work to be described as 'blind-alley'. He also thought the term inappropriate when applied to many of the occupations which were traditionally regarded as 'dead-end', such as errand-boy work, since the industrial biographies of adolescents compiled for the Poor Law Commission showed that the skilled trades absorbed large numbers of these youths. Freeman's rejection of the blind alley as the source of the problem was motivated by his principal concern which was 'the lack of training and the manufacture of inefficiency in the *majority* of boys between school and manhood'. Hence the title of his book: *Boy Life and Labour. The Manufacture of Inefficiency.*[29]

An elaborate analysis of the 'blind alley' was made by Dearle who, in common with others, related it to learning opportunities. He began by defining the issue as 'those who do not learn at work', with subdivisions into the blind alley proper, the partial blind alley and 'wasteful recruiting of trades and occupations', which referred to skilled employment. Blind alley proper applied to those branches of a skilled trade where the work was performed entirely by adolescents, usually where semi-automatic machinery was in use; to unskilled factory work of the type done mainly by boys and girls; to errand, messenger, and warehouse work; and to general labour. The logic of this classification was determined by the prospects offered by the occupations. The partial blind alley occurred in those trades where there was a difficulty in obtaining the correct proportion of boys to men. Consequently, while they provided entry to a significant proportion of young workers, there was also a significant proportion who would not be kept on, and for them the trades were nothing more than a dead end. One important difference between the ordinary and the partial blind alley was that in the former dismissal occurred in early adolescence—at 15, 16, or 17, whereas in the latter it was

[29] Freeman, *Boy Life and Labour*, pp. 200–3. He cited a chart from Jackson's *Special Report*, p. 48, which showed that the 'skilled trades' took only 8% of boys aged 14 but 28.4% of those aged 20. This meant, said Freeman, that these trades absorbed 'the bulk of the errand boys; and this is well known to be true', p. 203. See also his remarks on the 'evil' of boy labour being in the 'conditions of employment', pp. 3, 5.

usually at 18 or 19 when, claimed Dearle, (in agreement with
Tawney) it was much more difficult to find other employment.
The third category, wasteful recruiting, involved boys in
occupations where they failed to learn the trade, unlike those
in the other two categories who had little or no opportunity to
learn. The result, however, was the same: no definite employment at manhood.[30]

Dearle was critical of the simple-minded view of unemployment which placed the cause in blind-alley labour,
preferring instead to focus on what he called the 'Blind Alley
Character':

> If a permanent livelihood is to be found in manhood, a job must not
> only lead to a definite occupation, but must fit a person to fill one. In
> other words, it must bring him up as a steady, regular and disciplined
> workman. This, indeed is the crux of the whole matter. *It is less
> important that a boy's work should lead directly to a man's work,
> than that it should prepare him properly for it.* If it does, the shifting
> should not be difficult when the right time comes. The great evil of
> Boy Labour is that it produces a type of character which unfits him for
> it, and tends to make him casual and undisciplined and lacking in
> steadiness and perseverance ... The danger is ... far greater in the
> Blind Alley than in a skilled trade ... [where] the learner is more
> under control, has a more definite objective and will have his skill to
> fall back upon. To the boy labourer of the Blind Alley, his steadiness
> and regularity are likely to be his all. Hence we have to face not only
> the problem of the Blind Alley trade, but the derived one of the Blind
> Alley character in all trades. An occupation, therefore, must not be
> classed as boy labour simply because it does not lead to skilled work,
> but only when it fails to fit a lad for any kind of employment at all.[31]

Clearly, the emphasis here—'the crux of the whole matter'—is
on steady, regular, disciplined workmanship. Thus, rather than
being the 'blind alley' as such, the issue was really one of the
quality of the supply of juvenile labour.

Whatever qualifications might be made about the nature of
the 'blind alley', no one doubted either its general importance or
that there was a relationship between it and unemployment,
regardless of the complexities involved. It was certainly true

---

[30] Dearle, *Industrial Training*, pp. 369–413.
[31] Ibid., 372–3. (emphasis added). See also Jackson, *Special Report*, pp. 27–8
for references to 'character' and the 'serious economic loss to the community'.

that many young people were compelled to change jobs during their teenage years. It was also true that many of the unemployed had been in dead-end jobs during their adolescence. And yet, as Freeman noted when he made the fairly obvious, though neglected, point, 'an overwhelming majority of boys graduate from boy labour to regular adult employment'.[32] In other words, it was fundamentally a matter of supply and demand: there existed a demand for low-skilled workers which meant that boy labourers could expect to become adult labourers, if not in the same industry or occupation. This was often the case in the provinces, where in manufacturing towns, for example, boys in factories had more chance of continuing in adult employment.[33] Nevertheless, the phrase 'blind alley' was useful in explaining why 'boy labour' was *a* factor in the wider social problem centring around unemployment and poverty. The nature of the work— the employment conditions—in creating the 'Blind Alley Character' was responsible for the inability of youths to work 'steadily'; 'they know nothing'; and this together with occupational mobility and the excessive numbers entering 'blind-alley' employment led to a surplus of labour and consequently to unemployment.[34]

Making sense of the phrase is difficult; it was for contemporaries. Perhaps it is worth recalling Greenwood's remark that it was used 'as a means of characterizing the chief evil of juvenile labour' and that it was 'loosely interpeted to convey a multitude of sins'. As with other phrases in the debate on the 'boy labour problem' it lost much of its meaning in specific circumstances. In general, however, it raised questions about character, unemployment, skill, the transition from school to work, and, of fundamental importance, the organization of the juvenile labour-market in its entirety. The phrase seemed to capture all the anxieties associated with young workers, and this was its descriptive value.

[32] Freeman, *Boy Life and Labour*, p. 3; see also Booth, *Life and Labour* vol. v, p. 51.
[33] Dearle, *Industrial Training*, p. 419. In Liverpool and Leeds there was also opportunity for 'suitable' work, although there was a 'big leakage' in woollen and cotton mills: Jackson, *Special Report*, p. 27.
[34] Dearle, *Industrial Training*, pp. 419–20.

4. 'THE APPRENTICESHIP QUESTION'

The 'decline','decay', or 'break-up' of apprenticeship was central to the 'boy labour problem'. The cause of the decline was usually attributed to 'modern industrial conditions', of which the most frequently cited were the subdivision of labour and specialization of process; the impact of new machinery; the reorganization and growth of the production unit as workshops gave way to small factories which in turn were superseded by larger factories; and the rise in rents for workspace which apparently discouraged employers from investing in apprenticeship when they could recruit skilled workers from elsewhere, or alternatively substitute machinery for human labour.[35] The apprenticeship question, in some form or other was older than the Industrial Revolution, and throughout the nineteenth century there had been numerous complaints and warnings from trade unionists. Writing in 1912, Olive Dunlop, the historian of apprenticeship, thought that in its 'old style' it had come to an end by 1800.[36] But, as a recent study has remarked, given that there were hundreds of thousands of 'apprentices' in Edwardian Britain, clearly there is a problem of definition.[37] While this may be true, the belief that apprenticeship had been fundamentally altered in form and content was widespread among social scientists and reformers, though as with other aspects of 'boy labour', there were varied and often conflicting interpretations.

The 'question' had been of acute concern since at least the publication of the Reports and Minutes of the Royal Commissions on Technical Instruction (1884) and on the Depression of Trade and Industry (1886) when trade-union witnesses made clear their fears.[38] According to these witnesses modern

[35] See, for example, Bray, 'The Apprenticeship Question', p. 413; *Poor Law Commission*, evidence (Urwick), p. 351 and (Webb), p. 184, Q. 96938; *Consultative Committee on Continuation Schools*, p. 33; Gibb, *Boy and his Work*, pp. 8–13, 52; Cloete, 'Boy and his Work', pp. 114–16; Booth, *Life and Labour*, vol. ix, p. 222; LCC, *The Apprenticeship Question* (1906), 1.

[36] J. O. Dunlop and R. D. Denman, *English Apprenticeship and Child Labour* (1912), 224–36.

[37] C. More, *Skill and the English Working Class, 1870–1914* (1980), 41.

[38] *Royal Commission on Technical Instruction*, C. 3981.II (1884), iii, see especially evidence of G. Skipton, 3858; on decline of apprenticeship see minutes 1942–4, 2108, 2130, 2159, 2246, 3789–91, 3829–30, 3858 and 3920.

developments often resulted in a lower standard of workmanship and the decline of proper apprenticeship as youths were confined to a single process and, therefore, never obtained a comprehensive knowledge of the trade. As the spokesman from the Shipley branch of the Amalgamated Society of Engineers reported, employers kept the boys 'at one class of work; consequently, when they are supposed to be a man, they can do nothing else with credit.'[39]

The most damning evidence against apprenticeship in relation to overcrowding, specialization, machine work, and two- to three-year engagements, came from trade-union testimonies given before the Royal Commission on Labour in the 1890s. In trade after trade—boilermaking, engineering, printing, cabinet-making, tailoring, building, bolt and nut, and the boot and shoe trades—apprenticeship was said to have either declined or decayed. For example, the union representative from the Midland hosiery industry feared that as apprenticeship declined, juvenile machine-workers would supersede adults; in the boot and shoe industry it was said to result in certain departments being overcrowded with boys; witnesses from the paint trade argued that apprenticeship had almost broken down, while in the London cabinet-making trades, it was known to be almost obsolete, as machinery allowed boys to do men's work.[40] Robert Knight, the general secretary of the Boilermakers Union, reported few boys being bound in the shipbuilding and engineering trades; increasingly they entered the employment at different ages, where they remained for two or three years before moving on to work for more money as 'improvers' and were then replaced by new boys. It was, he said, a bad system because it produced a class of inferior workmen, reduced wages, and overstocked the labour-market.[41]

The first authoritative account of the state of apprenticeship

---

[39] *Royal Commission on the Depression of Trade and Industry*, C. 4715 (1886), xxi. *Second Report*, P. II, App. D, pp. 7–98; for further details in relation to skill levels see W. Knox, 'Apprenticeship and De-Skilling in Britain, 1850–1914', *International Review of Social History*, pt. 2 (1986), 172–3.

[40] *Royal Commission on Labour*, C. 6795. III, (1892), ii, 'C', pp. 15, 22, 24, 42.

[41] Ibid., C. 6894. VII (1893), iii, 'A', Q. 20, 683, see also C. 6894. 1X, iii, 'A', p. 25. See also the Midland Bolt and Nut Trade, ibid., C. 6795. iv (1892) XXXVI, Pt. I, Qs. 17,799, 17,800 and 17,885.

had come in Sidney and Beatrice Webb's *Industrial Democracy* where they warned that in many trades 'the actual conditions of entrance' were 'so unregulated that the ranks . . . are largely recruited by men who have not come in by the recognized gate.' The engineering and printing industries provided typical instances where 'picking-up' and 'improvers' were widespread. In the Webbs' view: 'Over by far the largest part of the limited field in which apprenticeship prevailed, the system has gone practically out of use.' 'The abandonment of apprenticeship', they wrote, 'as a form of technical training is not due to the discovery of any satisfactory alternative.' On the contrary, there was a 'remarkable consensus of opinion among "practical men" that the situation was highly unsatisfactory'.[42] One of those men was Charles Booth who concluded that in London 'the system of apprenticeship is either dead or dying'.[43]

By common consent the two most important developments affecting apprenticeship (and industrial training in general) were the break up of processes and the new machinery. The main criticism was that specialization lessened the opportunities for boys to learn the skills of their trades in such a way as to make them 'adaptable' to different types of work in the same trade, and to the particular demands of different firms.[44] Entrance into trades involved a 'leap into the dark'.

Rapid changes of process, the ingenious development of mechanical methods, a revolution in organisation to correspond, are not only—though this is their first and most obvious result—making industrial training while at work more and more uncertain and more and more fractional, but are also continually superseding trades which were once promising; it is impossible to predict what further changes of this radical sort are on the way.[45]

Or, as Tawney wrote, the growing specialization of processes

---

[42] S. and B. Webb, *Industrial Democracy* (1897, 1920 edn.), pp. 464–5, 471–2, and 476.

[43] Booth, quoted in J. Springhall, *Coming of Age: Adolescence in Britain 1860–1960* (1986), 82.

[44] See, e.g. Tawney, 'Economics of Boy Labour', p. 521; *Poor Law Commission*, evidence (Sadler), p. 225, Q. 93455 and (Urwick), p. 349, Q. 96921; Freeman, *Boy Life and Labour*, pp. 163–7; Cloete, 'Boy and his Work', pp. 115–17, and Dunlop and Denman, *English Apprenticeship*, p. 328.

[45] Gibb, *Boy Work*, p. 51.

makes it increasingly difficult for a boy who enters a workshop as an apprentice . . . to obtain a knowledge of the trade which he means to follow sufficiently general to make him a good all-round workman . . . he tends to become unduly specialised at a very early age, with the result that if he is displaced from the particular job he finds more difficulty in getting another than he would if he knew all sides of his trade.[46]

Employers, he said, told him that

Boys are kept as a rule in their own departments. They are not taught; they are made to work . . . Boys are specialised from the beginning; to shift a boy proficient in one department to another would not pay . . . To put an apprentice on a valuable machine means a waste of money unless he is specialised to it, and in all trades the longer a boy is kept at one process the sooner does he begin to be economically profitable.[47]

Tawney concluded, as did other investigators, that just as 'each process now had its machine', and the machine-minder appeared to be replacing the mechanic, so the boy labourer was replacing the boy learner.[48]

Popular opinion among the 'boy labour' reformers saw the combination of 'simplification of manual processes' and specialization as leading to an increase in the number of unskilled workers and machine-minders, and not only in London where labouring could be said to predominate with so much employment in docks, transport, and retail, but also in cities such as Coventry, with its numerous skilled workshops

[46] Tawney, 'Economics of Boy Labour', p. 521.
[47] Tawney, 'Memorandum', pp. 304–6; see also Jackson, 'Apprenticeship and the Training of the Workman', p. 415; S. and B. Webb, *Industrial Democracy*, pp. 477, 472 and 482.
[48] Tawney, 'Memorandum', p. 521; S. and B. Webb, *Industrial Democracy*, p. 483; *Poor Law Commission* evidence (Sadler), Q. 93455 and (Tawney), Qs. 96649 and 96651; C. S. Loch (ed.), *Methods of Social Advance* (1904), 127. The increase in adolescent machine-minders was said to be a national trend in the engineering trades: in the drilling, milling, slotting, punching, band-sawing, and screwing departments; in branches of the electrical and mechanical engineering industries; and in woodworking, cabinet-making, and the boot and shoe industry. See Tawney, 'Economics of Boy Labour', pp. 521–2, and his evidence to *Poor Law Commission*, Q. 96649; see also Sadler, Q. 93455; Bray, 'The Apprenticeship Question', p. 413; Cloete, 'Boy and his Work', p. 116; Jackson, *Special Report*, p. 186 and B. Cunningham, 'Apprenticeship', *Charity Organization Review* (July 1905), 40.

and in Birmingham, where according to a report from the Chamber of Commerce

in a few trades only is it possible to take apprentices now, owing to the large scale of production, the sub-division of labour has been carried to a minute degree and automatic and semi-automatic machines are installed in most industries; the worker being now a specialist in the production of a few articles on machines devised for their rapid and economical production.[49]

Perhaps not much more than one quarter of the manual labour of Birmingham could be described as 'skilled' since it was possible to 'pick up' so many factory operations in a few days or months at most. The problem, however, was not machinery *per se*, but the use of cheap boy labour to supplement the use of the 'inadequate development of machinery'.[50] When more efficient machines were introduced, as in the northern woollen and worsted industries, boy labour declined.[51] But where no such introduction occurred, the demand for young workers would continue to be unsatisifed.

However, as with the 'blind alley', the 'apprenticeship question' was more complex than it appeared, for while all the critics agreed that apprenticeship was changing, and that this was cause for concern, they differed over meanings and consequences. The first qualification, which often passed unnoticed, was not so much that none of the new machines demanded any skill, but that there were so many different degrees of skill involved in the new processes. There was an enormous difference between the skill necessary to work a simple drilling machine or an automatic lathe and the work

[49] Freeman, *Boy Life and Labour*, p. 149; and *Poor Law Commission*, evidence (Urwick), Q. 96921, (5 and 6); Gibb, *Boy and his Work*, p. 60; C. Sandler, 'Working-Class Adolescents in Birmingham: A Study in Social Reform, 1900–1914', Oxford University D. Phil. thesis (1987), 120.

[50] Freeman, *Boy Life and Labour*, pp. 165–8 and his references to Marshall, the Webbs and Jackson. See also Jackson, 'Apprenticeship' *Edinburgh Review*, (Oct, 1912), p. 427.

[51] Freeman, *Boy Life and Labour*, p. 168 quoting *Yorkshire Post*, 19 Dec. 1911. The basic problem, however, was the existence of what Professor Chapman called 'a relative over-supply of unskilled labour, and this was keeping back the introduction of more complicated machinery'. Quoted by Freeman, p. 228. See also G. Stedman Jones, *Outcast London* (1971), 72, referring to over-supply of unskilled labour.

executed on an elaborate drilling machine. Progress from one to the other was possible via a number of intermediate grades, each one involving work on a slightly more difficult machine, until 'the boy becomes insensibly a qualified turner or fitter'.[52] Nevertheless, this graduated form of training still left the majority of 'apprentices' without a definite system of trade instruction. According to the Webbs, such a situation encouraged the disuse of apprenticeship 'as an educational system'. It also helps to explain why Tawney thought 'workshop training, taken by itself', to be 'inadequate', and why in Jackson's view, it left young workers to undertake 'monotonous and uninteresting work at a period in their lives when they should be learning and developing to the utmost their skill, their intelligence, and their character'.[53]

These observations point to additional features of apprenticeship besides the learning of a craft. The new methods might or might not be developing 'skill' (always remembering the ambiguities of the term), but the lack of proper supervision, the occupational mobility involved and the search for higher wages were all seen to be detrimental to moral education and to the growth of adolescent intelligence. Consequently, however confused reformers may have been about the reality of apprenticeship, most of them joined with Beveridge in seeing the task ahead as not so much to revive 'old-style' apprenticeship, but the revival of the principle underlying apprenticeship, namely, that no young employee should ever 'be regarded merely as cheap labour', and, furthermore, that he or she should 'be undergoing preparation for a future career'.[54] Beveridge is voicing an ideal here, but one which appeared to offer a solution to the problem of 'boy labour'; hence its popularity. While it is unlikely that he believed traditional apprenticeship had ever been a complete educational system, he certainly sought to provide a substitute suitable for modern conditions.[55]

[52] S. and B. Webb, *Industrial Democracy*, p. 472.
[53] Ibid., p. 476 and Tawney, 'Memorandum', p. 307; Jackson, *Unemployment and Trade Unions*, p. 55.
[54] Beveridge, *Unemployment*, p. 131.
[55] The most detailed scheme was given in Bray, *Boy Labour and Apprenticeship*, 'The New Apprenticeship', pp. 176–231.

Beveridge was also responsible for raising the second qualification when he informed his readers that problems concerning
the industrial 'quality of labour' did not arise from the decay of
apprenticeship, but from the 'development of trades and
processes to which apprenticeship had never been applied'.[56]
Many observers often failed to appreciate this distinction,
possibly owing to their inability to ascertain with any accuracy
the exact industrial location of the trend. Others, however.
including Bray, Tawney, and Sidney Webb, agreed that in
discussing the causes of, and solutions to, the 'boy labour
problem', attention should be directed away from 'old-style'
training methods. This explains their support for the revival of
the principle of learning while working. Unsurprisingly, the
debate soon opened out into a broader evaluation of 'industrial
training' (to include social and moral virtues) which focused on
three connected proposals: the technical education of those
who would become skilled workers (but this rarely figured in
'boy labour' writings); the vocational education of the machin-
ist or otherwise semi-skilled employee; and the versatility or
'adaptability' of the young worker—both labourer and apprentice. Each of these required some form of further education. No
wonder then that the reformers thought training wholly in the
workshop to be 'inadequate' and looked instead to compulsory
part-time day continuation schools.[57]

Given that there were many different degrees of 'skill', and
that many trades and processes had developed to which
apprenticeship had never been applicable, it was often difficult
to identify the difference between a 'decline' in 'apprenticeship' and the multiplicity of forms of instruction, few of which
were efficiently organized. No one was more conscious of the
'tide of industrial change' than Dearle who recognized that
since there were different forms of industrial training, the
problem was not simply one of decline of apprenticeship.
Industrial training, he said, could be divided into four categories.[58] First, there was 'regular service', which he subdivided
into formal apprenticeship, informal verbal agreements,

[56] Beveridge, *Unemployment*, p. 125; and *Poor Law Commission*, evidence,
(Tawney), p. 344 (15).
[57] These are discussed in Ch. 8.
[58] Dearle, *Industrial Training*, chs. 4–7.

'employment during good behaviour', and 'working and learning'. The common feature of these methods was 'learning from beginning to end by continuous and regular employment in a single firm'. The second route was 'migration' which could occur for the following reasons: because it was generally adopted in the trade; as a result of misconduct; and because some chance openings were taken advantage of. The movement might be from shop to shop, or from machine to machine, as the work became progressively more difficult. Thirdly, 'following up', also called 'learning following upon labouring', where the youth worked as a labourer or a 'helper'. And fourthly, 'picking up' which referred to semi-skilled work learned over a short period with little regular teaching; and in which sometimes the boy moved onto new processes as he got older, picking them up, too.

If, then, 'the apprenticeship question' is interpreted in terms of 'skill', clearly the problem was not the absence of 'training', but rather the great variety of means. The problem lay in assessing the value of each method and the extent to which it prevailed in a particular trade or industry; it was, as Dearle admitted, largely 'a matter of guesswork'.[59] No one doubted that many boys continued to be apprenticed in the orthodox manner and became fully trained tradesmen. But there were thousands of other boys whose 'instruction' was much more casual. Would their training protect them against the 'tide of industrial change' and its consequences? And if this was the position with respect to 'apprentices' and those in a similar position, how much worse was it, warned Tawney, in the case of the 'large class of boys who are neither learners nor apprentices, and who . . . constitute at once by far the most serious part of the problem of boy labour'.[60]

5. REGIONAL AND OCCUPATIONAL CONSIDERATIONS

Describing the economic critique generally is all very well, but

[59] Ibid., 140. In so far as it undermined any pretence at statistical accuracy, this was a significant admission, the implications of which were never investigated. The problem was especially difficult given the rise in the proportion of semi-skilled workers. By 1911 they represented nearly 40% of the labour force.

[60] Tawney, 'Memorandum', p. 308.

a little more clarification is required before a comprehensive and detailed picture can be developed. There are three relevant questions: how geographically widespread was the problem? What kind of occupations were involved? And to what extent was it a problem of industry *per se*? The brief answers are that the 'boy labour' issue was not felt to be peculiar to London, or even to large towns. It was marginally more prevalent in the North and Midlands than in the South, owing to the pattern of industry, transport, and commerce . In addition to the large group of apprenticeships, the occupations involved were numerous, and included those of errand-, messenger-, van-, office-, and shop-boys, junior clerks, machine-tenders, and the great variety of labourers and specialized factory employees.[61] The wide range of occupations was confirmation, at least from the reformers' perspective, with their concern for education, training, and character development, that the problem was prevalent throughout industry, especially in branches of the engineering trades, the boot and shoe trades, textiles, transport and distribution, retailing, railway workshops, miscellaneous factory manufacturers, such as box-making, soapmaking and confectionery, and in commerce, metals and printing.[62] (In fact, only in the armed forces, mining and quarrying, agriculture, and domestic service were young workers not a source of anxiety.) This omnipresence is the reason why 'boy labour' was never portrayed as either a local difficulty or one confined to a particular industry or group of trades. It also explains why it assumed such significance in the opinion of so many commentators.

Consequently, reformers were convinced that to all intents and purposes the problem possessed national urban dimensions. One has only to look at the better-known regional surveys and investigations to see that it featured in all of them. Apart from London, those cities and towns specifically considered included Oxford, Norwich, Cambridge, Manchester, Birmingham, and Glasgow.[63] In his study of social problems in

[61] See Table 5.
[62] The concern for education, training, and character development is evident in the previously cited writings of, for example, Jackson, Bray, Dearle, Freeman, and the Webbs.
[63] See Butler, Hawkins, Keynes, Russell, Freeman, and Tawney.

the North, which included blind-alley employment, C. E. B. Russell referred to Leeds, Liverpool, Salford, Manchester, and Newcastle.[64] Official inquiries, such as the *Special Report on Boy Labour* and the Department Committee which inquired into the hours and conditions of van- and warehouse-boys, took evidence from some of the cities already mentioned, and also from Bristol, Leicester, Bradford, Plymouth, Sheffield, Northampton, Hastings, Cheltenham, Chester, York, Nottingham, Dublin, Edinburgh, Cardiff and Newport.[65] While 'boy labour' tended to be regarded as an urban problem, it was clearly not restricted to large areas.

This kind of specificity is important, but it can be misleading when trying to understand the extent and nature of the juvenile labour-market in relation to what middle-class observers perceived to be a variety of difficulties arising from the economic and social condition of male working-class youth. The full range of the critique is made clear in the next two chapters, but for the moment it is worth keeping in mind Dearle's previously quoted views on blind-alley 'character', and those of Tawney with reference to the 'large class of boys who are neither learners nor apprentices'.[66] It was in this sense that the matter appeared as geographically pervasive and,

[64] Russell, *Social Problems of the North*, passim.

[65] Jackson, *Special Report*, pp. 4, 176–92 and app. IX. The van- and warehouse-boy aspect of the problem appeared to be limited to London, Sheffield, Salford, Manchester, Liverpool, Birmingham, Leeds, and Glasgow. There was less of a problem in Bristol, Leicester, Nottingham, Newcastle, Edinburgh, Cardiff, and Newport. See *Report of Departmental Committee on Hours and Conditions of Employment of Van Boys and Warehouse Boys*, Cd. 6886, (1913), xxxiii, pp. 5, 31. However, identifying the 'boy labour problem' as a whole was separate from identifying those areas in which there was either a high or a low demand for juvenile labour. See A. Greenwood and J. Kettlewell, 'Some Statistics of Juvenile Employment and Unemployment', *Journal of the Royal Statistical Society* 75, (June 1912), 750–1, tables 5a-d. An enquiry by Factory Inspectors in 26 towns indicated that street-sellers, at least, would have difficulty in moving on to other employment in Blackburn, Bristol, Cardiff, Hull, Ipswich, Leicester, Northampton, Nottingham, Plymouth, and Sheffield. But there were plenty of opportunities in Manchester, Dundee, Glasgow, Southampton, Newcastle, Stoke, Swansea, Edinburgh, Leeds, Lincoln, and Wolverhampton. See *Report of Departmental Committee on Employment of Children Act, 1903*, Cd. 5229, (1910), xxxviii, pp. 13–14 and app. XX. But even in those areas where a certain amount of juvenile unemployment was a factor, the essential character of the 'boy labour problem' remained.

[66] See above n. 38 and below n. 67.

therefore, the consequences, which are described below, were thought sufficiently serious to justify a national response.

6. THE ECONOMIC AND SOCIAL CONSEQUENCES

In her study of unemployment and social policy, José Harris tells us that social scientists saw the problem in terms of its effect on individual standards of living; its role in either the creation or the exacerbation of ill-health and bad housing; and its malevolent influence upon the 'character' of the unemployed.[67] As many of the same personalities were also actively involved in investigating 'boy labour', it is easy to understand how they related one set of problems to the other. The substance of their fears was that the *laissez-faire* condition of the juvenile labour-market contributed to the over-supply of unskilled workers and to the perpetual creation of a class of casuals, the consequences of which, in addition to those concerning the adolescents themselves, were adult unemployment, poverty, and the demoralization of workmen and their families.[68] It is important to be clear about this from the outset: reformers always saw the effects of 'boy labour' extending well beyond the adolescent stage of life; in all their comments, the demands and responsibilities of the working-class family were never far from their thoughts.

The relationship between unskilled and casual labour and unemployment was most extensively examined by witnesses appearing before the Poor Law Commission where Webb, Bray, Tawney, Urwick, and Michael Sadler emphasized the national importance of safeguarding the economic, social, and educational life of young people. Sidney Webb expressed the

[67] J. Harris, *Unemployment and Politics: A Study in English Social Policy 1886–1914* (1972), 34.

[68] *Poor Law Commission, Report of the Effects of Employment or Assistance Given to the Unemployed since 1886 as a Means of Relieving Distress outside the Poor Law*, by C. Jackson and J. C. Pringle, Cd. 4795, (1909), xliii, pp. 6–7, 7–9. See also *Poor Law Commission, Minority Report*, ch. 4, and Harris, *Unemployment and Politics* p. 31. The importance of the family from the standpoint of social and political order was well illustrated by Helen Bosanquet, when she wrote: 'Nothing but the combined rights and responsibilities of family life will ever rouse the average man to his full degree of efficiency, and induce him to continue his work *after* he had sufficient to meet his own personal needs' (emphasis added): *The Family* (1906), 222.

dominant view when he claimed that the growth in the number of van-boys, messengers and errand-boys in London and in large provincial towns, was leading to the recruitment of 'a chronically excessive army of unskilled, casually-employed, merely brute labour', while the 'growing up of hundreds of thousands of boys without obtaining any sort of industrial training, specialised or unspecialised' was 'a perpetual creating of future pauperism, and a grave social menace'.[69] Tawney agreed, but he had in mind occupations far beyond those of the messenger class, which led him to argue that the 'large mass of chronically unemployed, or half-employed, low-skilled labourers' was recruited 'by a stream of young men from industries which rely upon unskilled boy labour'.[70] Sadler pointed to the 'industrial and commercial conditions which now prevail' making it easy for the young worker to secure employment, but which left the boy 'at the very time when he want a man's subsistence, out of line for skilled employment and only too likely to recruit the ranks of unskilled labour'.[71] Urwick spoke of the growth of adolescents' occupations which were either 'uneducative' or 'unpromising' in the sense of leading 'to no permanent occupation during adult life'.[72] Similarly, though Bray focused on the detrimental effect of juvenile wage-earning on 'character', he also saw it as being 'largely responsible' for the unemployment problem.[73] The Commission was sufficiently impressed with the seriousness of the issue to appoint Cyril Jackson to make further enquiries. In his report, Jackson concluded that there was indeed a connection between ' boy labour', unskilled work, and unemployment. Those who failed to find permanent jobs during their adolescence, he said, grew up to swell 'the army of general labourers who form the class from which the casual, the under-employed and the unemployed are drawn'. [74]

When the Commission prepared its final reports, it was

---

[69] *Poor Law Commission*, evidence, (Webb), p. 183.
[70] Ibid., (Tawney), pp. 329 (2, a, b) and 331 (6, 7).
[71] Ibid., (Sadler), Q. 93386 (3).
[72] Ibid., (Urwick), Q. 96921 (1).
[73] Ibid., (Bray), Q. 96218 (VI, b).
[74] Jackson, *Special Report*, pp. 1, 52 and his book, *Unemployment and Trade Unions*, p. 62. See also Jackson and Pringle, above n. 69.

evident that the matter had attained the status of a major social problem. In the words of the majority:

The great prominence given to boy labour . . . leads us to the opinion that this is, perhaps, the most serious of the phenomena which we have encountered in our study of unemployment. The difficulty of getting boys absorbed, through gradual and systematic training, in the skilled trades is great enough; but when to this are added the temptations, outside organised industries, to enter at an early age into occupations which . . . give no opportunity of acquiring skill, it seems clear that we are faced by a greater problem than that of finding employment for adults who have fallen behind in the race for efficiency, namely, that the growth of large cities had brought with it an enormous increase in occupations that are making directly for unemployment in the future . . . The almost universal experience is that . . . there is a regular drift from such boys' occupations into a low-skilled labour market.[75]

And the *Minority Report*, in recommending the 'Halving of Boy and Girl Labour as a means of reducing unemployment', was equally certain that

There is no subject as to which we have received so much and such conclusive evidence as upon the extent to which thousands of boys, from lack of any sort of training for industrial occupations, grow up, almost inevitably, so as to become chronically unemployed, or under-employed, and presently to recruit the ranks of the unemployable.[76]

Numerous other commentators added their voice to these sentiments, emphasizing the 'abuse' of young wage-earners.[77] Even Beveridge, who doubted the wisdom of attributing all unemployment to 'deficiencies of industrial training' and to

[75] *Poor Law Commision, Majority Report*, pp. 326.

[76] Ibid., *Minority Report*, Part II, ch. v, B i and pp. 1165–6.

[77] W. M. Lightbody, 'The Problem of Unskilled Labour', *Economic Review* (Oct. 1909), 423; Revd S. J. Gibb, 'The Choice of Employment for Boys', *Economic Journal* (Oct. 1914), 439; E. Lesser, 'Boy Labour and Unemployment', *Toynbee Record* (March 1909), 98–9; F. W. Baggallay, 'Child Labour in Factories and Workshops', *Economic Review* (July 1909), 293, 299–300; K. I. M. Medley, 'Van-Boy Labour', *Economic Review* (1911), 57; Thomas Jones, 'Unemployment, Boy Labour and Continued Education', *Socialist Review* (July 1909), 859. See also enquiries into conditions of van-, warehouse- and post-office boys: *Report of D. C on Vanboys and Warehouse Boys*, and *Reports of the Standing Committee on Boy Labour in the Post Office*, Cd. 5504, 5575, 6959, and 7556 (1909, 1911,1913, and 1914), vols. xxxix, xxxviii, xlix.

the overcrowded labour-market, saw the time at which boys
passed from juvenile to adult work as 'a point of stress' from
which there was 'a constant discharge into the pool of casual
labour'.[78]

The consequences of unemployment were, of course, plainly
discernible. But there was also disquiet felt about other
influences on the long-term stability of the individual and the
family, in addition to those arising from a temporary loss of
work. The most directly relevant influences were thought to
be the nature and 'character' of the unskilled who, it was
feared, could easily degenerate into casuals (or the unemployable); irregular employment; and low wages. Indeed, when
considering middle-class perceptions of 'boy labour' the
significance of the spectre of the casually employed labourer
struggling to maintain his wife and children on an inadequate
income can hardly be exaggerated. Contemporary investigations seemed to justify the sense of alarm, illustrating as they
did that economic and social distress involved not only 'a vast
amount of personal suffering and physical and mental degeneration', but also 'great waste of productive power'. These
echoes of the 'national efficiency' debate, including the threat
of physical deterioration, served to underline the basic fact of
working-class life, as revealed by the surveys: without proper
financial support, families were forced into over-crowded and
insanitary housing; sickness and disease were never very far
away; children were ill-clothed and inadequately fed; and
infant mortality was higher among this group than any other.[79]

Both Booth and Rowntree had pointed to low wages as 'a
fundamental cause of urban poverty', though irregularity
appeared to be the more important factor in London. Similarly,
in their survey of provincial towns, Bowley and Hurst identified
'half of the households below the poverty line at Warrington

[78] Beveridge, *Unemployment*, p. 131.
[79] *Poor Law Commission, Minority Report*, p. II, pp. 163, 191; *Majority Report*, pp. 128, 134; Jackson, *Special Report*, p. 28; Revd H. S. Pelham, *The Training of the Working Boy* (1914), p. 74; G. Shann, 'The Effect of the Non-Living Wage upon the Individual, the Family and the State'. *Industrial Unrest and the Living Wage* (1913), 87–105. See also W. Leslie Mackenzie, 'The Family and the City: Their Functional Relations', *Sociological Review* 1/2 (Apr. 1908), 118; L. G. Chiozza Money, *Riches and Poverty* (1905), ch. 14 and 16; H. Bosanquet, *The Family* (1906); and the standard works by Maud Pember Reeves, Lady Bell, and S. Rowntree.

and Reading, nearly one half at York, and one-third at Northampton' as 'living in poverty because the wages of the head of the household were so low that he could not support a family of three children or less'.[80] Booth's emphasis on irregular employment was endorsed by Beveridge, and by a national inquiry which found that besides it and low wages, the other main causes of pauperism were bad housing and unhealthy trades.[81]

While reformers certainly appreciated the consequences of the economic realities deriving from financial insecurity, they were equally confident that unskilled and casual labour could lead to a pauperized 'character'. This view was articulated by the Webbs when they claimed that, where labouring merged with casual work, the perpetual discontinuity of employment weakened the desire and the ability 'to work regularly'; it encouraged 'loafing habits' which led to gambling and drinking; furthermore, 'zeal, fidelity, and even honest effort' were lost sight of as the man went from one employer to another. As the husband was demoralized, so too was the wife in the home: casual labour and underemployment produced an 'inferior character' weakened by the 'paralysing uncertainty' associated with irregular weekly earnings; the woman failed to make 'thrifty' use of her budget, and the accumulating depression often resulted in excessive drinking and child neglect. Such children, said the Webbs, were more likely to be sent to reformatory or industrial schools, and when they grew up, more likely to find themselves without a trade, doing casual jobs, and thus the cycle of deprivation would ensnare another generation.[82]

Victorian and Edwardian reformers are renowned for their obsession with the moral qualities of individuals, and even the rise of the new social analysis, exemplified by Booth's enquiries, did not altogether lessen their inclination, except that they became more cautious and circumspect in their

[80] A. L. Bowley and A. R. Burnett-Hurst, *Livelihood and Poverty* (1915), 41–2. In place of York, read Stanley. For a general discussion of these points see J. H. Treble, *Urban Poverty in Britain 1830–1914* (1979), 16, 54, and ch. 1 and 2.

[81] Harris, *Unemployment and Politics*, p. 36.

[82] *Poor Law Commission*, evidence (Webb), pp. 186 and 195, Q. 93129, and *Minority Report*, pp. 191–3.

judgements.[83] But there was little such hesitancy with respect
to young workers and, therefore, few dissenting voices were
raised when the Revd Gibb proclaimed: 'The problem of boy-
work is not alone a problem of economics. It is a problem also
of character.' The work, said Gibb, 'becomes the strongest
formative influence' just at the time when the boy 'is most
plastic to receive impressions', and when the influences that
surround him were moulding his disposition. The existing
condition of adolescent employment was dangerous because in
addition to producing a 'casual labourer in the economic
sense', it encouraged a 'mean estimate of all that work
implies'.[84] The significance of this was explained by Beveridge
when, in agreeing with Booth, he confirmed that 'character'
and 'capacity' were inextricably interwoven with other causes
of unemployment. This amounted to saying that the supply
features of labour were relevant. Individual quality could help
the worker to resist unemployment (by virtue of possession of
'good' qualities) and also to maintain his 'efficiency' on those
occasions when unemployment was inescapable.[85] In this
respect, 'character' served a number of precise economic
purposes and was not meant merely to exhibit moral worth for
its own sake. Thus 'boy labour' was a problem not only
because it left the majority of youths without clearly defined
'skills' and aptitudes, but also because it could lead to the
creation of a casual class (exhibiting 'immoral habits of life'),
many of whom were 'unemployable'.[86]

7. SIGNIFICANCE OF THE 'BOY LABOUR PROBLEM'

The fact was that while the labour-market itself could be better
organized (and, as we shall see, the labour exchanges were an
attempt to do this), not much could be done about the nature of
the short-term demand for labour and, therefore, the ability to

[83] Stefan Collini has referred to the emphasis on character as a 'primary aim
of politics' in the period; see his *Liberalism and Sociology: L. T. Hobhouse
and Political Argument in England, 1880–1914*, (1979), 28.
[84] Gibb, *The Boy and his Work*, pp. 76, 78–9.
[85] Beveridge, *Unemployment*, ch. 7, *passim*.
[86] B. Webb, cited in Harris, *Unemployment and Politics*, pp. 44, 46; see also
S. and B. Webb, *Industrial Democracy*, pp. 784–5; Beveridge, *Unemployment*,
ch. 7, 'The Personal Factor'; Booth, *Life and Labour*, ix. 393.

withstand the vagaries of the purchase and sale of labour power was critically important, especially at a time of social and political change as well as economic uncertainty. So at one level, then, the significance of the 'boy labour problem' for contemporaries, lay in the fact that the work was 'uneducative'; it offered 'little mental or moral discipline'; no proper occupational movement; and, in one way or another, it created inefficient and unskilled labourers and excessively specialized apprentices. In addition, however, these same factors also hindered the development of a different kind of labour demand from employers, thereby compelling them to rely on the existing quality of young workers. Consequently, the problem appeared to be perpetual.

It must now be clear that at another level, the debate on the juvenile labour-market was not simply a matter of economics for there was a social dimension to the critique which did so much both to create new images of youth and to consolidate many of those already in existence. When reformers referred to the 'boy labour' issue, no one doubted that they were also expressing concern about alleged indiscipline, precocious independence, immorality, potential delinquency, lack of self-control, thriftlessness, and so on. The evolution of the image of youth, however, was not just a matter of two separate but related critiques,—the economic and the social,—it also depended, as is shown below, upon the 'discovery' of 'adolescence', in particular working-class adolescence, principally through child psychology, as a distinct stage of life during which 'influences' were of enormous importance. In this way, with the help of a freshly painted psychological portrait, which was used for illustrative purposes, reformers were able to offer a comprehensive definition of, and explanation for, the economic and social behaviour of young people.

Finally, the question needs to be asked whether or not in mounting their critique, reformers were describing a new situation. In some respects, much of what they perceived had been a feature of the juvenile labour-market for most of the nineteenth century: the 'haphazard' transition from school to work; the 'excessive' amount of occupational mobility; 'blind-alley' jobs; and anxieties about the 'decline' of apprenticeship. To this extent, the 'problem' had a long paternity. The difference between earlier expressions of unease, and the critique that began to appear in the 1880s, reaching a crescendo in the Edwardian era, lay partly in the economic and social circumstances of the latter period: the rediscovery of poverty; the new awareness of unemployment, casual labour, and low wages; the 'labour problem' and the implications of technological change; and, a not inconsiderable influence, the fear of urban degeneration and racial deterioration. The difference was also to be found in intellectual and political ambitions: the 'revolution' in the social sciences; the reinterpretation of individualism and collectivism; the emergence of class politics and the search for political order.

Of course problems of any description are never separate from their environment. However, it was not just that this had changed; the objective condition of juvenile labour had also been altered. There had been a substantial increase in the numbers of adolescents employed in apparently dead-end clerical and messenger-type occupations; the growth of a semi-skilled work-force was affecting the distribution and nature of 'skill'; and, similarly, the condition of apprenticeship was evolving under the impact of increasing mechanization and specialization of process. Reformers were often confused, they often misunderstood and exaggerated the extent of the problem, but, nevertheless, their perceptions were not entirely misconceived.

4. Social Science and Working-Class 'Adolescence': From Idea to Social Fact

The observation that 'charting the way in which concepts long available come to acquire a new prominence and resonance . . . would require a major effort of intellectual history' is especially apposite to 'adolescence'.[1] But no such grand aspiration is intended here. Instead, what follows is an attempt to put the concept into its Edwardian context, and to identify the different means by which it was popularized, notably the social sciences, in particular child psycholgy. The aim is to examine the sources from which the images of youth were in part derived, and through which the critiques could be sustained.

John R. Gillis places the 'discovery' of adolescence in the period 1870-1900 and attributes it to the greater dependency of middle-class youth in their reformed public schools, in contrast to the 'freedom' of young wage-earners who were regarded as precociously independent.[2] After 1900, he says, reformers imposed adolescence on the working-class in an attempt to enforce their own norms.[3] There is no denying that the concept achieved an extraordinary popularity among Edwardian social scientists, educationalists, and youth workers. Victorian observers, however, though they may have grasped the significance of the teenage years were not fully aware of the conceptual implications of the term. And Gillis says as much when he writes that their discovery corresponded 'to what *we now call "adolescence"* '.[4] This amounts to an admission that they did not use the word and, therefore, it seems reasonable to

---

[1] S. Collini, 'The Idea of "Character" in Victorian Political Thought', *Transactions of the Royal Historical Society* (1986), 38.

[2] J. R. Gillis, *Youth and History: Traditions and Change in European Age Relations, 1770—Present* (1974), ch. 3 and 4.

[3] Ibid., p. 133.

[4] Ibid., p. 102. My emphasis.

say that the 'popular' understanding of the term as a concept had far less to do with public schools (though without denying their importance in this respect) and, as is argued below, far more to do with the economic and social critiques of young wage-earners, and with the Child-Study Movement, especially the work of the American psychologist G. Stanley Hall and his British followers. The fact is that recognition of the concept's analytical uses occurred among Edwardian rather than late Victorian commentators, and was principally concerned with working-class youth.[5]

Lawrence Stone, however, has claimed that the debate about the nature and emergence of 'adolescence' is far more about 'boundaries and definitions than about concrete social realities', and that the difference between 'youth' and 'adolescence' is 'mainly one of terminology'.[6] In some respects, Stone is correct. The debate is concerned with the definition of a certain kind of phenomenon, but perceptions (or the perception) of social realities are always conditioned by definitions and boundaries; after all, it is these which make the realities 'real' and comprehensible. The argument presented here suggests that the definitions and boundaries of the ' boy labour' reformers were inseparable from their perceptions of social realities on at least two levels. First, the evolution of the concept of adolescence was part of the process by which they sought to understand certain attitudes and behaviour patterns, including precocity, delinquency, and what was always known as 'character'. Secondly, once young people began to be perceived in terms of a psychological perspective, then 'social reality' was changed—if only because research findings from the field of child psychology in part altered, and in part confirmed, but also enlarged contemporary knowledge of the condition of youth.

Broadly speaking, during the Edwardian years the professional middle classes came to have a precise notion of the 'working boy' who was rapidly being scientifically and socio-

[5] This point is well made in the case of America by J. Kett, *Rites of Passage: Adolescence in America 1790 to the Present* (1977), ch. 8.

[6] L. Stone, 'The Family in the 1980s. Past Achievements and Future Trends', *Journal of Interdisciplinary History*, 12/1 (Summer 1981), 69.

logically defined as an 'adolescent'.[7] This is not to say that previous generations had no understanding of either the medical or psychological characteristics of adolescence, rather it is to emphasize that during the period a nineteenth-century 'idea' evolved into a twentieth-century 'social fact'.[8] One of the main causes of this transformation was the series of well-known debates on the social problem, which began in the 1880s with the rediscovery of poverty and specified the effects of bad housing, ill-health, inadequate wages, and unemployment on the racial, social, and political constitution of the urban population. The examination of these issues helped to identify the young worker in economic and social terms, especially in relation to adult casual labour and the responsibilities of husbands, fathers, and voters. Consequently, young people, 'adolescents', were no longer seen simply as an irritant to the efficient functioning of the social organism, but as an integral feature of it. The other main cause was the new psychology (itself the product of social and scientific developments) which served to stimulate a new awareness of and a new interest in the biological and psychological constituents of youth. The transformation, however, could not have occurred if the psychological research had been purely 'scientific'. But Hall's picture of adolescence had a surfeit of social appeal which made it irresistable to youth workers, sociologists, educationalists, moralists and others; it was they who really 'discovered' the working-class adolescent. In effect, they took the portrait painted by Hall and his disciples and, ignoring its theoretical applicability to youth *per se* as a universal stage of growth, they used it to focus on young workers, on youth in the streets, on delinquents, on 'visible', that is, working-class youth.

1. THE SOCIAL SCIENCES

The basic framework for this part of the argument is derived from the writings of Reba Soffer who maintains that between

---

[7] For a feminist account of some attitudes toward girls, see C. Dyhouse, *Girls Growing Up in Late Victorian and Edwardian England* (1981).

[8] D. Bakan, 'Adolescence in America: from Idea to Social fact', *Daedalus* (Fall 1971), 979–95.

1880 and 1914 there was 'a genuine, vital revolution in the contents, methodology, and purposes of social thought'.[9] The exact nature of this revolution has been questioned,[10] but it is useful for our purposes because it draws attention to the role of social science in formulating knowledge and in making it relevant to social policy. It also emphasizes the dynamic nature of these sciences; they are shown as developing, debating, and investigating. Soffer chooses as 'revolutionaries' Alfred Marshall, William James, and Graham Wallas; and as 'revisionist' (élitist) she selects William McDougall and Wilfred Trotter.[11] There were, of course, many other important figures who were also revolutionizing social thought to a greater or lesser extent, such as Booth and Rowntree, Beveridge and the Webbs, and Hobhouse, Pearson, and Hobson. Nevertheless, her inclusion of James, Wallas, Trotter, and McDougall illustrates the significant role played by social psychology in the formation and expression of political and social attitudes and heralds its importance in the evolution of certain family welfare and penal reform schemes after 1918. And even prior to this date it was evident that the work of psycho-medical professionals was becoming central to the portrayal of young people as being by definition in need of 'care and protection'.

The social sciences in general, however, were able to command an audience because they could be used as 'an ordering tool for imposing rational and moral imperatives upon the given anarchy of economic, social, and political conflict.'[12] Practitioners were attempting to shape a disparate body of phenomena; they were trying to understand new forces about many of which they were apprehensive, and they were also striving to confront, for a mixture of personal, professional, religious, and political reasons, a society that was evolving in ways which were in some respects as equally dramatic as the

[9] R. Soffer, 'The Revolution in English Social Thought, 1880–1914', *American Historical Review* 75/7, (1970), 1938; a fuller discussion is given in her book, *Ethics and Society in England: The Revolution in the Social Sciences, 1870–1914* (1978).

[10] For a criticism, see S. Collini, 'Political Theory and the "Science of Society" in Victorian Britain', *Historical Journal* 23/1,(Mar. 1980), 223–36.

[11] On McDougall and Trotter, see R. N. Soffer 'The New Elitism: Social Psychology in Pre-War England', *Journal of British Studies*, 8 (1969), 111–40.

[12] Soffer, ' Revolution in Engish Social Thought', p. 1941.

first phase of the Industrial Revolution. Mid-Victorian social thought was of little use in diagnosing the multi-faceted problems of mass urbanization, industrial reorganization, poverty, and unemployment; and, as it could not diagnose them, so it could not be used to conceive of remedies. As Soffer says, the revolution began after 1880 'in response to the inadequate content of existing social theory, the inadequate condition of social reality, and the inability of nineteenth-century social science to deal with these inadequacies systematically and successfully'.[13] The impact of the 'revolution' was to lead to a redefinition of what was considered to be relevant to social science by 'enlarging the narrow concerns of earlier reformers with individuals or small groups and by limiting theoretical analysis to the specific social anomalies that demand immediate and critical attention'.[14] Perhaps most important was the belief in planning so that 'irrationality' and 'inhumanity' could be defeated. Those involved disagreed about many things, 'but they shared the conviction that no part of society could be left to develop haphazardly'.[15] Or, put another way, they believed the world was knowable and could be controlled. This revolution, like others, was born out of optimism.

All this may seem far removed from the 'boy labour problem' and psycho-medical perceptions of young workers as 'adolescents': it is not. The reformers and social scientists (and they were often one and the same) who investigated and debated boy labour, albeit in some cases as part of larger inquiries (as did, for example, Booth, the Webbs and Beveridge), were themselves activists in the movement for change in the contents, methodologies, and purposes of social thought. Thus their analysis of the juvenile labour-market and their social critique of the young wage-earners was directly related to what has been called in another context, 'the search for order'.[16] It is significant that throughout the debate the theme which constantly recurs is that of disorder, fickleness, irregularity,

---

[13] Ibid., p. 1952. See also P. Ford, *Social Theory and Social Practice* (1968), pt. 2.

[14] Soffer, 'Revolution in English Social Thought', p. 1953.

[15] Ibid., p. 1961.

[16] R. H. Wiebe, *The Search for Order, 1877–1920* (1967).

indiscipline, and lack of self-control, in short, a life-style characterized by apparently irrational mental and physical behaviour. The concept of adolescence as the social psychologists developed it and as other social scientists and educationalists adopted it, was important for categorizing knowledge of youth: it delineated reference points; it established norms; and, moreover, it facilitated a more precise age-structuring of the urban population at a time when commentators were eager to know as much as possible about what they regarded as the pathology of urbanism.

1.1 Socio-economic studies

Between 1880 and 1914 British working-class life and labour was described and examined on a scale not witnessed since the early Victorian years. Numerous publications examined the living and working conditions for men, women, youths, and children within the context of the family, unemployment, housing, health, education, recreation, and crime.[17] Probably the majority of these accounts originated in the desire to know and to understand at least the relationship between poverty and progress, if not something more. And the roll-call of sociological thinkers who participated in the search for a solution (or solutions) to the social problem is impressively self-evident from the list of authors who appeared in the pages of the *Sociological Papers* and later the *Sociological Review*.[18] At the time, few of the members of the Sociological Society were 'sociologists', but rather 'a mixed bag of historians and philosophers, biologists, journalists, politicians and clergymen, town planners, geographers and businessmen'.[19] Out of

[17] See e.g. almost any issue of the *Sociological Review* and the *Eugenics Review*. A selection of the investigative literature would include, in addition to Booth and Rowntree, the work of the Charity Organisation Society and its various reports, such as *The Unskilled Labour* (1908); reports by local statistical societies, e.g. *How the Casual Labourer Lives* (1909); and E. G. Howarth and M. Wilson, *West Ham, A Study in Social and Industrial Problems* (1907); Mrs Pember Reeves, *Round About a Pound a Week* (1914); Lady F. Bell, *At the Works* (1907); C. B. Hawkins, *Norwich, A Social Study* (1910); C. V. Butler, *Social Conditions in Oxford* (1912), and the writings of such prolific theorists as the Webbs and Helen Bosanquet.
[18] See especially the three volumes of *Sociological Papers* and the professional status of contributors to the *Sociological Review*.
[19] P. Abrams, *The Origins of British Sociology, 1834–1914* (1968), 101–43,

the jamboree of ideas, there came a kind of coherence, or at least an agreement that what was needed to 'revolutionize' social thought (and incidentally to match the economic and social critique of Marxian socialists such as Hyndman) was a form of analysis which appreciated 'the interconnections of poverty and wealth, work and the market, law and welfare'.[20] In their search for an 'organic conception of society' these theorists and activists not only gave meaning to individual experiences by translating them into 'a language of social progress and social organization' but also sought to translate the disparate elements within classes, sexes, and age-groups into a similar organic conception.[21]

Many of those who worked in the spirit of sociological investigation were foremost in identifying 'youth' as figuring in the social problem. In precise terms this meant seeing youth in relation to the structure of the family, to the organization of the labour-market, to employee efficiency, and to racial health. In one of his first papers Booth had signalled the importance of understanding social organization, and not just adding new information to old. There was, he said, a general state of 'helplessness' among all sections of society—the workers were helpless to obtain better wages, the manufacturers were confined by thoughts of competition, the rich wanted to relieve suffering without risk to themselves, and the legislature was helpless in the face of closely circumscribed limits of legal intervention:

To relieve this sense of helplessness, the problems of human life must be better stated. The a priori reasoning of political economy . . . fails from want of reality. At its base are a series of assumptions very imperfectly connected with the observed facts of life. We need to begin with a true picture of the modern industrial organism, the interchange of service, the exercise of faculty, the demands and satisfaction of service.[22]

and J. R. Halliday, 'The Sociological Movement: The Sociological Society and the Genesis of Academic Sociology in Britain', *Sociological Review*, 16/3, (Nov. 1968), 377–98.

[20] Abrams, *Origins of British Sociology*, p. 84.

[21] Ibid., 84–5.

[22] *Journal of the Royal Statistical Society* (1887), quoted in Abrams, *Origins of British Sociology*, p. 85.

During the course of the inquiries it became obvious that youth had its place in the 'true picture', and that it had definite characteristics which could be sociologically, economically, educationally, and psychologically defined.

The inquiries of the period are too familiar to require further description, but it is worth remembering that several of them gave special consideration to adolescents. We have only to think of Booth's volumes, throughout which there is an appreciation of young people as actively involved in economic and social life: there are frequent references to their work as apprentices and labourers, to their role as supplementary wage-earners and to the insulation of the juvenile labour-market.[23] Rowntree also considered the teen-aged employee as a contributor to the family income; the survey of Norwich devoted a whole chapter to 'Boy Labour and Industrial Education', besides referring to the economic relationship between parents and their female children; the majority of the tables in Bowley and Hurst's study of six towns aimed to distinguish between adult wages and those of 'lads and boys under 20'; and Violet Butler's account of working-class life in Oxford gave extensive coverage to the boy labour question and to voluntary youth organizations.[24] Apart from these studies, numerous other socio-economic texts identified the specificity of youth. We have seen that the Webbs' *Industrial Democracy* provided the first detailed examination (outside the Labour Commission) of apprenticeship and the machinery issue; Rowntree and Lasker's inquiry into unemployment opened with a chapter on youth unemployment; Will Reason's *Poverty* examined boy labour within the context of the family income; Helen Bosanquet provided a similar account in her book,*The Standard of Life*, where she discussed 'Little Drudges and Troublesome Boys'; and Beveridge gave a fairly detailed exposition of

[23] C. Booth, *Life and Labour of the People of London* (1897 edn.), vol. ix. This deals with age distribution of occupied classes, pp. 43–52; introduction of boy and girl labour; trades with exaggerated proportions of juveniles in them; wages and cost of living and apprenticeship; pp. 45, 350, 369, 400, 423–4; and (1902 edn.), vol. i, p. 43 for family earnings.

[24] S. Rowntree, *Poverty: A Study of Town Life* (1901), pp. 30, 59–60; Hawkins, *Norwich* , pp. 83 and 193–214; A. L. Bowley and A. R. Burnett-Hurst, *Livelihood and Poverty* (1915), 62, 123–4, 167; Butler, *Social Conditions* pp. 59–61.

juvenile labour in relation to the 'blind alley'.[25] In addition to these principal writings, the influence of socio-economic enquiry was most obvious in those of the leading 'boy labour' reformers.

It will now be seen that by 1914 there was a substantial literature on the social and economic problems associated with the juvenile labour-market. The first important Edwardian text, emanating from Toynbee Hall, and edited by E. J. Urwick, was the collection of essays, *Studies of Boy Life in Our Towns* (1904). But it was 1909 before the stream of books and articles began to appear.[26] The popularity of 'boy labour' at this time stems from the reports and hearings of the Poor Law Commission (and from the Consultative Committee on Continuation Schools).[27] During early 1908 the Commission heard evidence on the matter from Sidney Webb, Bray, Urwick, Sadler, and Tawney (who submitted a memorandum, based on an investigation he had conducted in Glasgow). As a result of their testimonies, which claimed to reveal a thoroughly disorganized juvenile labour-market together with the fearful economic and social consequences, Cyril Jackson began work on his special report. The fact that 'boy labour' was the subject of

[25] S. and B. Webb, *Industrial Democracy* (1897, 1920 edn.) chs. 8 and 10; W. Reason, *Poverty* (1909), 8, 82, 84, 150; S. Rowntree and Bruno Lasker, *Unemployment, A Social Study* (1910), ch. 1; H. Bosanquet, *The Standard of Life* (1898), 174–82; W. H. Beveridge, *Unemployment. A Problem of Industry* (1909; 1917 edn.), 125–31. In addition Alfred Marshall considered technical education, noting that the old apprenticeship system had fallen into disuse, and commenting on the 'growing demand for boys'; and A. C. Pigou, Professor of Political Economy at Cambridge, discussed young workers in relation to unemployment. See A. Marshall, *Principles of Economics* (1890; 1961 edn.), 181–2, 549–50, and 570; and A. C. Pigou, *Unemployment* (1913), ch. 5.

[26] In addition to official publications and the definitive studies of Jackson and Tawney, between 1909 and 1914 the standard works of the period included Bray's *Apprenticeship and Boy Labour*; S. J. Gibb, *The Boy and his Work*; A. Paterson, *Across the Bridges*; F. Keeling, *The Labour Exchange in Relation to Boy and Girl Labour*; A. Greenwood, *Juvenile Labour Exchanges and After-Care*; C. E. B. Russell and L. Rigby, *Working Lads' Clubs*; B. Baron, *The Growing Generation: A Study of Working Boys and Girls in Our Cities*: J. H. Whitehouse (edn), *Problems of Boy Life*; H. S. Pelham, *The Training of the Working Boy*; A. Freeman, *Boy Life and Labour: The Manufacture of Inefficiency*; and N. B. Dearle, *Industrial Training*. So large was the documentation that in his bibliography, Freeman listed over 50 books and pamphlets, more than 80 articles and 10 conference reports on various aspects of juvenile labour.

[27] For the importance of this Committee, see below ch. 8.

such special interest is indicative of the importance with which it was regarded by contemporaries. The government inquiries, then, not only provided a focus for familiarizing the public with the problem of juvenile labour in relation to poverty and unemployment, but also reinforced the occupational and social specificity of youth, with page after page of illustrative detail. In this respect, the debate on 'boy labour' may be said to have exemplified the 'discovery' of the working-class adolescent.

1.2 'National Efficiency': Eugenics, race, and physical deterioration

The importance of the national efficiency campaign in helping to shape and direct debates and policies concerning social reform programmes has already been mentioned, and attention was drawn to the centrality of 'the matter of physical efficiency'.[28] Consequently, socio-biological studies, popular and otherwise, did much to accustom contemporaries to a new awareness of young people. Nowhere was the need to be precise about the biological nature of youth more urgent than in racial matters, and nowhere was this more clearly demonstrated than in the eugenics movement, founded by the eminent psychologist Francis Galton, in 1904. The membership of the Eugenics Society was composed largely of statisticians, biologists, and sociologists and, via their journal *Eugenics Review* and the closely associated *Sociological Review*, they were in an excellent position to propagate their central belief, which was that the single most important element in the reproductive process was inheritance, or, put another way: 'nature' was more relevant than 'nurture'. The basic eugenic demand was that the fertility of the 'best stocks' should be stimulated, while that of the 'worst' should be reduced.[29] Eugenists were not all of one voice on the matter, being divided between those who emphasized either 'negative' or 'positive' eugenics, described as the 'discouragement of unworthy parenthood' and the 'encouragement of worthy parenthood' respectively.[30] Regardless of the emphasis, however, all those

---

[28] See Introduction.
[29] G. R. Searle, *Eugenics and Politics in Britain, 1900–1914*,(1976), 72–73
[30] On eugenics see Searle, *Eugenics and Politics, passim*; and C. W. Saleeby,

involved looked to young people as future parents and in so doing drew attention to the nature of adolescence.

But to appreciate fully the significance of eugenics in relation to 'adolescence' in particular, and to the changing image of youth in general, it is worthwhile recalling the climate of opinion in which the movement campaigned. In the words of G. R. Searle: 'The Boer War panic about possible physical deterioration, the preoccupation with "National Efficiency", and despondency about the apparent failure of "environmental" social policies, had between them created a political atmosphere highly congenial to eugenics.'[31] There was hardly a more typical feature of middle-class anxieties than the thought of physical deterioration and the accompanying racial themes of infant mortality and the class differentiated birth-rate. The frequently-cited failure of so many recruits to pass the army medical examination during the Boer War seemed to crystalize fears concerning the physical condition of the urban working class. In 1902, Maurice's alarmist claim that 'no more than two out of five of the population below a certain standard of life are fit to bear arms' confirmed the worst fears of those who were already acquainted with the critical comments of Rowntree on the physical conditon of army recruits in his study of poverty in York.[32] No doubt these revelations helped to establish the Inter-Department Committee on Physical Deterioration with a brief to enquire 'into the allegations concerning the deterioration of certain classes of the population'.

The Committee, which considered evidence on, among other topics, the health of schoolchildren, infant morality, physical exercise, youth clubs, and urban conditions, concluded that there were no grounds for believing that deterioration

The Progress of Eugenics (1914) and *Parenthood and Race Culture* (1909). See also *Report of the Inter-Departmental Committee on Physical Deterioration*, vol. 1, Cd. 2175, (1904); A. Davin, 'Imperialism and Motherhood', *History Workshop*, 5 (Spring), 5–95; J. Lewis, *The Politics of Motherhood* (1980); G. Newman, *Infant Mortality. A Social Problem* (1906).

[31] Searle, *Eugenics and Politics*, p. 9.
[32] 'Miles', 'Where to Get the Men', *Contemporary Review*, 81, (January 1902), 85; A. White, *Efficiency and Empire* (1901), 102–3; George F. Shee, 'The Deterioration of the National Physique', *Nineteenth Century*, 53 (May 1903), 797–805; Rowntree, *Poverty*, pp. 216–221.

generally prevailed.[33] Nevertheless, its report, published in 1904, recommended a school medical inspection service, free school meals for needy children, provision for infant welfare, and compulsory physical education for young people.[34] Such recommendations served to emphasize the importance of children and youths as guardians of the future generation. Moreover, in a section headed 'Risks of Contamination during Adolescence', the report specifically considered this age-group. There was no doubt, it stated, that 'the period of adolescence is responsible for much waste of human material and for the entrance upon maturity of permanently damaged and ineffective persons of both sexes'; all in all, it was a period 'of which too little account is taken'.[35] Here was one of the first calls for adolescence to be regarded as both racially and socially integral to the social organism, and in using the term itself, the report was heralding a new awareness of youth's biological condition.[36]

Despite the main conclusion of the Committee, much of the evidence it heard, together with its recommendations, seemed to confirm the popular view that an urban problem existed. But physical deterioration was only one feature of the race issue, the other concerned the declining birth-rate, especially the class inequality of the decline. This was the subject of Sidney Webb's famous Fabian pamphlet of 1907 in which he quoted the warning of the leading eugenist, Karl Pearson, that 25% of parents—Jews, Irish, and the casual labour class—were producing 50% of the next generation.[37] The fact that economic priorities were encouraging the 'servant-keeping class' to reduce their family size worried social reformers and encouraged them to campaign on behalf of education for working-class 'parenthood'. Eugenic doctors and educationalists, for example, argued for the domestic training of adolescent girls in preparation for their role as wives and mothers.[38]

---

[33] Even so, the debate continued and often in panic terms. Searle, *Quest for National Efficiency*, p. 61.

[34] *Report of the Physical Deterioration Committee*, pp. 84–93.

[35] Ibid., pp. 72–6.

[36] Nor should it be overlooked that the interest in youth and physical efficiency led to several calls for either military or physical training programmes.

[37] S. Webb, 'The Decline of the Birth Rate', *Fabian Tract* No. 131 (Mar. 1907); Searle, *Eugenics and Politics*, ch. 4, esp. p. 35.

[38] M. Scharlieb, 'Adolescent Girls from the View-Point of the Physican'.

No one among the eugenists had a keener appreciation of
the significance of adolescence than Caleb Saleeby, prolific
author and medical journalist, ardent disciple of Galton, and
self-proclaimed inheritor of his mantle.[39] Saleeby was eager to
impress upon his readers the scientific arrival of the concept:
'Those who know that the proper study of mankind is man
would certainly put down *the discovery* and the promised
recovery of adolescence as one of the great beginnings made in
our young century . . . This discovery has had no headlines,
even in the best papers, but it has had many in the best
heads.'[40] Adolescence, as a stage of life, was central to his
theory of biological progress. The very word, he wrote, meant
'*the birth of the adult*', and 'the adult, biologically and
eugenically speaking, is he or she who can become a parent'.[41]
Thus there was nothing coincidental about his reference to
Stanley Hall as the pioneer in the scientific study of 'this long-
neglected department of biology, anthropology, and psychology'.[42]

For Saleeby, 'the fundamental truth' was that 'adolescence is
preparation for parenthood'.[43] This, he wrote, was its 'natural
meaning and function'; and, therefore, it was 'the central
phenomenon of the life of any individual'.[44] The eugenist
could never know too much about it, nor ever exaggerate the
amount of care it needed in the scheme of 'national eugenics',
either in protecting young people in preparation for parenthood, or the 'feeble-minded' adolescent from parenthood.[45] It

Child, 1/12, (Sept. 1911), 1013–31 and her 'Recreational Activities of Girls
during Adolescence', *Child*, 1/7, (Apr. 1911), 571–86; and 'Adolescent
Girlhood under Modern Conditions with Special reference to Motherhood',
Eugenics Review, 1/3, (Oct. 1909), 175. See also A. Ravenhill, *Special Reports
on Educational Subjects*, vol. xv, 'Training for the Home Duties of Women',
Pt. 1, Cd. 2498 (1905), xxvi; and Dyhouse, *Girls Growing Up*, ch. 4.

[39] Searle, *Eugenics and Politics*, pp. 18–19; in addition to works listed in n.
29 above, Saleeby's other books on the subject included *The Methods of Race
Regeneration* (1911) and *Woman and Womanhood* (1912).
[40] *Progress of Eugenics*, p. 91.
[41] Ibid., p. 90.
[42] Ibid., 92.
[43] Ibid. For writers such as Saleeby, 'parenthood' also meant 'fatherhood' as
well as 'motherhood', though the latter always had a special significance. See
his *Parenthood and Race Culture*, pp. 145–59.
[44] *Progress and Eugenics*, p. 92.
[45] Ibid.

followed, then, that 'If ever nurture be worthwhile, surely it must be now, when the young being for whom we care becomes capable of bearing young on its own.'[46] Education was deemed to be of crucial importance in this context: it was the 'great question'.[47] This explains why 'nurture' in all its forms was considered to be so important: the newly discovered 'adolescent' was projected as being indispensable to the programme of racial regeneration; with proper guidance, the boy and the girl would be harbingers of a more efficient system of procreation and child-rearing.

So youth found itself strapped to a new image as guardian of the race. The first essential of nurture, however, was that young people 'must learn self-control'; but, bemoaned observers, how difficult it was to teach. Never, warned Saleeby, was eugenic philosophy more necessary 'than today, when the whole ethic of control and responsibility and keeping your promises and bargains and not being hustled along by the crowd, seems to be imperilled by modern forces and tendencies'.[48] In these circumstances, it was more urgent than ever before that 'the nation must discover and recover its adolescence' if the future progress was to be guaranteed and the gains of the past maintained. In practice this meant school lessons in mothercare and sex hygiene. And while the girls would learn the virtues of 'motherhood', the boys would be instructed in 'patriotism and fatherhood', since true patriotism, according to Saleeby, understood that the most lethal disease of nations was the '*decay of parenthood*'.[49]

Clearly, the eugenists envisaged a special role for 'adolescence', seeing it as important in itself in terms of the biology of the race and, allowing for its proper development, as the agent of healthy propagation. The specification of adolescence was part of the process whereby the different component parts of the social problem—in this case physical deterioration and racial superiority—were made into what Nikolas Rose has called 'visible units'.[50] The process involved entering into the

---

[46] Ibid.

[47] Saleeby, *Parenthood and Race Culture*, pp. xii–xiii, 120–44. See also *Methods of Race Regeneration*, pp. 33–8.

[48] Ibid., 98.

[49] Ibid., 98–108.

[50] N. Rose, *The Psychological Complex: Psychology, Politics and Society in England 1869–1939* (1985), 85.

'inaccessible corners of social life in the cities',[51] and one way
of doing this was to be more precise in identifying and thinking
about young people, for only then could a hygienic reform
programme proceed. And as eugenics was the intellectual
creed of so many social scientists and reformers, so the
particular nature of 'adolescence' became an important
consideration in public debates on issues concerning physical
deterioration, the birth-rate, and racial efficiency. If economic
and sociological enquiry helped to create a new image for
youth within the context of the social problem, eugenics gave
this image another dimension, ostensibly one of enormous
significance. But in linking the importance of the adolescent
stage to 'education', Saleeby and others further reduced the
opportunity for independent action (real or imagined) on the
part of youth; its very 'nature' was to be the justification for
adult control in order to ensure racial progress.[52]

2. THE SCIENCE OF PSYCHOLOGY: G. S. HALL AND HIS FOLLOWERS

The psychological perception of 'age' is a critical but neglected
aspect of the intellectual history of the late Victorian and
Edwardian periods. The present aim, however, is not to
examine the ramifications of that perception in relation to the
entire spectrum of social policy, but to show that child (and
social) psychology was principally responsible for the 'discovery'
of adolescence and, therefore, for the creation of the new image
which depended on the concept for its viability. Furthermore,
as far as the creation of the youth problem is concerned, the
significance of the psychological portrait is that, in allowing
the critics to draw upon those psycho-medical writings which
were popularizing the specificity of adolescence, it helped to
give their social and economic critique coherence, substance,
and status.[53]

The three principal participants in the production of a
psychologically constructed adolescent were G. Stanley Hall,

---

[51] Ibid.
[52] Saleeby, *Progress of Eugenics*, p. 87, and his *Parenthood and Race Culture*, pp. 120–44. This perhaps explains his enthusiasm for the Scouts and Guides in their pursuit of 'citizenship, character, discipline and patriotism'.
[53] See below, ch. 6.

J. W. Slaughter and Sir Thomas Clouston.[54] Stanley Hall, the American psychologist, was well known for his pioneering work on child development, for his theory of recapitulation, and for his ponderous but extremely influential and widely quoted two-volume study of adolescence. J. W. Slaughter, his pupil and disciple, lived in England where he was chairman of the Eugenic Education Society and secretary of the Sociological Society. These positions gave him access to important contemporary debates, and allowed him to disseminate Hall's views. But it was his desire to spread these views among the rank and file of all those who worked with youth 'in whatever capacity', that led him to write a slim volume, *The Adolescent*, first published in 1910 and reprinted three times by 1919. Sir Thomas Clouston, eminent Edinburgh psychiatrist and founder member of the British Child-Study Association, publicized his interpretation of adolescence through books, articles, and lectures.

While eugenics provided contemporaries with ideas, information and frames of reference, it could not offer an apparently neutral scientific language because its programme (or programmes) was always controversial. Psychology, on the other hand, at this time was not obviously associated with any particular political analysis and had made few, if any, forays into the public arena, except for an interest in the measurement of intelligence in schoolchildren. Since the 1880s a 'new' psychology had developed in Germany and the United States, and to a lesser extent in France and Britain.[55] During our period psychology established itself as an academic subject in several British (mainly Scottish) universities; the British Psychological Society was founded in 1901 by James Sully, the child specialist; and a few years later the *British Journal of Psychology* began publication.[56] Besides these institutional

[54] Other important medical contributors included T. N. Kelynack and Mary Scharleib.

[55] J. Ben-David and R. Collins, ' Social Factors in the Origins of a New Science: The Case of Psychology', *American Sociological Review* 31/4 (Aug. 1966), 452–3. See also Rose, *Psychological Complex* pp. 114–17.

[56] L. S. Hearnshaw, *A Short History of British Psychology, 1840–1940* (1964), ch. 11. Urwick thought that the importance of psychology lay in showing the 'social relations among individuals': 'A School of Sociology' in C. S. Loch (ed.), *Methods of Social Advance* (1904), 185.

beginnings, the other important landmark was the development of social psychology, building upon social anthropology and coming to its first fruition in the works of William McDougall, *Introduction to Social Psychology* (1895), and Graham Wallas, *Human Nature in Politics* (1908).[57] These books introduced a timely emphasis on 'instincts' and 'character' (two recurring topics in the psychological literature on adolescence) and, along with Gustav Le Bon's *The Crowd* (1895), sought to explain forms of human behaviour, thereby giving a new dimension to the debate on 'the city', the urban masses, and prospects for the 'new democracy', which was developing in Britain between 1880 and 1918.[58] These and other psychological studies were rapidly assimilated into the essential reading lists of reformers and social scientists, and from the 1890s there was also a growing interest in child psychology, pioneered in part by James Sully with his *Studies of Childhood* (1895), which followed on from some of the work of Darwin and Galton.[59] Undoubtedly the onset of compulsory schooling and the opportunity it afforded of bringing together large numbers of children was an impetus to scientific enquiry, as was the decision of the British Medical Association to establish in 1888 a committee to enquire into the 'average development and condition of brain power' among pupils.[60] By the late 1890s the British Child-Study Movement had been established, beginning with the formation in 1894 of the Child-Study Association, founded as a result of a meeting between a group of women teachers and G. S. Hall.[61] The Association,

[57] Hearnshaw, *History of British Psychology*, pp. 112–19, 185–96. See also J. Flugel, *A Hundred Years of Psychology* (1933, 1951 edn.), 134–53, 272–8.

[58] Hearnshaw, *History of British Psychology*, pp. 117–18, and Soffer, 'The New Elitism', *passim*.

[59] Hearnshaw, *History of British Psychology*, p. 268, and Flugel, *Hundred Years of Psychology*, p. 134. See also G. Murphy who stresses the importance of evolutionary theory, *Historical Introduction to Western Psychology* (1929), 389–90. The best introduction is in A. Wooldridge, 'Child Study and Educational Psychology in England, *c*.1880–1950', Oxford University D.Phil. thesis (1985), 19–63.

[60] Hearnshaw, op. cit., p. 268.

[61] Ibid. 269; Flugel, *Hundred Years of Psychology*, p. 134; R. J. W. Selleck, *The New Education, 1870–1914* (1968), 278. For the history of the Child Study Movement, see Wooldridge, 'Child Study', pp. 19–63, and A. G. Caws, 'Child Study Fifty Years Ago', *Quarterly Bulletin of British Psychological Society*, 1/3 (Jan. 1949), 104–9.

under Hall's influence, concerned itself with the 'natural development of individual children rather than the condition of the child population as a whole.'[62] It began in Edinburgh with the support of Clouston, while Sully acted as chairman of the London branch; and by 1899 it had its own journal, *The Paidologist*.[63] In 1896, however, stimulated by a Charity Organization Society report, and an international inquiry into physical and mental retardation among children, a Childhood Society was formed to continue work in this area, emphasizing the scientific study of the mental and physical conditions of children. In 1907 it merged with the Association to become the Child-Study Society with a new journal called *Child Study*.[64]

Despite the official independence of the domestic movement, it seems that most of the important research was carried out in the United States, while the British groups, for the most part, publicized and popularized the findings of Hall and his colleagues.[65] Thus from the earliest days there was a fairly intimate connection between child psychology, education and Stanley Hall. So it was not without reason that Sir John Adams, the Herbartian educationalist, proclaimed in 1912 that 'education has captured psychology', and that it was providing the main area of research.[66] There was, then, throughout the period an awareness on the part of those involved in educational and social welfare practice that child and social psychology were redefining old problems in new ways, posing new questions, and offering new answers. Given this to be so,

---

[62] Wooldridge, 'Child Study', p. 43; and for Hall's role in initiating the Child-Study Movement, see Dorothy E. Bradbury, 'The Contribution of the Child Study Movement to Child Psychology', *Psychological Bulletin* 34/1 (Jan.1937), 249–72 and W. Dennis, 'Historical Beginnings of Child Psychology', *Psychological Bulletin* 46/2 (Mar. 1949), 224–35.

[63] Hearnshaw, *History of British Psychology*, p. 269 and Selleck, *New Education*, p. 278.

[64] Hearnshaw, *History of British Psychology*, p. 269; and *Child*, 1/1, (Oct. 1910), 86 and *Child-Study* 1/1, (Apr. 1908), 1–3. See also Wooldridge, 'Child Study', p. 32.

[65] This is the opinion of Selleck, *New Education*, p. 279. But a different impression is given by Wooldridge, 'Child Study', pp. 19–63.

[66] Quoted in Hearnshaw, *History of British Psychology*, p. 254; and for education and psychology, see pp. 134–6 and 254–75. Sully was certainly both known to educationalists through his *Outlines of Psychology* (1884), and *The Teacher's Handbook of Psychology* (1886) which had run to five editions by 1909, when it was rewritten and enlarged.

it is reasonable to assume that when Hall came to release his 'great work', an audience was ready and waiting, especially in the Child-Study Movement whose members were drawn largely from among psychologists, educationalists, doctors, biologists, school inspectors, teachers, and parents. [67]

2.1 G. S. Hall

In 1904, after ten years preparation, Hall published his 'crowning effort in child study', the two-volume *Adolescence*, subtitled *Its Psychology and Its Relations to Physiology, Anthropology, Sociology, Sex, Crime, Religion and Education*.[68] The full title is significant because it illustrates the breath of his conception of adolescence as a stage of life as well as its implicit appeal to other social scientists, educators, youth workers, and parents.[69] What did Hall have to say about young people that so transformed the image of youth and led to the 'discovery' of the working-class adolescent? He was tremendously impressed by Darwin (he wanted to be the 'Darwin of the mind') and sought to apply his evolutionary theory to psychology and philosophy. Hall's particular adaptation of Darwinism was to resurrect the theory of recapitulation which argued that 'every phase of a person's growth represents one of the different levels at which the human race was once mature; hence, every person recapitulates or repeats the history of the race in his development'.[70] The idea of recapitulation was a favourite theme of the European Romantic movement, as was the concept of adolescence as a period of 'storm and stress' during which the sexual

[67] See K. Stevens, 'Child Study' in F. Watson, *Encyclopaedia and Dictionary of Education* (1921), 309. On membership see Wooldridge, 'Child Study', pp. 17, 33, 45, 54, and British Psychological Society Archives. Child Study Society Papers, *Minute Books*. On Hall's reception and his audience see D. Ross, *G. Stanley Hall: The Psychologist as Prophet* (1972), ch. 15, 16.

[68] Hall's other works in this area were *Youth: Its Regimen and Hygiene* (1906) and *Educational Problems* (1911).

[69] Kett, *Rites of Passage*, pp. 145–52 and ch. 8; and S. L. Schlossman, 'G. Stanley Hall and the Boys' Club: Conservative Applications of Recapitulation Theory', *Journal of the History of the Behavioural Sciences* 9 (Apr. 1973), 140–7.

[70] R. E. Grinder and C. E. Strickland, 'G. Stanley Hall and the Social Significance of Adolescence', *Teachers' College Record*, 64 (Feb. 1963), 391. See also R. E. Grinder, 'The Concept of Adolescence in the Genetic Psychology of G. Stanley Hall', *Child Development* 40/2 (June 1969), 355–69.

passions were aroused. In language strongly reminiscent of Rousseau, Hall described adolescence as 'a new birth, for the higher and more completely human traits are now born'.[71] What Hall did was to put these old ideas into 'the framework of post-Darwinian biology' so that 'the turbulence of adolescence' was linked to 'a wide spectrum of physiological and psychological changes determined by evolution'.[72] Henceforth adolescence was sanctioned with the mantle of evolutionary progress, with all the mysticism that this implied for youth as the standard-bearer of the future.[73]

Drawing upon a whole range of psychological and medical writings (his index of names had nearly 2,000 entries), Hall portrayed the adolescent stage as characterized by a number of unique features, among which two of the most important were a rapid acceleration of physical, mental and emotional growth and a new investment of energy. His own prose is more colourful: 'The floodgates of heredity seem opened and we hear from our remoter forebears, and receive our life dower of energy . . . Passions and desires spring into vigorous life.' Development, in all senses, he said, was far less gradual, 'more saltatory, suggestive of some ancient period of storm and stress when old moorings were broken and a higher level attained'. The comprehensiveness of the changes and their intensity were signals for a new birth: 'The functions of every sense undergo reconstruction, and their relations to other psychic functions change, and new sensations, some of them very intense, arise, and new associations in the sense sphere are formed.'[74]

Of all the characteristics attributed by Hall to young people perhaps the most socially debilitating was his emphasis on the apparent emotionalism of their behaviour and mental processes. The emotions were described as being liable to 'instability and fluctuation', which, he said, was *natural* during adolescence, and he claimed that these states were

---

[71] G. S. Hall, *Adolescence* (1904), vol. i, p. xiii. Rousseau had said 'We are born twice over; the first time for existence, the second time for life; once as human beings and later on as men or as women': W. Boyd, *Emile for Today: The Emile of Jean Jacques Rousseau* (1956), 96.

[72] Ross, *G. Stanley Hall*, p. 333.

[73] Ibid. 333–4.

[74] Hall, *Adolescence*, vol. i, pp. xiii–iv, and Ross, *G. Stanley Hall*, p. 326.

expressed with Hegelian logic as each one developed '[b]y contrast and reaction into the opposite'. Ardour, for example, in any form was followed by 'feeling limp, languid, inert, indifferent, fatigued, apathetic, sleepy, lazy'; similarly, depressive and expansive states existed side by side: 'self-feeling' and arrogance were often signs of bravado to hide 'distrust of self and sinking of heart'; and likewise with altruism and selfishness. Moreover, this condition could be exacerbated by immature reasoning. Youth, argued Hall, had a passion for 'callow ratiocination' as 'the tender intellect sometimes crepitates and grows dizzy in the orgy and flux and loses its orientation . . . in unifying the irreconcilable, in elaborating distinctions that have no existence . . . and a kind of reasoning mania is easily possible'. Adolescence, especially the early years, was also a period when psychoses and neuroses were more common than at any other time of life and when it was extremely difficult to suppress the 'morbid impulses'. These illnesses manifested themselves via great 'emotional strain . . . which some have described as a kind of repressed insanity that is nevertheless *normal at this period'.*[75]

One of the important features of Hall's portrait is his insistence on the normality and naturalness of the conditions he describes. This allowed him, and others, to present youth as the prisoner of its own nature. Even the healthy boy could be led into crime and immorality as a result of a 'blind impulse' on which 'consciousness does not act at all'. The significance of consciousness for self-control and for the development and recognition of moral and social 'principle' will be considered when the social critique is discussed, but for the present it is sufficient to register the claim being made by Hall, namely, that impulse could overcome consciousness and, therefore, some form of 'education' was necessary to protect the young person (and society) during the adolescent period. Of course, in his references Hall was introducing, or rather reintroducing, a psychiatric perspective in support of his essentially social criticism. And his middle-class audience had little difficulty in visualizing a progression from 'morbid' and 'blind' impulses to

[75] Hall, *Adolescence*, vol. ii, pp. 75 (my emphasis), 77, 533, and vol. i, pp. xiv–v.

the spectre of adolescent insanity, repressed or otherwise. So it was not merely coincidence that led him to cite Henry Maudsley, the great Victorian medical authority, who argued that such insanity rested on 'the conception that reason is an apparatus of restraint, superimposed upon intense and brutal impulses, and that in characteristic outbursts this curb is broken', and when this happens, savagery ensues, or 'dehumanization'; once the 'high social reflex' associated with self-control was lost, 'diffidence and reserve give place to pertness, self-will, turbulence [and] aimless iteration'.[76] Such was the threat posed by adolescence.

Put simply, the problem of adolescence, said Hall, was that it had awakened to 'a new world and understands neither it nor itself'. Without protection, guidance or care, 'every step of the way is strewn with the wreckage of body, mind and morals'. In some respects this alleged lack of self-knowledge (and self-control) was said to exemplify the very 'nature' of the age-group. Young people found themselves imprisoned by their own physiological and psychological development since, according to their critics, they had not yet learned how to control either their bodies or their psyches; they were forever being buffeted back and forth across a chasm of stimuli, and all the while they were unconscious of what was happening to them. However, the obverse of this vulnerability was that left to themselves, they posed a number of social, economic and racial threats. [77]

In order to understand Hall's theory of recapitulation, we have to appreciate his fears (which were widely shared) about the detrimental influence of the urban environment. One of the worst dangers, so he claimed, came with 'modern civilisation', which was putting 'unknown obstacles' in the path of adolescents who were themselves 'leaping rather than growing into maturity'. Such precociousness was seen as the harbinger of disaster, for if young people were to be properly developed through education, then adolescence had to be prolonged for as long as possible. But late nineteenth- and early twentieth-century American society was making this difficult to achieve:

[76] Ibid., vol. i, pp. 265–6, (my emphasis) 284, 293, 297.
[77] Ibid., vol. i, pp. xiv–v.

Never has youth been exposed to such dangers of both perversion and arrest as in our own land and day. Increasing urban life with its temptations, prematurities, sedentary occupations, and passive stimuli just when an active, objective life is needed, early emancipation and a lessening sense of both duty and discipline, the haste to know and do all befitting man's estate before its time, the mad rush for sudden wealth and the reckless fashions set by its gilded youth . . . [78]

In this context the (American) 'boy labour problem' was of particular importance:

The vast majority of American children now leave school near the dawn of adolescence . . . it is precisely this nascent and most educable period that under our present conditions we fail to reach . . . The decay of the apprentice system, the general uselessness of boys and girls under new city conditions, the specialization of industry, the utter inadequacy of the manual training movement . . . to cope with the present situation . . .make a grave situation involving inestimable moral and economic waste . . . [79]

The environment was significant for Hall because in common with many other social scientists he believed that its influence in 'producing acquired characteristics transmissible by heredity' was greatest during the years of youth, and this implied a certain licence for 'nature' which had to be allowed, within limits, to exercise its evolutionary prerogative. This meant that the cathartic experience was crucial: each stage of growth had to have full expression if it was to lead onto the next stage, and frustration of the former might damage the latter. During the catharsis, however, the 'barbaric aspects of the recapitulatory sequence' came to the fore; the young person experienced simultaneously emotional and psychological turmoil; this was a crisis moment: 'The whole future of life depends on how well the new powers now given suddenly and in profusion are husbanded and directed.'[80] Anything was possible, for while character and personality were taking form, 'everything is

[78] Ibid., vol. i, p. xv. See also J. Addams, *The Spirit of Youth and the City Streets* (1910), 3–21; and Kett, *Rites of Passage*, pp. *passim*.
[79] Hall, *Adolescence*, vol. i, p. 54. See also Addams, *Spirit of Youth, passim*; W. B. Forbush, *The Boy Problem: A Study in Social Pedagogy* (1902), *passim*; and Kett, *Rites of Passage*, pp. 215–44.
[80] Hall, *Adolescence*, vol. i, pp. xv, 50; Ross, *G. Stanley Hall*, pp. 310–11.

plastic'.[81] Educators were presented with a wonderful opportunity: 'No age is so responsive to all the best and wisest in adult endeavour.'[82] Left entirely to themselves, however, adolescents 'tend to disorder and triviality, and controlled too much by adults they tend to lose zest and spontaneity; thus the problem is to find the golden mean between both'.[83]

Stanley Hall's study is nearly 1,400 pages of half-digested references to the physiological and psychological history of young people. In the opinion of his biographer, Dorothy Ross, the ideas it contained 'were tied to biological speculations that were barely plausible, at best, and were constantly embellished with lyrical references to the psychological truth of the Christian doctrine', as well as numerous 'unctuous comments about sexuality'. And yet, emerging out of this, at times, incomprehensible mess, there was, in her words, 'a vivid portrait of the adolescent stage of life'.[84] In fact, it was the 'first systematic portrayal of adolescence' in the modern world', even though most of its components were 'already fairly commonplace in the nineteenth century'.[85] But the picture was to cast an uneasy shadow over youth as its strongest lines emphasized upheaval, instability, confusion, and plasticity, all of which necessitated sensitive handling in a carefully controlled environment: nature had to take its course, but not entirely untrammelled.

2.2.   *J. G. Slaughter*

The publication of *Adolescence* met with an immediate welcome, for Hall's sympathies were 'so well attuned to the needs of the day and so widely scattered among them'.[86] He directed his concept at contemporary anxieties and appeared to confirm what to many observers seemed to be a truism: 'Modern life is hard, and in so many respects increasingly so, on youth. Home, school, church fail to recognize its nature and needs and, perhaps most of all, its perils.'[87] There is no doubt

[81] Hall, *Adolescence*, vol. i, p. xv.
[82] Ibid., vol. i, p. 54.
[83] Ibid., vol. ii, p. 432.
[84] Ross, *G. Stanley Hall*, pp. 310–11.
[85] Ibid., 333.
[86] Ibid., 336.
[87] Hall, *Adolescence*, vol. i, p. xiv, and Kett, *Rites of Passage*, p. 221.

that Hall's message was enormously popular, as was evident from the demand for him to address meetings of parents, teachers, youth workers, and fellow social scientists. All the same, it remained a fact that his writings were very difficult to absorb and were often impenetrable. It was in an attempt to remedy this situation that J. W. Slaughter published his rather prosiac but more accessible account, *The Adolescent*. The significance of the book for our purposes is twofold: first, it was deliberately written to familiarize a lay audience with a psycho-social approach to young people, which indicates the growing importance of psychology in Edwardian age relations; and, secondly, by simplifying Hall's views, it projected into the public arena a few fundamental and comprehensible ideas which could easily be incorporated into the social critique and more generally into the realm of ageism.

The chief characteristic of adolescence, according to Slaughter, was 'emotional change', since intellectual trans-formations followed and were subsidiary to those of an 'emotional character'. Similarly, the main distinction between savagery and civilization, in individual terms, was largely 'a matter of the emotions', especially their organization and orientation. Youth, he claimed, found life difficult because it brought 'a higher intensity' to its daily experiences by the use of artificial stimulants which resulted in the alternation of excitement and depression. Indeed, 'the melancholy of adoles-cence' was seldom able to define itself, 'it covers like a fog the whole landscape of the spirit and it is intensified by a vague longing, the objects of which are unknown.'[88]

The emphasis on emotionalism, confusion and mental instability was further extended by Slaughter in his chapter on 'Pathology and Hygiene', where he explained certain forms of undesirable behaviour by relating physiological and psycho-logical traits to each other. As adolescence was clearly a stage of physical growth, with every part of the body having its own 'proportions of disease and its own accelerations and retarda-tions', so there occurred 'disproportion in growth', which meant that 'each organ and system has its time of undue strain with consequent liability to disarrangement of function'. One

---

[88] J. G. Slaughter, *The Adolescent* (1910), 24.

of the most important consequences of this growth phase was
its effect on the 'large muscles' which incited youth to 'activity
of a violent kind'.[89] The control of the muscles was crucial
because, as Hall had argued, they were 'the organs of the will'
and participants in the development of 'mind and morals'.
'Muscles', he wrote, 'are the vehicles of habituation, imitation,
obedience, character, and even of manners and customs.'[90]
Apart from the moral damage, violent activity could put undue
pressure on the heart. But Slaughter felt that the strain of
growth was most obviously reflected in the digestive system,
especially in the numerous ailments of the alimentary canal,
and these had 'psychological manifestations', some causal and
others consequential: youth rejected children's diet and developed an appetite which was 'capricious', showing a tendency
towards 'unwholesome' foods with a love of seasoning, pickles,
and sweets; there was also a craving for alcohol, tea, coffee, and
other drugs, including tobacco, to aid the process of contributing to the 'feeling of independence'.[91] Slaughter, like Hall,
vividly relates mind and body to morals and character. Notice
how swiftly the presentation moves from physiology, through
psychology and into social comment, and at each point the
image of youth becomes more pejorative.

   The rejection of wholesome food was only one aspect of
what Slaughter termed the 'perpetual inclination to rebel
against established order', which he saw as an impatience with
restriction and a desire for freedom. Echoing Hall and the
Romantics, adolescents were, he said, adrift from their 'old
moorings', and new ones had not yet been found. It was during
these years that 'degenerate tendencies of all kinds assert
themselves', and even a normal tendency or characteristic
could easily lead to crime. He was anxious, however, to remind
his readers that the source of all outbreaks of so-called anti-
social or criminal behaviour lay in 'the general psychological
condition already described . . . when new emotions and
impulses bring about an upheaval and re-formation of the
whole moral situation'. This 'condition' was inescapable
because it was regarded as inherent in the nature of adoles-

[89] Ibid., ch. 7, *passim.*
[90] Hall, *Adolescence*, vol. i, pp. 129–32.
[91] Slaughter, *Adolescent*, pp. 60–2.

cence and, therefore, 'years of discipline' were required before 'the newly made character possesses sufficient stability to keep it from being overturned in any one of many directions.'[92]

2.3. Sir Thomas Clouston

While Hall and Slaughter embroidered their treatises with romanticism and mysticism, Sir Thomas Clouston was direct and to the point. Adolescents, he claimed, were liable to 'indolence, laziness, ineptitude or even immaturity'; they had difficulty in digesting food, they were subject to 'foolish and impulsive actions' and were often possessed by 'cravings'. Moreover, it was at this time of life that hysteria, epilepsy, asthma, dipsomania, megrim, neurasthenia, and insanity first appeared, as did 'pathological, mental and moral conditions' such as 'perversions of the moral sense, of volition, uncontrollable impulsiveness, tendencies to law-breaking and crime, unteachableness, stupidities, morbid pessimism and melancholy', as well as 'perverted sexual and reproductive instincts'. Every normal adolescent, he said, 'showed a want of respect for law, a contempt for age, and a restiveness to routine'.[93] Such a breathless condemnation of young people made no allowance for either their integrity, their conscience or their reasoning powers. If want of virtue was 'normal' in adolescents, then this could be explained, once again, by their 'nature'.

Although little or none of this was new, the particular importance of Clouston lay not only in his status as a respected pathologist and author, who was aware that 'adolescence' as a subject was 'now attracting enormous attention by psychologists',[94] but also that his views were aired before the interested and 'progressive' members of Child-Study circles, which gave them a special relevance. There were two features of his description which were attractive to commentators in support of their own analyses. First, he drew attention to the developing brain cells which, he said, had to be trained because

[92] Ibid. 60–2, 72.
[93] Sir. T. Clouston, 'The Psychology of Youth', in T. N. Kelynack (ed.), *Youth* (1913), 3O, and his 'Adolescence', *Child Study* 5/2 (July 1912), 96–7. For more detailed treatment see his *The Hygiene of Mind* (1906), 154–96 and *Unsoundness of Mind* (1911), 199–206.
[94] *Hygiene of Mind*, p. 156.

all the complex qualities, summed up as 'character', resided there.[95] The significance of these cells (when properly 'trained') lay in their ability to act as the 'inhibitory or controlling centres of the brain'; although there was always the danger that while being stimulated, they would become ' "too explosive" '—'keenness' in youth was necessary, but it had to be 'regulated by sufficient inhibition'. The adolescent was regarded as being susceptible to unregulated stimulation, for at no other stage of life was the power of the cells to receive 'impressions' greater than during these years. The second feature, also involving restraint, was Clouston's emphasis on the 'faculty of inhibition'—it was 'the crux of all practical moral conduct'.[96] The faculty began to develop in childhood but at adolescence it was not yet able to order 'impulse and desire, passion and temptation.' Recognition of this limitation was crucial given the precarious development of the 'critical years' during which the maximum pressure was exerted in various and often conflicting and perilous directions: adolescence was not only a 'new birth', the 'crux of life' and the most important stage in relation to the 'hygiene of mind', but also it brought on a real 'crisis' in individual development.[97] Here, then, were reasons for imposing education, discipline and control on young people: physiological and psychological fact appeared to confirm the importance of regulating both their environment and their behaviour and, therefore, provided an active role for teachers, parents, youth workers, and social administrators.[98]

3.   THE IMPACT OF G. S. HALL AND CHILD PSYCHOLOGY

It would seem to be indisputable that between the 1890s, certainly by 1904 when *Adolescence* was published, and *circa*

[95] For the importance of the brain in relation to moral development, see his *Morals and Brain* (1912), 15–16, 21–4. See also *Unsoundness of Mind, passim*. On the problem of mind and brain in Victorian science, see R. M. Young, *Mind, Brain and Adaptation in the Nineteenth Century* (1970).

[96] *Morals and Brain*, pp. 17.

[97] D. M. Taylor, quoting Clouston at the Child Study Conference of 1911: *Child* 12, (Sept. 1911), 1044; and Clouston, 'Adolescence', *Child Study* 5/1, (Apr. 1912), 3–4, 7, and *Child Study* (July 1912), 90, 95; *Hygiene of Mind*, pp. 51, 154.

[98] On preventive measures, see Clouston, *Morals and Brain*, pp. 50–5.

1911 when Slaughter and Clouston were writing, the concept of adolescence as a physiological and psychological state ceased to be an 'idea' confined to medical practitioners and became a social fact of popular concern among various social and professional groups within the middle class. The significance of Hall was that he brought together the numerous professional perspectives on youth and synthesized them into a visionary concept with a multiplicity of aspects. Nevertheless, the question remains as to the direct influence of psychology on the development of the concept: how did 'adolescence' become a 'social fact' of public concern, and with what results for the image of youth?

The claim made here is that the ideas and views of Hall and his followers were consciously received by several of the most respected and widely-quoted 'boy labour' reformers, including youth workers and educationalists. Three themes in particular were influential: the notion that adolescence was in fact a separate stage of life with its own requirements; the psycho-medical features of the concept; and the psycho-social behaviour that was said to characterize it. R. A. Bray, for example, remarked: 'We are coming to understand that the period of adolescence forms a critical epoch in the development of the lad', and he quoted Hall on the struggle between sin and virtue for the 'youthful soul' and on the dangers of 'modern life'.[99] It was in some respects the most important period in the development of a human being. It is during these years that physical health demands the most careful attention; and it is during these years that . . . there is no real supervision or, under existing conditions, any hope of it.'[100] The same sentiments were expressed by C. E. B. Russell, whose definitive *Working Lads' Clubs* opened with a quotation from Hall:

Those who believe that nothing is so worthy of love, reverence and service as the body and soul of youth, and who hold that the best test of every institution is how much it contributes to bring youth to the ever fullest possible development, may well review themselves and the civilisation in which we live to see how far it satisfies this supreme test.[101]

---

[99] Bray, *Apprenticeship*, pp. v–vi. [100] Ibid., p. 198.
[101] Russell and Rigby, *Working Lads' Clubs*, frontpiece.

In a later lecture, he regretted that there was no subject 'more generally neglected or so little understood' as was adolescence. How many people, he asked, had read Hall's 'great standard work', and he urged teachers and social workers to realize and provide for the new conditions which separate adolescence from childhood.'[102] Barclay Baron shared this sense of urgency, warning that it was a period 'of which too little account is taken'; it was necessary to recognize that it 'is not an arbitrary division. In the physical life it stands out most distinctly, and in the mental and spiritual spheres also it will be found to have its special character.'[103] In putting the psychological condition of the young worker at the centre of his inquiry into boy labour in Birmingham, Arnold Freeman showed that he, too, regarded an appreciation of the teen-aged years as indispensable to an understanding of the problem: 'The growing boy's reaction to social and industrial circumstances is totally different from what a man's would be; it is only by understanding something of adolescence that we can understand the boy's behaviour amid industrial conditions, or estimate the force of the social influences brought to bear upon him.'[104] It was, he said, 'essential to have in mind' what the psychologists call 'adolescence', and he went on to quote liberally from Hall and Slaughter, emphasizing their views on physical, cognitive, and social development, in particular the 'Imperfect Development of Reason and Will', the 'Liability to Vice and Crime', the 'Susceptibility to Religious and Educational Influence', and the 'Sovereignty of the Environment'.[105]

The impact of psychology on the 'boy labour' group was

[102] C. E. B. Russell, 'Adolescence', *Converging Views on Social Reform* (1913), 44–5.
[103] B. Baron, *The Growing Generation. A Study of Working Boys and Girls in Our Cities* (1911), vii, 5.
[104] Freeman, *Boy Life and Labour*, p. 9. There was an interesting review of his book in which the reviewer called for closer study of adolescents in order to fit them for proper work. The review referred to the success with adult workers of F. W. Taylor's, *The Principles of Scientific Management* (1913) and to H. Munsterberg's *Psychology and Industrial Efficiency* (1913) which showed that selection was possible. The reviewer commented: 'The general good demands that there be established something in the way of a science and art of youth-culture, for the period of adolescence is most critical and rooted in the history of the individual, and therefore a matter of the highest concern to the community': *Charity Organisation Review* 36/214 (Oct. 1914), 290.
[105] Freeman, *Boy Life and Labour*, pp. 93–4, 100–7.

fairly profound in so far as it helped to both shape and sharpen their perceptions of the problem. But it was the use of the concept among educationalists which did so much to transform the 'idea' into a 'social fact'. The important role played by the Child-Study Movement has already been described, in particular the relationship between psychology and education. F. H. Hayward, a government inspector and a leading exponent of Herbartianism, was explicit in his admiration for experimental psychology and for the work of Hall and the social psychologist William McDougall. Under the influence of Hall, Hayward claimed to have 'broken with an English tradition', and that in setting forth just the barest outlines of his theories, he was making 'a useful contribution to English thought and life'.[106] It was, he said, important that teachers, parents, and employers should know something about adolescence, in particular the emergence of personality—a combination of will, reason, and conscience—because 'the great practical problem of the next two or three decades will be the problem of how to educate and train and provide for the adolescent'.[107] At present, however, youth was 'free from adult control', while being 'extremely suggestible, extremely open to the influence of ideas'.[108] Consequently, in order to exert the proper influences it was essential to understand the psychology of adolescence. Similarly, J. J. Findlay, Professor of Education at Manchester University, and an early member of the Child-Study Association, in his commissioned study of 'the school' for the Home University Library, devoted a chapter to a description of the stages of growth in which he quoted Hall, 'the chief investigator in this field' on adolescence.[109] Although Findlay portrayed young people as naturally 'difficult', he warned against exaggerating the 'storm and stress' of the period, 'unless his environment arouses the storm'.[110] This was a crucial consideration, certainly for those social theorists influenced by a psychology which had always

[106] F. H. Hayward, *Day and Evening Schools with Special Reference to the Problems of Adolescent Education* (1914), v, 1–2.
[107] Ibid. 6–7.
[108] Ibid. 15.
[109] J. J. Findlay, *The School: An Introduction to the Study of Education* (1911), 73–4. See also his *The Education of the Young Wage Earner* (1918).
[110] Findlay, *The School*, p. 76.

viewed the mind of the child as being in an interactive relationship with its environment.[111] Hence the vital importance of education in the broadest sense, via teachers, social workers and others in the caring services, all of whom would help the individual make the necessary adjustments.[112]

Nowhere was an awareness of the concept more self-consciously and more influentially displayed than in the writings of Michael Sadler, beginning with his editorship of a collection of essays which was a landmark in the sustained campaign for compulsory part-time day continuation schools. Sadler left no doubt as to what was under discussion: 'We realise, more clearly than hithertofore, how critical, alike in their effect upon physical health and upon character, are the years of adolescence, and how much more might be wisely done, by private effort and by public authority, to ward off the perils by which, in unwatched and unguided lives, those years are beset.'[113] In his position as chairman of the subcommittee which collected evidence for the Consultative Committee on Continuation Schools, Sadler was responsible for drafting much of its report. More than any other educational document, with its emphasis on the 'urgent and complex' nature of 'Adolescence' and 'Modern Industrial Conditions', the report identified youth in relation to a particular developmental period; its pages are full of references to the social, political and economic importance of the 'critical years', in particular the need to care for the young in order to rear efficient, adaptable citizens.[114]

In addition to its influence on individual and prestigious educational figures, psychology made its presence felt at conferences and in reports where, time after time, the call came for more control of, and protection for, the 'critical and perilous age that comes between immature childhood and

[111] V. Bailey, *Delinquency and Citizenship: Reclaiming the Young Offender, 1914–1948* (1987), 15.
[112] Though Findlay wanted teachers to 'restrain their hand . . . from a larger trust in human nature, and a sounder confidence in the wisdom of the coming race'. *The School*, pp. 79–80.
[113] M. E. Sadler (ed.), *Continuation Schools in England and Elsewhere* (1907), 711–12. See also pp. xii and 709.
[114] *Report of Consultative Committee on Continuation Schools*, ch. 5 and p. 39.

mature manhood'.[115] Perhaps it is an open question whether education 'captured' psychology, but leaving aside who captured whom, the two disciplines were establishing a close working relationship with each other prior to 1914. This is well illustrated by the appointment in the previous year of Cyril Burt as educational psychologist to the London School Board, the first such post in the country, and by the influence of the Child-Study groups as a means of popularizing the 'necessity' for psychology.[116] It is fair to say that the Movement (and the BMA's research into the physical and mental health of elementary schoolchildren) helped to familiarize, partly through a lecture programme, the teaching and the growing child-care professions with contemporary psychological research, and with the social and educational significance of identifying the stages of human growth in psycho-medical terms.[117] One reason why Hall was so well received among professionals of this kind, was that he offered an analysis which provided a comprehensive explanation of youth while simultaneously telling the professions that they were imperative for its proper development.[118] 'Adolescence' was a handy image; a set of compressed references which enabled certain groups of adults to persuade themselves that they understood young people, especially young wage-earners who were deemed both to be most at risk, and to pose a far greater threat than middle-class youth.

But there was another aspect to the impact of psychology

[115] For example, *School Government Chronicle* 16. Apr. 1910, 364; Ogilvie Gordon, 'The Social Organisation of Adolescence', *National Conference on the Prevention of Destitution* (1911).

[116] L. S. Hearnshaw, *Cyril Burt, Psychologist* (1979), 33–9; Rose, *Psychological Complex*, p. 199; Bailey, *Delinquency and Citizenship*, p. 33; Dr C. W. Kimmins, chief inspector of schools in London was not only an important member of the Child-Study Association, but also helped to initiate the appointment of Cyril Burt to the LCC.

[117] British Psychological Society Archives. Child Study Society Papers. Several lecture programmes are stuck in the Society Minute Books, *passim*. On psychology setting out to 'make sense' to the layperson, see Young, *Mind, Brain*, pp. vii–viii.

[118] In the USA, his influence extended to four distinct groups: youth workers; the writers and readers of parents' manuals for middle- and upper-middle-class homes; educators; and vocational guidance workers: Kett, *Rites of Passage*, p. 221.

which concerns its effect on the vocabulary of social observation. The writings and lectures of Hall, Slaughter, Clouston, and lesser-known figures were full of medical words and phrases used in conjunction with those which were commonplace and, therefore, easily understood, so that the former more or less altered the meaning of the latter. As a result, critics were able to use to their own advantage familiar terms which now had a new authority invested in them by virtue of seemingly more precise and scientific definitions: 'passions', 'desires', 'intensity', 'perversions', 'melancholy', 'confusion', 'mania', 'emotions', 'instincts', and so on. Furthermore, the accuracy of these popular descriptive nouns was also validated by the technical vocabulary which, spoke, for example, of 'motor power', 'functions', 'muscle culture', 'brain cells', 'the faculty of inhibition', and the 'psychological manifestations' of the digestive system. In effect psychology supplied a language which enabled social criticism of adolescents to appear an objective description of their condition. With the new consciousness of adolescence, commentators now had ready to hand a text laden with scientific references. In providing a vocabulary for identifying and examining young people, psychology not only helped to 'discover' adolescence, but also to produce a new and generally incapacitating image of youth. And as psychology claimed a role in analysing child development and the allegedly accompanying problems, so it was able to project itself as being indispensable to the solution of those problems.[119]

Neither is it entirely irrelevant to observe that child psychology was only one branch of a burgeoning science in search of status, as it addressed itself to numerous social questions relating to mass society in an urban environment, at a time when racial, economic, and political issues concerning conflict between classes and nations were predominant. Nor is it fanciful to suggest that there was a close connection between the ambivalence of adolescence as Hall and his followers defined it, and the writings of social psychologists such as McDougall, Trotter, and Wallas (perhaps Le Bon, too) on 'the

[119] Hearnshaw, *History of British Psychology*, p. 211; Rose, *Psychological Complex*, pp. 4–5.

crowd' and urbanization; writings which found their most popular and literary expression in the pen of the radical liberal politician, C. F. G. Masterman.[120] Without trying to push the analogy too far, adolescents and the crowd, as we shall see, shared some of the same characteristics: they were full of potential for good as well as evil; they were easily led and, therefore, misled; and both possessed a vital 'energy'. There was also a comparison to be made between the adolescent who, while experiencing 'storm and stress', simultaneously brought the race to the brink of a new era, literally and metaphorically, and the crowd who also manifested signs of 'adolescent' fickleness and instability, but nevertheless represented the 'raw material' from which the new civilization would have to be forged.[121] Likewise, the description of the adolescent personality in terms of 'emotions' and 'instincts' was matched by the use of the same nouns to describe the crowd, the intention being to construct a theory of 'character' which would help to explain and guide 'social progress'.[122]

Needless to say, there were important differences between the concept of adolescence and the other concepts used by social psychologists with reference to the urban malaise. In spite of these, contemporary anxieties tended to blur distinctions rather than clarify them. After all, reformers knew that 'modern life'—industrially, socially, politically, economically, personally—was confusing and threatening, just as

[120] C. F. G. Masterman, *The Condition of England* (1909); W. McDougall, *An Introduction to Social Psychology* (1908); W. Trotter, 'Herd Instinct and Its Bearing on the Psychology of Civilised Man', *Sociological Review* 1/3, (July 1908), 227–48 and McDougall, 'The Will of the People', *Sociological Review*, 5/2, (Apr. 1912). G. Wallas used the principles of psychology in his *Human Nature in Politics* (1908). See also G. Le Bon, *The Crowd* (Eng. trans. 1895). Two recent studies which discuss these and related issues are A. Lees, *Cities Perceived. Urban Society in European and American Thought, 1820–1940* (1985) and S. Moscovici, *The Age of the Crowd* (1981, Eng. trans. 1985).

[121] R. H. Tawney, 'The Economics of Boy Labour', *Economic Journal* 19, (Dec. 1909), 536.

[122] On the theory of 'character' see Hearnshaw, *History of British Psychology*, p. 189; on importance of 'character' for social progress see, e.g. McDougall, *Introduction to Social Psychology, passim,* and his later work, *Character and the Conduct of Life* (1927); A. Shand, *The Foundations of Character* (1914); E. J. Urwick, *A Philosophy of Social Progress* (1912). See also Collini, 'Idea of "Character" ', *passim* and *Liberalism and Sociology, passim;* M. Freeden, *The New Liberalism: An Ideology of Social Reform* (1978), *passim.*

everyone knew that the spectacle was unfolding in 'the city' where youth seemed to be beyond restraint and without any kind of beneficial influence. These two different and separate phenomena,—urban life and working-class adolescence,— came together in a single cultural photograph, principally composed by perceptions derived from the social sciences, and in particular from psychology.

5. The Boy Labour Problem: the Social Critique

In the introduction to this study examples were given of the ageist criticism to which young people were subjected throughout the centuries, and few of the 'boy labour' reformers would have dissented from any of those views.[1] However, despite the similarity between the earlier critiques and that of the Edwardian era, there were some important differences, both in the kinds of behaviour condemned by adults and in the nature of the explanations (and occasionally justifications) of that behaviour, explanations which drew upon child psychology.[2] In particular, when early twentieth-century observers referred to the 'boy labour problem', they had in mind not only economic, but also social considerations.[3] The habits of the working life were felt to be inseparable from those of the social life: the casual 'thoughtless' way in which the transition from school to wage-earning was made; the indiscipline inherent in constant occupational mobility, made on a 'whim', and often motivated by 'greed' for higher wages or by lack of 'perseverance'; the 'blind alley' leading nowhere, encouraging apathy and resulting in the creation of unskilled and poorly paid labourers without either hope or stamina; the 'decline' of the 'old' apprenticeship system and with it the opportunity to instruct youth in the rudiments of social discipline and respect for order and authority.[4] Consequently, after, say, 1900

[1] Introduction, pp. 15–16.

[2] Ch. 4, s. 2.

[3] Strictly speaking this was not unique to the Edwardian period for there had been a great deal of economic and social criticism of apprentices since the sixteenth century. See e.g. A. Yarborough, 'Apprentices as Adolescents in Sixteenth Century Bristol', *Journal of Social History* (Fall, 1979), 67–81; S. R. Smith, 'Youth in 17th Century England', *History of Childhood Quarterly* 2 (1975), 493–516, and his 'The London Apprentices as Seventeenth Century Adolescents', *Past and Present*, 61 (No. 1973), 149–61; J. Rule, *The Experience of Labour in Eighteenth-Century Industry* (1981), 95–123; J. O. Dunlop and R. D. Denman, *English Apprenticeship and Child Labour* (1912), 189–191 ff.

[4] Ibid., and W. Knox, 'British Apprenticeship, 1800–1914', Edinburgh University Ph.D. thesis (1980), 280.

the social critique, which in the 1880s and 1890s had mainly focused on recreational patterns, resulting in the formation of religious brigades and the club movement, was compelled to take far more account of the worker status of youth and of the demand for its labour, notably when proposing new means of exercising control. It was not that adolescent leisure time was no longer viewed as a problem by reformers, but rather that its context, involving individual psychology, physical deterioration, unemployment, poverty, and the quest for 'efficient' workers and citizens, had changed, and this context was important because it helped to mould perceptions of youth and, therefore, its image.

1. INDISCIPLINE AND INDEPENDENCE

The usual point of departure for the critics was an extensive commentary on the allegedly twin 'vices' of indiscipline and precocious independence, both of which were regarded as the primary causes of imperfections in individual 'character'. As these deficiencies were said to be most clearly displayed in the leisure activities of the young, so nearly every aspect of their recreation met with unfavourable comment, including their taste in food and dress.[5] But there was a deeper and ultimately more sinister dimension to reformers' comments, for 'character' was seen as the expression of an adolescent personality, rooted in an apparently immutable psycho-medical condition, whose most conspicuous characteristics were irrational and emotional behaviour. All the same, it would be wrong to exaggerate the importance of psychology in giving support to what were basically ageist prejudices. Although the psychological specificity was crucial, it was always accompanied by, and in many respects actually determined by, the interests and attitudes of social class. Within this framework indiscipline and independence were seen to have a vivid reality, especially as wage-earning youth was believed to be free of parental supervision.

[5] The definitions of 'leisure' and 'recreation' have been taken from P. Bailey, *Leisure and Class in Victorian England: Rational Recreation and the Contest for Control, 1830–1885* (1978): leisure—'Time is that which lies outside the demands of work, direct social obligations and the routine activities of personal freedom of choice'; recreation—'those activities and interests that form the typical occupations of leisure time', p. 6.

At the centre of the critique, then, stood the young worker who, in the words of Sidney Webb, was 'indisciplined . . . precocious in evil, earning at 17 or 18 more wages than suffice to keep him, independent of home control and yet unsteadied by a man's responsibilities'.[6] It was essential, he continued, to save London and other large cities from this 'ever-increasing crowd of stunted, half grown, and desperate weaklings', who grew into manhood, 'undisciplined' and 'untaught'.[7] Other reformers, such as Bray, Paterson, and Greenwood, who were concerned about the effects of urban growth on family life, including the alleged failure of parents to control their sons, pursued this theme.[8] According to Bray, in the 'lowest' type of family, there was 'no supervision . . . the boy is self-supporting, and troubles little about the home'; parents, it seemed, were often afraid to exercise their authority, 'lest the lad should take his earnings and go elsewhere'. The boy was in the position of a 'favoured lodger' who had to be well treated. Even in the best of homes, the father's absence at work all day left the boy free of parental care during the greater part of the week.[9] Bray feared that modern industrial and urban conditions were under-mining all aspects of domestic government: the 'city-bred youth' was growing up in a state of 'unrestrained liberty'; the 'old patriarchal system is gone'; the family has 'become democratized; we have in it an association of equals in authority'.[10] The 16-year-old, warned Alexander Paterson, was 'openly independent'; he expected his tea when he came in from work, regardless of the time; often stayed out late at night; and only in prosperous homes was there any significant degree of discipline.[11] The 'more or less independent wage-earner' also worried Arthur Greenwood: 'all restraint is cast aside . . . and the young labourer, at the critical age of adolescence, becomes a victim of whim and impulse, finding

[6] *Royal Commission on the Poor Law and the Relief of Distress* (hereafter *Poor Law Commission*) , vol. ix, *Unemployment*, Cd. 5068, (1910), xlix, evidence (Webb), p. 183, answer vii.
[7] Ibid.
[8] See below, n. 9–12.
[9] R. A. Bray, *Boy Labour and Apprenticeship* (1911), 101. See also his evidence to the *Poor Law Commission*, xlix, appendix ix, Qs. 96433–4.
[10] Bray, *Boy Labour*, pp. 102 and 170, and his *The Town Child* (1907), 50–1.
[11] A. Paterson, *Across the Bridges* (1911), 22–3, 125–6.

an outlet for his newly awakened energies in some form of hooliganism, and in the excitement of the streets and the music-halls'.[12] These were by no means unique or exceptional remarks, but expressions of the common view among observers that 'boy labour' involved a 'moral evil': fundamentally, 'a lack of wholesome discipline', exacerbated by the allegedly high wages which 'flatter his [the boy's] sense of being independent'.[13]

Such hostility comes as no surprise, but the extent of it is worth recognizing, as it brought together two of the recurring themes of the debate: the failure of the urban working-class home, and the freedom that was said to come with wage-earning.[14] However, the fact that the problem was thought to originate with young people selling their labour-power in the market-place presented critics with a dilemma: juvenile labour was an economic necessity, yet apparently it not only contributed to the social problem in terms of helping to create unemployment and a casual class, but it also gave the young workers a premature adult status which, in view of the development of the modern city, exposed them to an untold number of undesirable influences, thereby weakening their character and encouraging them to defy authority.[15] In some respects this was not an entirely new dilemma since there had always been a tension in the age relationship once youth was within sight of financial self-sufficiency. The new factor was

[12] A. Greenwood, 'Juvenile Labour Problems', *Child* (Oct. 1911), 31–2. For a different view of the status of the young (female) worker in the family, see E. Roberts, *A Woman's Place: An Oral History of Working-Class Women, 1890–1940* (1984), 40–5, and her 'Learning and Living: Socialization Outside School', *Oral History*, 3/2 (Autumn 1975), 14–28. The general impression given by oral history accounts is that parents expected their teenaged children to be in by 10 o'clock. But at least one boy crept out again after coming home: 'you get a little bit more independent then, because you were earning'. Family and Work Experience Archive' (Essex), 'Home Life after Leaving School', No. 31 and 1–75 *passim*. For juvenile workers in general see J. Springhall, *Coming of Age: Adolescence in Britain 1860–1960* (1986), 62, 63, 88.

[13] C. E. B. Russell, 'City Lads', *Child* (April 1911), 593; M. E. Sadler (ed.), *Continuation Schools in England and Elsewhere* (1907), xii. See also Springhall, *Coming of Age*, pp. 88–9.

[14] In addition to Bray, Greenwood, Paterson, and Russell, see H. Bosanquet, *The Family* (1906), 310, and M. G. Barnett, *Young Delinquents* (1913), 6.

[15] For references to the city, see s. 3 below.

that during the 1890s and early 1900s, as the previous chapter has shown, the importance of parental control and other forms of supervision and guidance was reinforced by developments in child psychology which popularized the uniqueness of the adolescent stage, portraying it as one of great turmoil when all the faculties were finely balanced. Adult influence, therefore, in all senses of the word came to be regarded as essential if the proper course of mental and physical growth was not to be impaired.[16]

The urgency of re-establishing control of adolescents and enforcing their dependence was usually presented within the context of schooling and in relation to precocity. This was useful to reformers because it gave a certain logic to their comprehensive disapproval of working-class youth culture. The process worked something like this: since observers saw the elementary school as the single most important agency of socialization, they regretted the sudden ending of its authority once the pupil reached school-leaving age. It was the place where the child learned good 'habits' such as punctuality, regularity, accuracy, 'prompt obedience', 'attention', 'order', 'self-control', and 'cleanliness', while at the same time being subjected to a 'constant moral discipline'.[17] Education, reformers admitted, was required not for its academic content but for its 'extra-curricular effects'.[18] Helen Bosanquet was in no doubt that the

greatest influence in our parish outside the home is beyond doubt the school . . . For good or evil the rising generation is there receiving instruction and discipline . . . in the face of all criticism . . . our children are being firmly and gently brought into line . . . I do not think we attach nearly sufficient weight to this fact in estimating the advance that had been made towards reclaiming the 'submerged' classes of the community.[19]

[16] The psychological factors have been discussed in ch. 4, s. 2; but see also below, s. 3.

[17] Bray, Town Child, pp. 115–26; V. Butler, Social Conditions in Oxford (1912), 163; E. J. Urwick (ed.), Studies of Boy Life in Our Cities (1904), 294.

[18] R. I. McKibbon, 'Social Class and Social Observation in Edwardian England', Transactions of the Royal Historical Society 28 (1978), 194.

[19] H. Bosanquet, Rich and Poor (1896; 1908 edn.), 50, also quoted in McKibbon, 'Social Class', p. 194.

Once the boy left school, however, he showed his 'outrageous impertinence, conceit, and disrespect for us who are clearly his betters'.[20] The recurring complaint was that within a short time, the freedom of the streets coupled with lax control at home 'have played havoc with habits of attention and discipline'.[21] All previous 'training' of the boys was undone, so that after a year or two, 'you can do nothing with them; they will be sulkily stupid.'[22] At the time when it became so necessary, the education of the working-class child came to an end.[23] As the Consultative Committee on Continuation Schools reported, 'at the most critical period in their lives a very large number of boys and girls . . . are left without sufficient guidance or care. This neglect results in a greater waste of industrial efficiency, and in the lowering of ideals of personal and civic duty.'[24]

Bearing all this in mind, it is not difficult to see that the concept of precocity helped to reinforce the projection of adolescents as affluent, independent, irresponsible, and disobedient wage-earners. But it was the haste with which 'the status of manhood' fell upon the boy that most worried contemporaries: 'the lad goes to bed a boy; he wakes up as man.'[25] Or, in the words of the Revd Gibb, the ' "golden gates" of childhood close with a snap: the boy seems to spring at a bound into a youth that is in haste to become manhood. The average boy grows up too quickly; and the forcing agency is clearly the work.'[26] Accordingly, 'Boyishness is suppressed: mannishness, if not manliness, developed.'[27] Careful growth

---

[20] Urwick (ed.), *Boy Life*, p. 295.

[21] Paterson, *Across the Bridges*, p. 212.

[22] H. Dendy, 'The Children of Working London', in B. Bosanquet (ed.), *Aspects of the Social Problem* (1895), 42; see also P. Neuman, *The Boys Club* (1900), 11, and R. M. .Barrett, 'The Treatment of Juvenile Offenders', *Journal of the Royal Statistical Society* (June 1900), 184. The deterioration of the school-leaver was a common theme throughout the literature.

[23] *Report of the Inter-Departmental Committee on Physical Deterioration* (hereafter *Physical Deterioration Committee*), Cd. 2175 (1904), xxxii, p. 73.

[24] *Report of the Consultative Committee on Attendance, Compulsory or Otherwise, at Continuation Schools*, (hereafter *Consultative Committee on Continuation Schools*), I, Cd. 4757 (1909), xvii, p. 16.

[25] Bray, *Boy Labour and Apprenticeship*, p. 103 and A. Freeman, *Boy Life and Labour: The Manufacture of Inefficiency* (1914), 90.

[26] Revd S. J. Gibb, *The Boy and his Work* (1911), 76.

[27] Ibid., 77.

was being overtaken by a hurried 'leap' into maturity.[28] Many reformers, being ex-public-school men, were conscious of the concerted effort made in the schools to prolong boyhood; indeed, to glorify boyishness.[29] Urwick made this plain when he linked precocity to the early age at which working-class children became full-time employees in comparison with middle-class children who remained at school well into their teens. Early school-leaving, he wrote, led to the creation of

a species of manchild, in whom the natural instincts of boyhood are almost universally overwhelmed by the feverish anxiety to become a man. It is at this stage that he begins with a disagreeable precocity, to imitate the habits of his elders—smoking daily an unwholesome number of cheap and nasty 'fags', acquiring with painful pertinacity the habit of expectoration . . . and adding to his vocabulary the wealth of coarse and profane expletives which defile all his ordinary conversations with his mates'.[30]

Reformers were obviously engaged in constructing a negative image in the following manner. The basic premiss was that although elementary education had been successful in teaching the approved social and moral virtues, the years of compulsory schooling came to an end too soon and, therefore, the transition from school to work was made too quickly, and usually without careful thought. This meant that working-class adolescents began their working lives in a 'haphazard' fashion and, being without any regulated supervision, were pushed into precocious attitudes and behaviour; the years of obedience and order were suddenly replaced by excessive freedom, disorder, and lack of guidance, all of which contributed to the dissolution of personal character. Once the premiss on which the image was based had been accepted, the second part appeared to follow 'naturally'. The word 'natural' served a useful purpose as it was a most effective way of legitimizing the critique: assuming that adolescents behaved 'naturally', it then appeared 'natural' that in the absence of adult authority,

[28] G. S. Hall, *Adolescence*, 2 vols. (1904), preface.
[29] On public schools and their influence see F. Musgrove, *Youth and the Social Order* (1964), 46–57 and J. R. Gillis, *Youth and History* (1974), 102–5. References to the extensive literature can be found in B. Simon and I. Bradley (eds.), *The Victorian Public School* (1975).
[30] Urwick (ed.), *Boy Life*, p. xii.

and encouraged by their new-found financial status, they would be free to follow their own destructive 'impulses'.[31] In fact, so the argument ran, they could not be expected to do otherwise for the psychology of adolescence proved that during these 'critical years' all adolescents were liable to display the same characteristics.[32] Among middle-class youth, however, such 'characteristics' were watched over and controlled by parents and teachers and, therefore, did not pose a problem.

2. LEISURE

Nowhere, it seemed, were the dangers of adolescent freedom and independence more manifest than in their choice of leisure pursuits. It was not simply the nature of the recreations themselves which concerned the critics, but that they exposed young people to thriftless and dangerous habits, while encouraging them to mix with friends of their own choosing (including undesirable adults). Generally speaking, disapproval was voiced against 'aimless' street life; the visiting of music-halls and the cinema; smoking and gambling; reading a 'low' type of literature; playing games in the wrong spirit, which meant lying and cheating; and, more ambiguously expressed, the social intercourse between the sexes, when 'coarse' behaviour was often too much in evidence. While there was some disagreement between reformers as to whether or not these activities were positively harmful, no one dissented from the view that they were at best 'unelevating'.

Whatever the specific matter of leisure activities, each occurred within the urban environment, which was always a determining factor in the social critique. Many social scientists saw the city as a kind of grand metaphor for society: they felt it had an organic and often diseased life of its own, and they shared in the universal recognition of it 'as the centre of modern social problems'.[33] The cultural significance of the

[31] See below s. 3 and ch. 5, s. 3.
[32] See ch. 5, s. 3.
[33] For a typical account of middle-class perceptions of adolescent leisure-time see Paterson, *Across the Bridges*, pp. 139–66. See also Springhall, *Coming of Age*, pp. 109–56. There is a vast literature on the city, but see H. Meller, *Leisure and the Changing City, 1870–1914* (1976), and (ed.) *The Ideal City* 1979); B. I. Coleman (ed.), *The Idea of the City in Nineteenth-Century Britain* (1973); A. Lees, *Cities Perceived* (1985), *passim*.

city is obvious when we remember, as E. J. Hobsbawm has reminded us, that the so-called 'traditional' working-class culture was made in the last thirty years or so of the nineteenth century.[34] If the social surveys of Booth and Rowntree showed a high proportion of people living on the poverty line, there was an even higher proportion who were experiencing a rising standard of living. And as material life changed, so too did patterns of recreation, with the booming popularity of football, the day excursion, the fish and chip shop, the new style music-halls, and, even more exciting, the picture-palaces.

Since the 1880s the theory of urban degeneration had held that cities were responsible for the physical (and mental) deterioration of their populations.[35] The town child was described as 'excitable and painfully precocious . . . neurotic, dyspeptic, pale and undersized in its adult state'.[36] Bearing in mind the impact of the Boer War, the *Report of the Physical Deterioration Committee*, and the scare over the birth-rate, it is not surprising to find that Sidney Webb's condemnation of 'boy labour' for creating 'a "weedy", narrow-chested, stunted weakling . . . who succumbs to disease', reflected a widespread contemporary anxiety.[37] Throughout the Edwardian period, the racial deterioration factor, or at least urban ill-health, continued to inform discussions about imperial security, economic competitiveness, and social stability. The consequences of urban conditions were most dramatically, and famously, articulated by C. F. G. Masterman, one of the leading 'New' Liberals, in the well-known collection of essays under his editorship, *The Heart of the Empire*, with its significant subtitle, *Discussions of Problems of Modern City Life in England*. As the new century opened, 'we are', he prophesied, 'face to face with a phenomenon unique in the world's history':

Turbulent rioting . . . [h]ooliganism, and a certain temper of fickle excitability [have] revealed to observers during the past few months

---

[34] E. J. Hobsbawm, *Industry and Empire* (1969), 11.
[35] G. Stedman Jones, *Outcast London* (1971), ch. 6.
[36] Ibid., p. 127.
[37] *Poor Law Commission*, evidence (Webb), p. 183, ans. vii. On physical deterioration as a political and social issue see G. R. Searle, *The Quest for National Efficiency* (1971) and B. Semmell, *Imperialism and Social Reform* (1960), esp. ch. 11.

that a new race, hitherto unreckoned and of incalculable action, is entering the sphere of practical importance—the 'City Type' of the coming years; the 'street-bred' people of the twentieth century; the 'new' generation knocking at our doors.[38]

The result, he claimed, in language similar to Webb's, was 'the production of a characteristic *physical* type of town dweller: stunted, narrow-chested, easily wearied; yet voluable, excitable, with little ballast, stamina or endurance'.[39] The effect of education only served to expose the town-dweller to the 'baneful influence' of the 'new sensational press'. 'Fear', he wrote, 'rather than courage is the driving force of common humanity,' and in the city crowd, there was 'a note of menace' mixed with 'evidence of possibilities of violence in its waywardness, its caprice, its always incalculable mettle temper'.[40]

Masterman's writings, though often quoted, are rarely cited in relation to the youth problem. And yet, in so far as they were representative and after allowing for the exaggerated tone, they can help to place reformers' criticisms of youth in their social and political environment. Furthermore, there is a revealing similarity between the vocabulary Masterman used to depict urban inhabitants and that with which reformers described adolescents.[41] The young worker was, of course, a member of the city crowd which in the opinion of many observers, made him simultaneously threatening and vulnerable. It was common knowledge that young people had always been involved in crowd activity, having participated in a number of strikes, including school strikes, and the impact of this should not be underestimated in a period of industrial unrest.[42] The question facing reformers was how to harness 'the immense momentum

[38] C. F. G. Masterman (ed.), *The Heart of the Empire: Discussions of Problems of Modern City Life in England* (1901), 7.

[39] Ibid., 8; and his *Condition of England* (1909), esp. ch. 4.

[40] Masterman, *Condition of England*, p. 120.

[41] This will hopefully become obvious throughout this chapter. See also G. Pearson, *Hooligan: A History of Respectable Fears* (1983), 71.

[42] D. Marson, *Children's Strikes in 1911* (1973), Ruskin History Workshop Pamphlets, No. 9; S. Humphries, *Hooligans or Rebels? An Oral History of Working-Class Childhood and Youth, 1889–1939* (1981), ch. 4; H. Hendrick, 'The Leeds Gas Strike, 1890', *Thoresby Society Miscellany* 16, pt. 2, (1974), 93; and Pearson, *Hooligan*, pp. 156–63.

of city life' for the development of 'the highest type of character'.[43] In the present state of things, the city offered 'one vast field of temptation . . . it lays itself out to feed all that is most restless, and rash, and casual, and disorderly, and adventurous'; it 'bribes' the boy 'to live for the day, and forget the morrow'.[44] The numerous attempts to enlist urban youth in organizations such as the Boys' Brigades and religious and philanthropic clubs were intended to counter the 'temptation', but none had been able to do more than partially subvert what many commentators saw as the source of the problem, namely, the culture of 'the streets'. [45]

2.1. The streets

The street was usually condemned as the place for 'hanging around' or 'wandering about', both of which were deemed to be suspicious activities, if only because they were said to encourage loud and vulgar behaviour, the widespread use of foul language, smoking, and gambling, and generally acting in a 'wild' manner. In her study of Middlesbrough, Lady Bell described young adolescents as 'simply turned loose' to 'go about the streets at the mercy of any temptation that may come their way', leaving them to 'grow up into a generation which will bring down the average of the deserving and the efficient'.[46] Other observers emphasized the night-time character of street culture with dancing and singing going on 'up to ten or eleven p.m'.[47] One of the most vivid descriptions, which exemplified both the accuracy of the observation and the condescension of the interpretation, came from the pen of a Christian propagandist on behalf of clubs:

There, on these dark, drizzly evenings, stand a knot of big, rough lads. Work is over, they are enjoying rest and recreation—that is to say,

[43] Revd W. Hume Campbell, 'Growth of a Child's Mind and Character', in *Converging Views of Social Reform* (1913), 42.
[44] Canon Scott Holland, Introduction to Revd S. J. Gibb, *The Problem of Boy Work* (1906), ix; see also Dendy, 'Children of Working London', p. 42.
[45] For youth organizations, see below ch. 7.
[46] Lady F. Bell, *At the Works* (1907), 138–9.
[47] Revd J. P. Paton, 'The Moral Training of our Youth', in James Marchant (ed.), *The Cleansing of a City* (1908) 8–9; B. Baron, *The Growing Generation* (1911), 13; M. A. D. Scharlieb, 'Adolescent Girls from the Viewpoint of the Physician', *Child Study* 1 (Ap. 1912), 14.

they are lolling in an archway, smoking bad cigarettes, and jawing and chaffing in their vernacular. Now they gratify their babyish cravings by a raid into a sweetshop; now their more manly instincts by a stroll into a neighbouring bar. Then they are out again, cuffing and quarrelling with one another, and shouting low jokes and giving rude shoves to groups of girls.[48]

It was claimed that 'six months of the idle, undisciplined street life' undid 'all previous training . . . it is extraordinary how a course of lounging outside public-houses will change these lads'.[49] The enticements of the streets were a particular concern: after condemning the 'foul language' of the 'working lads of our city', the *Parents Review* commented on the ice-cream parlours and chip-supper bars, with their 'glitter and inducement . . . and . . . inviting aroma . . . It is perfectly appalling to think of the moral damage that is being done . . . in these places.'[50] A Scottish enquiry concluded in similar vein that ice-cream shops encouraged the free mixing of the sexes, drinking, smoking, and 'rough horseplay', and were often the haunt of prostitutes.[51] Sweet-shops were frowned upon because they offered 'cheerful gossip' and an 'infinite variety of sticky things to eat', which besides being of such poor quality that they injured the digestive system and ruined the appetite for 'wholesome' food, engendered the 'pernicious habit of constantly spending money'.[52] The commentary on the streets provides an excellent example of the way in which a vocabulary of abuse seeks to distort objective behaviour. Thus the horseplay was 'rough', the desire for sweets 'babyish cravings', while the sweets themselves become 'sticky things' in contrast to 'wholesome' food, and spending money becomes a 'pernicious habit'.

---

[48] M. A. Lewis, *A Club for Boys. Why Not Open One!* (1905), 4. Contrast this with accounts given by boys themselves in Freeman, *Boy Life and Labour*, pp. 110–19.

[49] Dendy, 'Children of Working London', p. 41.

[50] Robert Black, 'City Life for Working Lads', *Parents Review* (Au. 1907), 619; and *School Government Chronicle*, 11.Jan. 1908, p. 60.

[51] Cited in Baron, *Growing Generation*, pp. 14–15.

[52] Ibid., 13; on food, see pp. 12–13; also Paterson, *Across the Bridges*, p. 141; and Robert Hutchinson, 'The Diet of Youth' in T. N. Kelynack (ed.), *Youth* (1913), 55–62. The psychologists also had an interest in food—see J. G. Slaughter, *The Adolescent* (1911), 61–2 and Sir T. Clouston, *Hygiene of*

Not all reformers were hypercritical in their observations. The Revd Gibb understood that 'the rich movement of the streets' had an appeal to boys: 'the rumbling of the 'bus, the hoot of the motors, an imperious fire-engine or a fallen horse . . . and the opportunity to chat with other boys'.[53] Alexander Paterson, though patronizing, also appreciated that 'the pleasure of mere gossip at the street-corner cannot be easily exaggerated. A group of boys leaning against a wall, or over the counter of some ice-cream shop will discuss football or county cricket from nine o'clock to midnight.'[54] Urwick was another perceptive critic who saw the street, on the one hand, as 'the place of do-as-you-please', of licence, and of disorder; and yet, on the other hand, as 'so strange a mixture of good and evil, so complex an influence in the growth of the boy and girl, of youth and man'; and as 'by far the strongest influence in the life of our towns'.[55] On balance, he felt that the tendency was to raise, not lower, the standards of action and thought, but this was true only when the street was experienced as part of a more structured life: 'The chief evil . . . is that there is too much of it; it fills too many hours of a child's life, so that its freedom, sociability, and opportunities for play lead only to habits of aimlessly killing time by knocking about waiting for some diversion to turn up.'[56] Implicit in these remarks, of course, is the search for a more ordered pattern of leisure; the street had a useful purpose to serve, provided it could be dovetailed into more 'rational' recreations.[57]

2.2. The music-hall and the cinema

The main objections to the music-hall were the opportunity it offered for rough and immoral behaviour, and the political and vulgar nature of the songs.[58] The general view was that the

Mind (1911), passim; and *Morals and Brain* (1912), pp. 31–6. Eating was to be seen as an 'organic habit', and both 'good habit' and 'food conscience' were important aspects of 'self-control'.

[53] Gibb, *The Boy and his Work*, p. 12.
[54] Paterson, *Across the Bridges*, p. 43.
[55] Urwick (ed.), *Boy Life*, pp. 296–7.
[56] Ibid., p. 298.
[57] The idea of the 'rational' is taken from Bailey, *Leisure and Class*, passim.
[58] P. Summerfield, 'The Effingham Arms and the Empire: Deliberate

music-hall was at best a poor entertainment, and at worst 'the gate to every temptation', frequent attendance at which denoted 'a careless and irreligious life': it undermined the development of 'character'; it was coarse and unelevating; it taught nothing and undid much; it could lead the individual into bad company, and anyway, 'the best boys do not go at all'.[59] It was not so much that the acts themselves were 'harmful', but that the atmosphere of the halls was 'low'.[60] Young people were exposed to an environment of 'beer, tobacco and spirits', while the songs were 'polluting', not especially in the words, but in the 'suggestions and innuendos'.[61] These criticisms led to the charge that there was often more 'indecency' in the music-hall than in the cinema. Arnold Freeman, for example, condemned the 'unwritten language of vulgarity and obscenity' which, he said, was known to the audience, but his main objection was to the 'unrelieved silliness and superficiality of it all'.[62] This kind of condescending attitude was common among reformers who claimed that the halls demanded 'no concentrated effort of mind, no fixed attention for any length of time'.[63] The reference to lack of concentration was part of a much more comprehensive critique involving class and age which is discussed below.[64] For the present, however, it is sufficient to see it as an important feature of the hostile middle-class view of working-class recreation as thoughtless, trite, and offering only momentary satisfaction, and the conviction that young people

Selection in the Evolution of the Music Hall in London', in E. and S. Yeo (eds.), *Popular Culture and Class Conflict* (1981), pp. 231–4; Bailey, ch. 7; G. Stedman Jones, 'Working-Class Culture and the Working-Class Politics in London, 1870–1900: notes on the Re-Making of a Working Class', *Journal of Social History* 7, (1974), 460–508; J. R. Springhall, *Coming of Age* ch. 4.

[59] Paterson, *Across the Bridges*, pp. 153 and 135; Rev. H. S. Pelham, *The Training of the Working Boy* (1908), 50; J. Marchant, *J. B. Paton: Educational and Social Pioneer* (1909), 207.
[60] Paterson, *Across the Bridges*, p. 153.
[61] Paton, 'Moral Training', pp. 9–10.
[62] Freeman, *Boy Life and Labour*, p. 149.
[63] Baron, *Growing Generation*, p. 142, and C. E. B. Russell, *Manchester Boys* 1905), 96.
[64] See below, s. 3.

in particular lacked self-control, which was why they were unable to concentrate and to persevere with a situation.[65]

In many respects the cinema excited the wrath of moralists more than did the music-hall, although the boy labour group of reformers never exaggerated its influence. Nevertheless, Freeman reported the claim that the cinema had helped to cause the school strikes of 1911 when pupils struck after seeing newsreels of the industrial unrest which was widespread at the time. He also cited other claims, including those from Nottingham where the cinema was held to be responsible for falling attendance at Band of Hope meetings, for the decline in the number of library books borrowed, and for having incited gangs of boys, 'fired by the cowboy drama' to parade 'the streets armed with pistols'.[66] The two principal charges were that films displayed nothing of an 'elevating kind', and that they could encourage criminal actions such as stealing the money in order to gain the price of admission.[67] On the subject of whether films were morally and socially desirable, Freeman quoted an advertisement which, he said, summed up the impact of the cinema, and explained why its influence should not be overstated: 'To cause a smile, perchance a tear, but ne'er a blush'.[68] The report of a special inquiry into the cinema, conducted by the National Council for Public Morals, was predictably more alarmist in concluding that some films were 'helping to lower the standard of reverence for women, and familiarising the minds of young people with loose ideas of the relations between the sexes'.[69] At the same time, however, after hearing evidence from chief constables, it conceded that the cinema was unlikely to encourage criminality.[70] All in all,

[65] C. E. B. Russell, *Social Problems of the North* (1913), 75. See also below, s. 3.

[66] Freeman, *Boy Life and Labour* p. 135. For a recent interpretation of the impact of the cinema see D. Mayall, 'Palaces for Entertainment and Instruction: A Study of the Early Cinema in Birmingham, 1908–18', *Midland History* 10 (1985), 94–109.

[67] Freeman, *Boy Life and Labour*, pp. 135, 139.

[68] Ibid.

[69] *The Cinema. Its Present Position and Future Possibilities. Report and Evidence of the Cinema Commission of Inquiry.* National Council of Public Morals (1917), p. 143.

[70] Ibid., pp. xxxviii–ix, xl, xli, and 118. Teachers were the group most likely to exaggerate the effects.

the main argument against the music-hall and the cinema was that both were uneducative, carefree, thoughtless; they failed to offer a clear example of good behaviour, they were doing nothing positively to improve the character of adolescents, and they 'can hardly be said to train the boy to be a better husband or father or worker or citizen'.[71]

2.3. Gambling and smoking

It is difficult to know the extent of juvenile gambling, though gambling in general was felt to be on the increase and, among young people, it was regarded as an 'elusive evil', giving boys an 'unhealthy craving for excitement', turning them into bad workers and familiarizing them with 'a flashy and material order of life, which weakens the hold of moral principle and excludes the spirit of religion'.[72] At least one witness before the House of Lords Committee on Betting argued that among the young, it was 'a form of insanity' leading to 'all the aspirations and capabilities' being 'sacrificed on the altar of narrow and blind selfishness'; even bright youths were drawn into 'the vortex of this madness' where they developed 'low cunning instead of character' and became 'moral and intel-lectual wrecks'.[73] Leading youth workers were less extreme, though they agreed that sports and games, especially football, were being 'perverted' by petty gambling which was one of the boys' 'earliest vices'.[74]

Numerous reformers remarked on the prevalence of juvenile smoking. The most popular brand of cigarette was Woodbines, known to Birmingham boys as 'Coffin-Nails'.[75] The 'smoking habit' was regarded as a growing one with several 'extremely deleterious' consequences, which besides being passed on from generation to generation, led in general to national physical deterioration and in particular to the rejection of army recruits

---

[71] Freeman, *Boy Life and Labour*, p. 140. See also Baron, *Growing Generation*, p. 128, and Pelham, *Training*, p. 153.

[72] R. I. McKibbon, 'Working-Class Gambling in Britain, 1880–1929', *Past and Present*, 82, (Feb.1979), 148–9, and Paterson, *Across the Bridges*, p. 171.

[73] *House of Lords Select Committee on Betting, Report and Evidence*, v (389), 1902, p. 683 (evidence of a Newcastle magistrate).

[74] Baron, *Growing Generation*, p. 83; Russell, *Social Problems*, pp. 117–20; Freeman, *Boy Life and Labour*, pp. 152, 188; Urwick (ed.), *Boy Life*, p. 304.

[75] Freeman, *Boy Life and Labour*, p. 152.

on the grounds of 'smoker's heart'.[76] The main charge against
smoking was that in addition to facilitating 'the work of
disease', and leading to the 'habit of drink', it encouraged a lack
of self-control and even delinquency.[77] A typical description of
a schoolboy smoker, 'E. S.' was given by his teacher:
'Frequently sick—lazy—impossible to get the lad to make an
effort. Gets more backward in his work every day—impossible
to get him to do anything previously told... No moral
character.'[78] The reference to 'character' was obviously
intended to clinch the matter, so that such wild accusations
would be taken seriously. The reason why smoking was
viewed with such concern was that, in common with tea and
alcohol, it was seen as a brain stimulant and, as the psychologists had shown, uncontrolled stimulation could be extremely
dangerous.[79]

2.4 Literature

Perhaps less dangerous than gambling, but certainly more
pervasive and of dubious moral quality, was the 'cheap
literature' so popular among older schoolchildren and young
workers.[80] It is instructive to see here yet another instance of
the social critique being used to indict the adolescent personality.[81] Boys were said to look for 'excitement' in what they read
because they were 'not greatly interested in things of real life;
they want sensation... melodrama; they love romance, no
matter how fantastic or far-fetched'; their instincts were
receptive to what was 'weird or blood-thirsty'.[82] However,
though most young males (but apparently not girls) read
'penny-dreadfuls' and halfpenny comics, these were thought to
be less of an 'evil' influence than either the cinema or the

---

[76] *Report of the Physical Deterioration Committee*, p. 76; see also *Evidence*,
2346–9; 2369–72; 1766–9; 9261–4; 2954–9; and *Report of House of Lords
Select Committee on Juvenile Smoking Bill*, ix (1906), p. v.

[77] Ibid.,v, and Paterson, *Across the Bridges*, pp. 185–86.

[78] *House of Lords Select Committee on Juvenile Smoking*, p. 50.

[79] Clouston, *Hygiene of Mind*, pp. 259–61, 180–1.

[80] Springhall, *Coming of Age*, pp. 129–33; Patrick Dunae, 'Penny Dreadfuls:
Late Nineteenth Century Boys' Literature and Crime', *Victorian Studies* 22/1
(Winter 1979), 133–50.

[81] See below, s. 3.

[82] Freeman, *Boy Life and Labour*, pp. 144–51; Scharlieb, 'Adolescent Girls',
p. 14.

music-hall, as the majority of stories merely pandered to 'the most commonplace and futile sentimentality', even if sometimes those concerned with 'love' could degenerate into 'frank nastiness'.[83]

A far more determined and sectarian estimate came from the National Purity League Crusaders who were continually alert for sexual innuendo and what they considered to be other forms of immorality. Stories were condemned for espousing 'trickery, cheating, lying ... [and] laziness' as suitable for jokes, and for appealing to 'low instincts' and awakening 'low passions', by showing women 'scantily attired' in poses which were 'lewdly suggestive'.[84] But the real problem was less one of sexual immorality than of unedifying influences experienced during 'these years of adolescence' when the mind was 'sponge-like in its nature'. The picture-palace, the music-hall and cheap literature were regarded with apprehension because they represented 'the three great sources of *ideas* to the working-boy'. They wrote their langauge on 'the blank sheet' of the young mind:

The senses of the adolescent, now open at their widest, are opened not to Nature and Art, but to cheap and tawdry pantomime; his kindling imagination is not nourished with fine, heroic literature, but with the commonest rubbish in print; his emotions are fed, not with gracious and elevating influences, but with unnatural excitants. And all those great cravings that Nature has implanted in him, the intellectual curiosity, the longing for idealism, the hero-worship, the splendid ambition, the creative genius, the religious instinct—all of these are dying for lack of nourishment. Or, perhaps we should say that thorns are springing up and choke them.[85]

Here is expressed something of the ambivalence in the reformers' perception of the working-class boy: on the one hand attributing to him a number of fine qualities, but on the other hand arguing that these were being disabled by his

---

[83] Baron, *Growing Generation*, pp. 119–20; Freeman, *Boy Life and Labour*, p. 144.
[84] Marchant, *Paton*, pp. 219, 221; Paton, 'Moral Training', pp. 63–71; Marchant (ed.), *Cleansing of a City* 'The Need for Purity', p. 39; see also essays by William Barry and R. F. Horton. Marchant wrote in terms of youth 'feeding upon the offal of literature and learning the language of shame', p. xvi.
[85] Freeman, *Boy Life and Labour*, p. 151.

immaturity and by his 'natural' inability to discriminate between different kinds of stimuli.

2.5. *Sports and games*

By 1900, games, sports, and physical recreation of all kinds had become more highly organized and team-oriented than at any time in the past. The main authors of this development were the urban middle class who were guided and inspired by public-school practices, so that sport was seen to have crucially important social and moral attributes.[86] Working-class games were welcomed, but they elicited a mixed response from commentators: there was applause in so far as they encouraged healthy activities, usually of the outdoor variety, in which strenuous physical exercise matched with thought and stamina combined to produce what was theoretically an excellent form of character training. Unfortunately, however, working-class sporting attitudes lapsed seriously from the public-school ideal.[87] Football, said Russell, was very popular, but 'the standard of honour among the players is frequently but a low one'. Older boys, it seemed, lied about their age in order to get into Junior Leagues so that they could be more certain of winning medals; and the game itself was 'unfair, and too often foul and violent tactics take the place of strenuous play'.[88] The difficulty was said to stem from the lack of effective supervision of the kind given in the public schools which compelled boys to play in the 'spirit' of the game, for as these schools well understood, 'something more than sportsmanship is involved, and that is character'.[89] How different it was with working-class youth which was 'untroubled . . . by very strong feelings of discipline or nice regard of rule'.[90] And without discipline—'physical or moral'—critics felt there was little point to the game.

---

[86] Meller, *Leisure*, pp. 225–36; and the excellent studies, J. A. Mangan, *Athleticism in the Victorian and Edwardian Public School* (1981), D. Newsome, *Godliness and Good Learning* (1961), and N. Vance, 'The Ideal of Manliness' in Simon and Bradley (eds.), *Victorian Public School*, pp. 115–28; see also Bailey, *Leisure and Class*, ch. 6.

[87] Paterson, *Across the Bridges*, p. 173.

[88] Russell, *Social Problems*, p. 110.

[89] Baron, *Growing Generation*, p. 82.

[90] Urwick (ed.), *Boy Life*, p. 271 and his evidence to the *Poor Law Commission*, p. 353, Q.97001.

A jaundiced and detailed criticism of the young workers' approach to games and sport came from Barclay Baron who concentrated his remarks on the 'naturalness' of working-class attitudes:

> they adopt . . . the natural methods of play. The give and take of the streets, the hard law of each for himself carried on to the pitch or the football field. The fact of the greater 'naturalness' of working boys or girls must ever be in the forefront of any discussion of their behaviour on given occasions. They are not ashamed of naive methods in sport as in the other business of every day for the simple and sufficient reason that shame presupposes a recognition of transgressions, and of this they are often quite unconscious.[91]

All this was contrary to middle-class behaviour which exhibited an 'intensive culture' of games; 'the class as a whole has bound itself in vigorous discipline to a conscious ideal of "good form"'.[92] Thus, (in theory) the act of playing automatically incorporated its own ethical considerations—the ethos of the game (both sporting and otherwise) was dominant. The young worker, however, was accused of allowing 'outside factors' to influence him, and these disturbed 'the ideal of the game played for its own sake alone'.[93] Baron identified the problem as the desire of the boy 'to win something beyond the game itself' which in turn 'led to the doubtful methods of attaining it'.[94] And proof of the boys' inability to play the game properly could be found in the noisiness of their enthusiasm, for 'noise in sport betokens but too often confusion of purpose and lack of discipline', both of which were 'unpardonable weaknesses in a good game'.[95]

Baron's opinion, widely shared among reformers, was that 'from the "sporting" view of a game it is no appreciable step to the "sporting" view of the whole life'.[96] This belief, a profoundly middle-class perspective finely tuned by public-school education, lay at the heart of all the criticisms concerning working-class attitudes towards games and sport.

[91] Baron, *Growing Generation*, pp. 67–8.
[92] Ibid., 104.
[93] Ibid.
[94] Ibid., 84–5.
[95] Ibid., 92.
[96] Ibid., p. 106; and Russell, *Social Problems*, pp. 75, 101.

Put simply, it was meant to imply that young workers lacked that essential *esprit de corps*. No one, said Russell, could fail to be struck by its absence among the boys of Manchester.[97] At its best, the corporate feeling involved 'co-operation . . . subordination . . . [and] self-forgetfulness', as well as 'self-respect, good temper, cheerfulness . . . courage and persever-ence'.[98] In certain circumstances, each of these 'virtues' could be found in some aspect or other of working-class behaviour, but they never came together in anything like a coherent concept of 'sportsmanship'. This was partly explained by the difficulty working-class people of all ages were said to have with concepts—their lives were viewed as too fragmentary, too quick, and too thoughtless for them ever to conceptualize their own behaviour. Consequently, without the right kind of supervision and tuition, adolescents would never understand the principles behind the exhortation to 'Play up! Play up! And play the game!'[99] One of these principles, which helped to serve as the main thrust 'in the contest for control' of leisure activities was that of 'rational recreation'.[100] The urge on the part of reformers to make recreation 'rational' was a point of focus for the social critique. Contemporary awareness of the psychology of adolescence explains why the 'rational' was counterposed to 'instincts', which needed to be controlled. And as street play, in all its forms, expressed the 'natural instinct of boyish spirits', few critics doubted that there was an urgent need 'to provide some more rational outlet for it'.[101]

2.6. Delinquency

When all else failed, some reformers resorted to the threat of delinquency, especially when they sought to impress upon the public the importance of the 'boy labour' problem. Tawney was one of those who exploited popular interest in the topic. Several occupations, he claimed, in particular those of a 'casual and irregular' nature, were liable to lead youths into crime, and

[97] Russell, *Manchester Boys*, p. 82.
[98] Ibid., p. 83; Scharlieb, 'Recreational Activities of Girls during Adoles-cence', pp. 575, 584; Russell, *Social Problems*, p. 75.
[99] Quoted in Bailey, *Leisure and Class*, p. 127.
[100] Ibid., ch. 2 and *passim*.
[101] Gibb, *Problem of Boy Work*, p. 50.

for good measure he cited figures provided by the chief constable of Glasgow to show that messengers, van-boys, street-traders, rivet-boys, and young labourers were the most susceptible.[102] Other chief constables shared this view, as did the report of the Borstal Association which, after mentioning several causes of criminality, drew special attention to 'the absence of any system of control or organization for the employment of the young'.[103]

The majority of observers, however, agreed that the hooligan and the juvenile delinquent were comparatively rare; they were 'the most striking example of the fruits of an undisciplined boy'. Urwick specifically contrasted them with 'the average boy';—they were 'the exceptions at the other end of the scale'; while the Revd Pelham significantly remarked that the same offences committed by a public-school boy would be kept secret by his house-master.[104] Neither Paterson nor Russell, both of whom were actively involved with delinquents, exaggerated the scale of the problem. Paterson referred to 'boyish crime' and to the 'stream of high-spirited fellows . . . summoned for playing football, or swearing, or gambling in the street'—these were to be distinguished from the 'proper "youthful offender"' who was arrested on 'a more serious charge'.[105] And even in the midst of national concern over juvenile crime during the First World War, Russell maintained that the boy who is really 'a criminal at heart' was 'a rarity'; youthful crimes were 'expressions of animal vigour, of exuberance of spirits, of energy misapplied for want of legitimate outlet'.[106]

It is true that there had been something of a panic over hooliganism in the 1890s, and psychologists perceived adolescence as the most vulnerable period for criminal behaviour.

---

[102] R. H. Tawney, 'The Economics of Boy Labour', *Economic Journal*, 19, (Dec. 1909), 533.

[103] Quoted in Bray, *Boy Labour and Apprenticeship*, p. 169, see also p. 170.

[104] Urwick (ed.), *Boy Life*, p. 298; Pelham, *Training*, pp. 88–9. Paterson said that only 'a few drop from the straight course every year', *Across the Bridges*, p. 183; and Russell, *Social Problems*, pp. 75–6. Freeman confined himself to a single page in which he paraphrased G. S. Hall in saying that 'Vice and crime . . . are born during adolescence, p. 106.

[105] Paterson, *Across the Bridges*, pp. 183–96, especially pp. 184–9.

[106] Russell, 'The Problem of Juvenile Crime', *Barnett House papers*, 1 (1917), 5.

Nor was there a shortage of contemporaries who pointed to the criminal statistics, which showed the high proportion of convictions for adolescents. However, the fact that it appeared to be the age at which 'most criminal careers commence', did not mean that the majority of adolescents were delinquent.[107] The relevant point was the predisposition of adolescents to delinquency. Anyway, the panic failed to survive to become an Edwardian obsession.[108] Reformers were much more likely to use the term delinquency in a loose generic sense referring to a variety of behaviour patterns likely to offend against adult (and largely middle-class) sensibilities, and as a warning of what could happen were their predictions in relation to juvenile labour and leisure ignored. Although the subject makes good copy for historians, delinquency never involved more than a small minority of boys and its importance should therefore be kept in perspective. The overriding issues involving adolescent workers did not refer to their potential criminality, but to unemployment, family instability, poverty, industrial unrest, and to flawed character.[109]

3. AGE AND CLASS AND THE YOUNG WORKER'S PERSONALITY

The significance of defining the adolescent condition as 'natural' has already been remarked on, but in order to understand fully the nature of the critique, it is necessary to

[107] J. G. Slaughter, *The Adolescent* (1911), saw it as an 'urgent problem', p. 70; see also G. S. Hall, *Adolescence*, (1904), vol.i. 325.

[108] Pearson, *Hooligan*, claims that the 'Hooligan' figured centrally in the Edward era's deliberations on the 'boy labour' question, p. 197. This is an exaggeration. Pearson concentrates on establishing a continuity of concern with 'hooliganism' at the expense of examining the discontinuities involved. See also Humphries, *Hooligans or Rebels?*, p.174. Perhaps John Gillis is correct to argue that the perception of delinquency changed during the period, especially in the area of non-indictable crime. See his 'The Evolution of Juvenile Delinquency in England, 1890–1914', *Past and Present*, 67 (May 1975), 96–126.

[109] Ibid., 97. He claims that there existed a 'cycle of anxiety' which did not diminish until 1910 (what happened in 1910?), p. 98. Furthermore, he makes much of the idea that 'independent' and 'precocious' youth was 'stigmatized as delinquent', p. 97. This is an attractive but crude interpretation. Certainly 'independent' youth was viewed with suspicion and seen as potentially delinquent in so far as they were thought to be beyond the control of their parents, but reformers *et al.*, were much more careful in their analysis than this either-or approach implies.

examine the middle-class perception of what for want of a more accurate word might be described as the young worker's personality. This term has been chosen in preference to the more common noun, character, in order to emphasize the psycho-medical features of the social critique. 'Character' is usually defined in relation to moral values. 'Personality', however, is stressed here because commentators were concerned not only with personal ethical systems, but also with physical and mental display: clothes, gestures, speech, tastes, manners, attitudes and, most important, emotions and instincts. It was within these categories that reason, conscience and will developed and, as Hayward and others observed, all three together 'give personality'. [110]

The reformers' ambivalence toward working-class youth, which was mentioned above in relation to recreation, characterized much of their description and assessment of the physical and mental condition of adolescence. If the boy was loud and boisterous, he was also thoughtful and reflective; if he was rebellious and quarrelsome, he was also loyal and idealistic. It has been said, wrote E. J. Urwick,

that the heart of a boy is half angel, half savage. In the boys we are considering there are no half tints; the lights and shades stand out in strong relief; but though at first view the lurid lights of the savage element alone appear, there is a rich background formed of the finer shades of the angel element, waiting for the skilled hand to bring forwards and develop till the two unite to form a harmonious character. [111]

In his conclusion he optimistically identified the significant

---

[110] Kelynack (ed.), *Youth*, p. 4 quoting Hayward. For a discussion of the meaning of 'character' in Victorian times, see S. Collini, 'The Idea of "Character" in Victorian Political Thought', *Transactions of the Royal Historical Society* (1986), 32–34. Quoting from the *OED*, Collini shows that Victorians incorporated both evaluative and descriptive elements in their definition of the term. It could refer either to 'the sum of the mental and moral qualities which distinguish an individual' or to 'moral qualities strongly developed or strikingly displayed'. The properly developed character', as Collini suggests, was evidenced by self-restraint in all its forms, and the absence of such restraint among working-class youth condemned them in the eyes of most commentators. However, 'personality' has more of a psychological ring to it; and as Edwardian observers were especially familiar with the psycho-medical appraisal of youth, it seems appropriate to focus attention in this direction.

[111] Urwick (ed.), *Boy Life*, pp. xiii–iv.

features as being 'those of strong, healthy, and normal vitality, full of the possibilities of real and lasting progress, full of hope and promise for the future'.[112] This optimism, though usually accompanied by a sense of unease, was also a fundamental feature of the reformers' approach to the problem. At the same time, few of them doubted that without appropriate guidance from the 'skilled hand', the 'finer shades' would be swamped by the 'savage element'. Such an eventuality was unlikely to occur, but it was not impossible.

The focus on 'personality', however, is obvious in some of the better-known descriptions of the 'town-boy' who was 'sensitive to a degree', and

ready to fall into the depths of childish depression over trifles; yet quick to regain the almost abnormal buoyancy of animal spirits which are his undoubted birthright; disgracefully casual, but keen enough when his interest is aroused; a creature full of obvious shallows and unsuspected depths; superficially very sharp, though very seldom clever; unreasonably self-confident, but not yet self-reliant; exasperatingly suspicious, with that odd mixture of incredulity and credulity, both equally misplaced, which makes him so difficult to teach; such is the town boy's nature.[113]

Furthermore, echoing the contemporary interest in racial efficiency and urban degeneration, the lowest class of boys, in overcoming their environment and inherited disease, were said to exhibit 'a remarkable toughness of fibre, a sort of India-rubber capacity of recovery from fatigue or injury . . . as well as an alertness and quickness of movement' together with 'a superficial and mercurial versatility'; they were, 'under the stress of city life', developing into 'a new type of humanity'. [114]

The 'city type' will be referred to again, but it is worth pausing to say that this vocabulary (Urwick's) was to be found over and over again in the years after 1904. Not that it was unique to the Edwardian era, far from it. But the deluge of 'boy labour' publications gave it a new prominence and, in its psycho-social context, it continued into the inter-war years and well beyond. One very important consequence was to

[112] Ibid., 255–6.
[113] Ibid., xiii; see also Paterson, *Across the Bridges*, pp. 169, 174.
[114] Urwick (ed.), *Boy Life*, pp. 265–6.

distance young people from ordinary society: so they became 'abnormal', 'animal', 'misplaced', and, so it was asserted, had a particular 'nature'. Of course, this was meant to imply that it was natural for urban youth to display certain personality traits—or, stripped of rhetoric, that they could not help but be what their class and their age determined for them.

The same implication was also to be seen in the writings of the Revd Gibb, who saw young workers as 'eager, light-hearted, volatile'; they lived 'for the day', with little thought for the future. In the friendly but patronizing tone, so common among reformers, he described the young man as 'living on friendly terms with all the world; companionable and ready for a chat; faithful and loyal to his chums . . . his feelings and thoughts on serious things of life and religion are unfathomable to others, and, while he is . . . wholly inarticulate . . . he is not without his depths'; his conversations 'consist of the non-essential with the essential wrapped up in a remote corner'; he was 'sensitive and magnifies small grievances; hopeful, and expects an Eldorado elsewhere'. However, though youth was fickle, this did not imply any 'uncommon instability of character, but is merely the combined result of boyish thoughtlessness, boyish expectations, boyish restlessness, and the total absence of any clear guidance'. Some guidance was necessary, because without it 'our boy' with his 'cheerfulness, activity, vim, and pluck; with his inexperience, aimlessness, and natural irresponsibility' was 'fatally adapted' to 'fall victim' to the most undesirable influences.[115] Here again is the emphasis on 'nature'—'boyishness' becomes self-explanatory within the framework provided by the notion of 'natural irresponsibility'.

Charles Russell also drew attention to the 'mercurial' temperament of 'city lads' who were 'quicker, more active' than village boys. While urban youth were often wild, disordered and reckless, they were also often 'merry, jolly . . . full of fun, and with a certain dare-devil spirit', although they were ruined by growing up in an anti social environment. Russell thought that as a species, boys were stern critics:

[115] Gibb, *The Problem of Boy Work*, pp. 1, 2, 5, 6; *The Boy and his Work*, pp. 3, 4, 12; and his 'Choice of Employment for Boys', *Economic Review* (Oct. 1904), 447.

'Forgiveness—of all virtues the most difficult perhaps—is most rare.' Nevertheless, he acknowledged that many street-boys were 'loyal, generous, open-hearted, exceedingly self-sacrificing'. On matter of religion, their 'shyness and diffidence' were signs of 'delicacy and refinement of feeling' for which they too seldom received the credit. When all was said and done, however, Russell regarded the adolescent as suffering from 'flabbiness and want of grit' and was 'indeed a puzzling, inconsistent, exasperating creature . . . a strange peculiar creature; sometimes one would think, hardly accountable for what he does'.[116]

In his famous book *Across the Bridges* (which was made compulsory reading at Eton), Alexander Paterson claimed that the London boy was 'more vicious and neurotic' than his fellows in the North, the reason being 'a lifelong diet of tea, cheap jam, and fish'. The boys were said to be 'quicker' in their speech; their ideas were 'more chaotic' and their motives 'a more inconsequent series'. Temperamentally, London youths were 'emotional and affectionate', but there was a 'quick transience of mood and motive' which made their character 'the more difficult to gauge or mould'. In conversation, their 'conclusion and moral judgement are rarely or never original'; their wit was usually borrowed from the music-hall, and they were not 'naturally reflective'. Even so, he warned his readers not to describe the youths as 'fickle' for 'behind these rapid changes there is, as a rule, no attempt to deceive; they merely reflect the chaos and inconsequence of a boys' motives.'[117]

It is clear from the initial statement of ambivalence, illustrated by the first quotation from Urwick, that through the welter of abuse and condescension, there was an observable procedure which did so much to lock adolescents into a series of negative images. Disregarding, for the moment, the psychological assessment, the social identity of adolescence as constructed by the critics clearly denied young people any capacity for either serious thought or rational action. Moreover, the manner in which the identity was created is important because it shows how in the hands of skilled

---

[116] Russell, 'City Lads', *Child*, (Apr. 1911), 587–93, and his *Manchester Boys*, pp. 1–3, 49, 122.
[117] Paterson, *Across the Bridges*, ch. 9 & 10.

practitioners, and before a sympathetic audience, a certain kind of language was used to produce a verisimilar account of mental and physical behaviour. The process was in three parts: it began with the youth portrayed as a sort of hybrid—human but with personality traits more akin to those of other species; hence the boy was an 'odd', 'strange, peculiar creature', with an 'abnormal buoyancy of animal spirits', a 'creature full of obvious shallows and unsuspected depths'. The second stage was to associate young people with unreliability, unreasonableness, emotionalism, and often neurosis, by the constant use of such adjectives as 'fickle', 'puzzling', 'thoughtless', 'volatile', 'depressive', 'difficult', 'inarticulate', 'unfathomable', 'inconsistent', 'irresponsible', 'reckless', and so on. The third element, which relied on psychological references, suggested that their behaviour and attitudes were 'natural', and that this was a clinical feature of 'boyishness'. The last stage was critical in so far as it revealed the others as transitory— provided, that is, the individual escaped permanent mental and moral injury during the adolescent period. This is why Hall's critique of the environment and his emphasis on proper influences were such integral features of both his and the reformers' analysis. Furthermore, the psychologically informed view that there was such a 'natural' condition was necessary for the intellectual coherence of the critique, for by juxtaposing the critical adjectives with 'the town boy's nature', the vocabulary appeared to confirm its own perspective by virtue of identifying and explaining this 'natural' state. In this analysis, 'bad' behaviour ceased to be the work of the devil and became that of the psyche—a comforting transition for social scientists and their followers who now felt confident of their abilities to solve all aspects of social problems.

There is no suggestion that commentators deliberately invented and manipulated language. It seems much more likely that they drew upon a tradition of class-based social commentary with its roots in nineteenth-century religion, politics and science. But, as has been shown, there was also the older, ageist-inspired tradition dating back at least to Aristotle. Both forms of observation came together (probably with the beginnings of the organized youth movement between the 1860s and 1880s), and were subsequently joined by the new and potentially more systematic observatory techniques of child and social psychology, which enhanced and expanded the vocabulary (and the understanding) of all those with an interest in the 'boy labour problem'.

So far little has been said about social class, but as a conditioning and often determining factor, it was rarely absent from Edwardian age relations. In their examination of the adolescent personality, observers were acutely aware of the influence of 'station in life'.[118] Sometimes their awareness was explicitly expressed, as when they criticized the role of parents in helping children to make the transition from school to employment. On the other hand, their frequent comparisons of the working-class 'character' with that of the middle class were usually more implicit. Nevertheless, it is well known that the sociological literature of the period is full of accounts of the supposed mental and moral weaknesses which were said to characterize all but the most respectable members of the lower orders. Two popular sentiments were that they lacked personal self-control and that they were either unable or unwilling to abide by ethical principles, possibly because they could neither recognize nor formulate them.[119]

Unsurprisingly, then, almost all observers made some reference to the failure of the young worker to exercise self-restraint. Club managers constantly referred to the charge, claiming that boys came with 'weak wills, little power of self-control, strong temptations, undisciplined natures, much emotion, and little principle'.[120] Russell thought it was essential that the club teach not only cleanliness, order and obedience, but also 'self-respect and self-control'.[121] Generally speaking, the 'boy labour' group was prone to equate the absence of restraint, perseverance, and discipline with wage-earning independence, which explains why they usually cited 'excessive' job-changing as one form of evidence. A provincial investigator, writing in praise of youth organizations, and calling for compulsory part-time day continuation schools, hoped they would make adolescents 'more self-controlled and resourceful than the present "general labourers" ' for then it

---

[118] Gillis, 'Juvenile Delinquency', p. 97. See also above, n. 102.
[119] McKibbon, 'Social Class and Social Observation', *passim.*
[120] Violet Brooke-Hunt, *Clubs for Boys and Young Men* (1897), p. 15.
[121] C. E. B. Russell and L. M. Rigby, *Working Lads' Clubs* (1908; 1932 edn.), 15.

would not be so difficult 'to induce them to "stick to" anything that involves effort'. As it was, the boy had 'a perpetual ache for change and adventure . . . He cannot keep his mind for any length of time on any end . . . he is capable only of casual and disjointed tasks.'[122]

But it would be a mistake to attribute the emphasis on self-control to a crude mixture of ageism and class prejudice since much more was involved. It is important, for instance, to understand the widespread anxiety aroused by the apparent consequences of urban living and to remember the graphic descriptions provided by the likes of Masterman, with his references to 'hooliganism', the 'fickle excitability' of the crowd, the 'City Type', and the ' "street-bred" people'.[123] Such images help to account for the views of, for example, eugenists such as Caleb Saleeby, who saw the education of the adolescent as crucial if racial integrity was to be maintained. [124] Many commentators feared that the 'town-bred' adolescent, with either his 'animal' or 'mercurial' temperament, could succumb to degenerate moral and physical influences (and would almost certainly do so in the absence of proper guidance). If Masterman's 'new generation' should be found without the 'ethic of control and responsibility', what, asked contemporaries, would this augur for the future of 'Progress'?[125]

There is another reason why we need to resist an historically naïve interpretation of the critique: middle-class reformers

---

[122] Butler, *Social Conditions in Oxford*, pp. 90–1 and 181.

[123] Masterman, *Heart of the Empire*, pp. 7–8; *Condition of England*, p. 120 and ch. 4.

[124] C. Saleeby, *The Progress of Eugenics* (1914), 92–8.

[125] On 'Progress' see S. Collini, *Liberalism and Sociology*. L. T. Hobhouse and Political Thought in England, 1880–1914 (1979), *passim*, and M. Freeden, *The New Liberalism: An Ideology of Social Reform* (1978), *passim*. See also P. Clarke, *Liberal and Social Democrats* (1978, 1981), 14–18. with references to T. H. Green, Clarke writes: 'Morality was essentially the working of reason within a rational world. The rationality of the world was the premise for an unshakeable belief in human progress.' p. 14. Much of the social (and economic) critique of youth assumed a basic 'natural' irrationality. And though it would be very difficult to prove a direct relationship between Green's philosophical Idealism and the critique of youth, it is reasonable to assume that many of the critics were conscious of the wider intellectual universe in which their interest in 'boy labour' was situated. On this see below, ch. 8, section on citizenship.

were eager to educate urban youth in what they regarded as superior values because they themselves believed in these values; their own intellectual, spiritual, and material success seemed to be proof of the benefits of virtue. The notion of self-control, for example, was integral to their social philosophy. It was almost a tangible means of understanding the world: it made sense of time, relationships, desires, and, not to be underestimated, those fears that could threaten to unbalance a life. It was able to achieve these ends, so beneficiaries claimed, by introducing elements of order, thought, and hierarchy into a mass of sensations that were forever bombarding the individual. Such restraint (and the accompanying perseverance and self-discipline), however, did not come 'naturally', it had to be learned, as it was in the homes of the middle classes and, most conspicuously, in their public schools.[126]

The public school, of course, was one of the pivots on which middle-class culture turned; this was certainly true from the 1870s onwards when the schools had organized themselves into a coherent system of education with a shared common code and ethos. There is no doubt as to their influence on the organized youth movement, whose leaders constantly stressed their ability to provide a similar kind of educational experience for boys of the working and lower-middle classes.[127] It was widely understood that the overriding aim of the schools was to cultivate an *esprit de corps*, which was 'so difficult exactly to define, and yet so ennobling in its effect upon character'.[128] While on the larger stage of politics, 'character' was visibly manifested in imperial duties performed in distant parts of the world, on the home front it meant not only the proper management of personal affairs, but also a willingness to abide by certain rules. And no where were these rules better displayed than on the playing-fields where games made men. The playing of the game taught not only fair play, self-reliance, obedience, endurance and agility, but also self-control, as when compelled to work as part of a team, or not kicking wildly at

---

[126] On 'learning', see McKibbon, 'Social Class and Social Observation', p. 184; Mangan, *passim*; and Paterson, *Across the Bridges*, p. 173.

[127] See below, ch. 7.

[128] Simon and Bradley (eds.), *Victorian Public School*, pp. 10–11; J. Springhall, *Youth, Empire and Society* (1977), 123.

the ball and not lashing out with the fist during a boxing match. Games showed the boy 'how to take a beating'. Boxing, said Stanley Hall, had an educational value in so far as it could do 'moral work': 'At its best, it is indeed a manly art, a superb school for quickness of eye and hand, decision, force of will, and self-control. The moment this is lost stinging punishment follows. Hence it is the surest of all cures for excessive irrascibility, and has been found to have a most beneficient effect upon a peevish or unmanly disposition.'[129] So it was that games could shape 'undeveloped bodies and unformed characters'.[130]

From absence of self-control to lack of principle was but a short step for the majority of critics. The immorality of youth was so generally accepted that at least one medical authority defined 'moral instability' as a characteristic of adolescence.[131] The apparent failure to make proper moral distinctions was evident from the remarks of Barclay Baron who had referred to young workers being 'untroubled' by 'nice regard of rule'; they lacked an awareness of 'a recognition of transgressions' in the playing of games and, by implication, in life too.[132] This was tantamount to claiming that youth had no moral code: their behaviour and attitudes being 'natural' to a stage of growth which by definition had little capacity for either thought or reason. Likewise, self-restraint, forethought, reason, and regard for rules were seen as the prerequisites of 'principle'. The critics, then, had no doubt why it was that working-class adolescents were so morally deficient: they had been brought up that way by their parents. (How much responsibility was attributed solely to parents and how much to the psychological condition of adolescence is unclear. But as class and age were so closely connected in this particular middle-class perception of young workers, it is probable that the responsibility shifted back and forth between the two, depending on circumstances. Either way, however, the parental role was felt to be of great significance). These were the people who lived their lives

---

[129] Hall, *Adolescence*, vol. i, p. 218.
[130] Lewis, *A Club for Boys*, p. 5 and Russell and Rigby, *Working Lads' Clubs*, p. 138.
[131] Kelynack (ed.), *Youth*, p. 85.
[132] Baron, *Growing Generation*, pp. 67–8, 82.

closer to 'emotion' than to 'intellectual' experience. 'Generosity ranks far before justice, sympathy before truth, a pliant and obliging disposition before a rigidly honest one. In brief, the less admixture of intellect required for the practice of any virtue, the higher it stands in popular estimation.'[133] The specific complaint against the working-class home was that in it children were trained according to the dictates of 'personal comfort', rather than 'to any delicate distinction between right and wrong'; they were given no idea 'of the meaning of character', instead they learned by example that 'acts and not motives alone count for anything.' Or, as the health visitor Margery Loane remarked, among the poor, character depended on habits, having 'no conscious connection with principle'.[134]

An examination of the relationship between habits, principles, and character would go far beyond the scope of this study. However, it is important to see that Loane's readers would have recognized the implications of her reference to 'habits', for together with 'instincts', 'impulses', and 'energies', the word was part of the vocabulary of social science, in particular social psychology. In fact, Helen Bosanquet, one of the most influential of observers, had cited William James, the seminal psychologist, who warned against individuals making a hell on earth for themselves by 'habitually fashioning' their characters 'in the wrong way'. Could the young, he wrote, 'but realise how soon they will become mere walking bundles of habits, they would give more heed to their conduct while in the plastic state. We are spinning our own fates, good or evil, and never to be undone.'[135] The point being made here was not that habits per se were dangerous, but that care needed to be taken when forming them because of their psychological significance. Clearly, habits were not unproblematic. The implication seemed to be that without 'thought', 'habit' would be destructive of good character. This is probably what Loane meant when she noted the absence of principle in the lives of the poor. She no doubt understood, as did James, that habit

[133] Quoted by Masterman, The Condition of England, p. 115.
[134] M. Loane, The Next Street But One (1907), 103, and Bray, 'The Boy and his Family' in Urwick (ed.), Boy Life, p. 60.
[135] H. Bosanquet, The Strength of the People (1902), pp. 32–3, also quoted in Collini, 'The Idea of "Character" ', pp. 34–5.

could be 'insidiously corrosive'.[136] The anxiety was simply stated by Urwick: 'Habit . . . becomes . . . dangerous if it is allowed to usurp the place of thought as applied to the higher processes of life.'[137] Thus 'wrong' habits and too much habit were to be avoided since the former led to 'bad' actions and attitudes, while the latter was, to quote Urwick again, 'inimical to thinking'.[138] It is perhaps true to say that as far as reformers were concerned, habit, like instinct, could imprison consciousness by banishing forethought and the distinction between right and wrong, which were the assumed essences of principle. Without consciousness, conscience would lapse and a crude utilitarianism would prevail. Hence the relevance of the criticism of working-class parents for rearing their children according to the dictates of comfort, rather than to a principled distinction between different ethical values. This also explains why Barclay Baron was voicing a widely-held view when he referred to the 'naturalness' of young workers and their alleged failure to recognize 'transgressions'.[139]

It should now be obvious that while Edwardian social observation knew no age boundaries, the critique of youth was by no means merely a reflection of the general assault on working-class beliefs. The criticisms made against adults: their emotionalism, impetuosity, love of excitement, absence of forethought and momentariness—were ascribed to class culture, or, in other words, ignorance, economic circumstances, physical and mental demoralization, the environment, and organizational incompetence.[140] When these and similar characteristics were displayed by adolescents, however, they were explained primarily in terms of physiology and psychology. The behaviour and mental perspective of the young was said to arise from a specific stage of development, whose distinguishing feature was emotional turmoil. It was this state of adolescence, aggravated as it was by indiscipline, precocity, independence and urban chaos, which was held to be responsible for the young person's 'nature'.

---

[136] Collini, 'The idea of "Character" ', p. 34. The phrase is his.
[137] E. J. Urwick, *A Philosophy of Social Progress* (1912; 1920 edn.), 82.
[138] Ibid.
[139] Baron, *Growing Generation*, p. 67–8.
[140] McKibbon, 'Social Class and Social Observation', *passim*.

Prior to Stanley Hall and the Child-Study Movement, the use of the adjective 'natural', in relation to young people, usually referred to that which could be observed in their everyday behaviour. By the early 1900s these familiar observations had been clinically examined, as 'personality' was subjected to psycho-medical analysis, while the conclusions reached were regarded as the basis for further theoretical and empirical investigation. Not only did psychology explain adolescence as a developmental stage, but also it confirmed the traditional perceptions of youth: yes, it was a problem, and this being the case, it did require careful discipline, guidance, and education. Moreover, the concept of adolescence proved useful to the critics (reformers, educationalists, youth workers, doctors, clerics, social workers, social scientists, and assorted moralists) in assisting them to structure the youth problem or, to be more precise, a series of anxieties involving juvenile labour, further education, delinquency, personal hygiene, and moral and civic duty. The concept imposed a kind of coherence on these disparate elements and simultaneously suggested a number of solutions.

But the critique and the impact of psychology are misunderstood if seen in terms of pessimism. It is true that as adolescents stood poised for a 'new birth', they were exposed to numerous detrimental influences and, therefore, nature needed a helping hand, though delicately used. Indeed, Hall had warned of the difficulty in finding the 'golden mean' between too much and too little control.[141] There was, however, a fundamental optimism among reformers which arose from two sources: the new knowledge provided by the 'revolution' in the social sciences allowed them to feel that they understood social problems, and could conquer them; secondly, the demands for, and the early appearance of, a 'scientific' social policy, intended primarily to deal with unemployment, added to their confidence.[142] This is not to say that reformers were complacent in the face of industrial unrest and the developing mass democracy, both of which gave reason for serious disquiet, but not for despair.

[141] Hall, *Adolescence*, vol. ii. p. 432.
[142] On the 'scientific' policy, see J. Harris, *Unemployment and Politics: A Study in English Social Policy, 1886–1914* (1972) ch. 6.

While the alliance between lay commentators and the 'new' psychology identified adolescence and clarified its meaning and its 'nature', the prestige of adolescents themselves was in no way enhanced, except possibly by way of mystical rhetoric proclaiming them to be guardians of a racial inheritance. Rather the concept of adolescence imprisoned them in a personality image where the definitions and processes of definition were the property of certain forms of knowledge that lay well outside their jurisdiction. Working-class male adolescents found that as all their thoughts and actions could be instantly filed and catalogued under the appropriate social or psycho-medical heading, they were unable to participate in the debate about their own lives; they were disenfranchised from a consciousness of their own position, for in their 'natural' condition, it was axiomatic that they could not know who or how they were.

Part III

SOLVING THE PROBLEM:
PHILANTHROPY, COLLECTIVISM, AND CLASS

6. Youth Organizations: Organizing Boys and 'Making Men'

The purpose of this chapter is not to provide a detailed account of youth organizations, as their histories are easily available elsewhere.[1] Instead the intention is to describe a few of the salient features of the more relevant groups in order to show something of the motivations and workings of the voluntary youth movement prior to the introduction of collectivist measures after 1900, and to suggest why the 'boy labour' reformers were eager to incorporate several aspects of the movement's practice and ideology within those policies. It is important to stress that the differences between, on the one side, the personnel of the brigades, Scouts, and clubs and, on the other, the reformers, should not be exaggerated, if only because many of the latter were also active in one or more of the organizations. Nevertheless, the fact that the youth problem was being redefined in the early 1900s, led to the advocacy of new remedies which meant that the voluntary sector found itself regarded as only one part of the solution, rather than the whole solution.

---

[1] My debt to these studies will be obvious throughout most of this chapter. See, for example, J. Springhall, *Youth, Empire and Society: British Youth Movements, 1883–1940* (1977) and his 'The Boy Scouts, Class and Militarism in Relation to British Youth Movements, 1908–1930', *International Review of Social History* 16, pt. 2 (1971), 125–58; J. Springhall, B. Fraser, and M. Hoare, *Sure and Steadfast: A History of the Boys' Brigade, 1883–1983* (1983); W. McG. Eagar, *Making Men: The History of Boys' Clubs and Related Movement in Great Britain,* (1953); F. Dawes, *A Cry from the Streets: The Boys' Club Movement in Britain from the 1850s to the Present Day* (1975); F. Booton, *Studies in Social Education.* i; *1860–1890* (1985); A. Percival, *Youth Will Be Led* (1951); B. Harrison, 'For Church, Queen and Family: The Girls' Friendly Society, 1874–1920', *Past and Present,* 61 (No. 1973), 107–38; M. Heath Stubbs, *Friendship's Highway* (1926); M. E. Townsend, *The Girls' Friendly Society* (1977); P. Wilkinson, 'English Youth Movements, 1908–1930', *Journal of Contemporary History,* 4, 2 (1969), 1–23. See also H. J. Hendrick, 'The "Boy Labour Problem" in Edwardian England. A Study in the Relationship between Working-Class Adolescents and Middle-Class Reformers', Sheffield University Ph.D thesis (1985), ch. 5.

For about twenty-five years or more prior to the Poor Law Commission designating 'boy labour' a social problem, several attempts had been made to deal with the youth question by enrolling older children and young adolescents in a socially conservative youth movement, whose main features were discipline, religion, and organized leisure. The movement was enormously diversified, but there were three broad groupings which dominated this particular phase and area of the age and class relationship: the uniformed brigades, representing different religious denominations; the clubs, which had varied origins; and the Scouts.

The youth work practice which began to emerge in the 1870s and 1880s built upon a long tradition of mainly religious charitable activity among young people, usually in connection with Sunday schools, temperance societies and the Band of Hope. One of the most influential mid-century organizations was the Young Men's Christian Association (YMCA), 1844, whose members tended to be respectable workers in their late teens and twenties, employed in the retail and clerical professions. From about the mid-1870s the YMCA made a conscious effort to recruit more adolescent and working-class members, and extended its interests to include additional recreational and sporting facilities. In this respect the Association was an important influence on later youth workers who saw that a combination of religion, recreation and welfare could capture the allegiance of members, and thus provide numerous opportunities for their social education. It is certainly not without significance that the Association always maintained a link with the new youth movement by aligning itself with the Boys' Brigade and playing an active role in the formation of the Scouts.[2]

There is little doubt that the principal influence on those who

[2] On charitable work among children and adolescents see K. Heasman, *Evangelicals in Action. An Appraisal of their Work in the Victorian Era* (1962); S.P.C.K., *The First Forty Years. A Chronicle of the Church of England Waifs and Strays Society, 1881–1920* (1922); G. Wagner, *Barnado* (1979); F. K. Prochaska, *Woman and Philanthropy in 19th Century England* (1980), ch. 3; F. Smith (ed.), *The Band of Hope Jubilee Volume* (1897); L. Lewis Shiman, 'The Band of Hope Movement: Respectable Recreation for Working-Class Children', *Victorian Studies* 17/1 (Sept. 1973), 49–74; Revd H. Russell Wakefield, 'Church Band of Hope Work amongst the Young', *The Church's Care for the Recreation and Social Well-Being of the Young* (1908). On the YMCA and YWCA, see C. Binfield, *George Williams and the YMCA* (1973); J. E. Hodder Williams, *The Life of George Williams* (1906); Sheffield YMCA

worked among children and adolescents (and little distinction was made between the two) was organized religion, and, therefore, they were primarily concerned with temperance propaganda, opposition to secularism, the protection of girls and women away from home and, directly and indirectly, with sustaining the Christian family. The new youth movement of the 1880s shared many of these concerns in varying degrees, but it was motivated by several other ambitions which included keeping boys 'off the streets', actively teaching the value of discipline, spreading the public school *esprit de corps*, and generally advocating the intangible virtues of 'character'. In each of the new groups, religious belief and church attendance continued to be encouraged, but this was no longer the principal aim of the movement as a whole.

1. THE UNIFORMED YOUTH MOVEMENT

The new youth movement found its most dramatic expression in the religious brigades, the first of which was the Boys' Brigade (BB), founded by William Smith in Glasgow in 1883, followed by the Church Lads' Brigade (CLB) in 1891, and the Boys' Life Brigade (BLB) in 1899. Throughout the 1880s the Cadet Corps developed among working-class boys (having started in public schools), and in 1908–9 the non-denominational Scouts first appeared in substantial numbers. The religious and philanthropic development of Smith is well known, in particular his background as a missionary in the city and his membership of the YMCA and the Volunteer Force. But it was his experience as a Sunday-school teacher which left him wondering how discipline could be maintained with older boys and how they could be kept in touch with the Church once they became wage-earners and left the Sunday school. One solution was to provide an organization for the 13–17 age-group, such as the Working Boys' Brigades formed in the 1860s, and the Glasgow Foundry Boys' Religious Society.[3]

Undoubtedly the loss of so many young workers from the

publications, *Young Men's Magazine* (1893); Heasman, *Evangelicals in Action*, *passim*; YWCA *Jubilee Volume, 1855–1905* (1905); Anon., *A Study of the World's YWCA* (1924); L. M. Moor, *Girls of Yesterday and Today* (1911).

[3] The best full history of the BB is B. M.Fraser, 'The Origins and History of the Boys' Brigade from 1883 to 1914', Strathclyde University, Ph.D. thesis (981). See also Springhall, *Youth, Empire and Society*, ch. 1; Martin Barratt,

Church was the most significant factor in the immediate origins of the Brigade. As one of the first members recalled, 'When we reached thirteen most of us felt we were too big for the Sunday School, and there was a gap of a few years until we were able to join the YMCA at seventeen . . . During that gap period, many working-class boys ran wild, became hooligans and street-corner loafers.'[4] The BB was formed, wrote Smith, because of the need 'to improve the discipline of the Sunday School; to hold and interest the older boys, and to reach them and influence them, not only on Sunday, but all through the week'.[5] Smith looked to the discipline which he encountered in the Volunteer Force to be put to good use, while the programme of uniform, bands, drill, camps, recreation rooms, and religious instruction was intended to attract young adolescents so that their leisure time might be 'organized'.

The declared aim of the BB was 'The advancement of Christ's Kingdom among Boys and the promotion of habits of Obedience, Reverence, Discipline, Self-respect, and all that tends towards a true Christian manliness'. Smith, who summed up the philosophy as one of 'Discipline and Religion', hoped that by emphasizing masculinity and the becoming of 'Christian men', the boys would come to see the '*manliness* of Christianity' and that this would counter their tendency to regard it as 'effeminate and weak', an idea which seemed to be too popular.[6] The concept of

'The Early Years of the Boys' Brigade: Its Aims and Activities', in K. S. Dent (ed.), *Informal Agencies of Education* (1979); and Springhall, Fraser, and Hoare, *Sure and Steadfast, passim.*

[4] Quoted in Springhall, *Youth, Empire and Society*, p. 24. Sunday-school attendance varied between regions. Fraser says that 3 out of 4 working-class children attended, 'Origins of the Boys' Brigade', p. 25. However, writing about South London in early 1900s, Paterson claimed that only one-fifth attended and 'barely 1 per cent are to be found there after the age of fourteen'. A. Paterson, *Across the Bridges* (1911), 174; see also A. Freeman, *Boy Life and Labour: The Manufacture of Inefficiency* (1914), 264, and J. L. Paton, *Cleansing the City* (1908), 20.
[5] W. A. Smith, *The Story of the Boys' Brigade* (1888), 5; see also A. E. Birch, *The Story of the Boys' Brigade* (1959), 19; F. P. Gibbon, *William A. Smith of the Boys' Brigade* (1934), 32; Fraser, 'Origins of the Boys' Brigade', pp. 118–19; Eagar, *Making Men*, pp. 320–3.
[6] Quoted in R. S. Peacock, *Pioneer of Boyhood: The Story of Sir William Smith, Founder of the Boys' Brigade* (1954), p. 26, and Smith, *Story of Boys' Brigade*, pp. 8–9. For an account of membership in the Bristol Brigade see 'Bristol people's Oral History Project', R087, pp. 2–14.

'manliness' of course was derived from public-school culture, which also inspired Smith to bind 'the boys together and create an *esprit de corps* that would make them proud of their company, jealous of its honour, ashamed to do anything to disgrace it, and prepared to make any sacrifice rather than be dismissed from it'.[7] The ambition was to surround the youth with 'continued influence for good' at a critical time of his life: 'We try to make him feel that there is no part of his life that is beyond the range of God's love, and that everything should be done in God's sight.'[8] In the attempt to provide good influences, officers were advised to cultivate personal contacts: to become friends with the boys, to invite them home for tea and to visit their homes; they were to encourage their charges to have confidence in them and never to break faith; above all, they were told, never 'miss an opportunity of strengthening your hold over them'.[9] If discipline and religion were central to the BB philosophy, so too was friendship—it was the Trojan horse in which 'influence' hid, awaiting its opportunity.

One reason why officers were instructed to be friendly disciplinarians is that Smith, once again echoing public-school sentiments, consciously strove to prolong boyhood for as long as possible. 'Boys', he said, 'ought to be boys' and nothing else. 'We don't attempt to put old heads on young shoulders.'[10] This was a rejection of Arnold's view that the change from 'childhood to manhood . . . ought to be hastened' in favour of that expressed by Warden Sewell of Radley College: 'How I dread mannikizing a boy . . . No, keep boys boys—children children—young men young men.'[11] The Brigade was probably the first youth group to emphasize the specific nature of 'boyhood' and to develop a programme and a philosophy designed for this stage of life.

The BB had many imitators of which the most numerically significant was the CLB and the non-military BLB. The CLB, founded by W. M. Gee, an ex-Volunteer officer and secretary of the Junior Branch of the Church of England Temperance Society,

[7] Gibbon, *William A. Smith*, p. 81 and Smith *Story of Boys' Brigade*, p. 9.
[8] Quoted in Gibbon, *William S. Smith*, p. 82.
[9] *The Boys' Brigade Manual* (1913), 52–3; and Gibbon, *William A. Smith*, p. 53 and Peacock, *Pioneer of Boyhood*, p. 34.
[10] Smith, *Story of Boys' Brigade*, p. 15.
[11] Quoted in F.Musgrove, *Youth and the Social Order* (1964), 55.

saw itself as an Anglican institution for the 'care and training of
lads in Religion, Morals and Physique' during the important
years prior to manhood.[12] In its publications, it claimed to be
'one of England's Great Public Schools'; it was 'the "public
school" of the sons of the poor, where, for a short time, they are
trained in those qualities which make Public School boys so
healthy, *esprit de corps*, obedience, humility, a sense of responsibility, honour and truthfulness'.[13] Although the commitment to
religion was stressed from time to time, often in response to the
charge of militarism, the CLB always seemed to emphasize
matters of social discipline and conformity.

If the BB was intent upon creating Christian men and
displaying the manliness of Christianity, its Anglican counter-
part wished to create conservative and patriotic Christian men.
The political ambitions of the CLB can be deduced from its
interpretation of the Edwardian crisis: 'At so critical a period in
British history as the present, when there is so great and
unfortunate a tendency to slackness, ease, and carelessness as to
religion, morals, and work, when there is so great a craving for
pleasure's sake, when so serious a social problem as the great
army of the unfit and unemployed has become a national scandal
and a public danger', it was necessary to provide men of the
future with 'that spirit of self-denial, self-control and definiteness
of righteous purpose' which had put Britain in the lead among
nations. The Brigade claimed that it could offer both the spirit
and the purpose because it 'disciplines and controls our lads . . .
tames flippancy, quells impertinence, promotes chivalry,
encourages reverence, teaches ready obedience to all properly
constituted authority, and insists upon pure and clean English
and temperance in all things'.[14]

Of all the uniformed organizations, the Boys' Life Brigade

[12] Springhall, *Youth, Empire and Society*, ch. 2; *Twentieth Anniversary
Souvenir of the Church Lads' Brigade, 1891–1911* (1911), 1–11; Anon., *The
Church Lads' Brigade: Some Accounts of its Objects, its Work, its Needs*
(1908), 1. See also *Eighth Annual Report, 1899–1900* (1900) and *The Church
Lads' Brigade and the Church Scout Patrols . . . or . . . Our Men of a Few Years
Hence* (1912).

[13] *CLB Twentieth Anniversary Souvenir*, p. 87. See also *Eighth Annual
Report*, p. 3 and Revd Edgar Rogers, 'The Church Lads' Brigade', in *The
Church's Care for the Recreation and Social Well-Being of the Young*, p. 6.

[14] *The CLB: Some Accounts of its Objects, etc.*, pp. 1–2; Revd Edgar Rogers,
The Making of a Man in the CLB (1919), vii; and *The CLB and the Church*

founded in Nottingham by the Revd John Brown Paton, was the most distinctive in so far as it appeared to be non-military, committed as it was to the principles of life-saving, even though it had a BB-style uniform and a military command structure.[15] Paton shared Smith's belief that young people should be kept under the influence of the Church and that they required discipline and order. However, he was much more explicit in his references to the nature of 'adolescence', referring to it as the age of 'terrible peril' which had to be responded to; the 'wayward forces' had to be 'rightly directed', so that the 'new instincts and impulses, the new faculties and powers . . . shall be rightly exercised and trained, and that protection shall be given as far as possible against the temptations to which it is exposed'. Adolescence was to receive a suitable . . . [and] . . . spiritual education' from the application of Christianity to 'common life'.[16] In practice this included compulsory attendance at either company Bible class or Sunday school, but the unique feature of the BLB was its adherence to life-saving drills (fire, water, and stretcher), with an emphasis on gymnastics, swimming, first-aid and hygiene, in order to 'prepare for helpful service to others', while simultaneously training the body in 'healthful vigour' and 'moral discipline'.[17]

The most militaristic of all the uniformed groups was the Cadet Corps.[18] The Corps originated in 1859 when the Volunteer Movement was formed as a result of the panic over the threat of a French invasion. By the 1870s several public schools had their own cadet or rifle corps, though within the schools it was not until the Boer War that they achieved real popularity. In the 1880s, however, working-class boys began to

---

Scout Patrols, etc. p. 2. For an account of membership in the CLB see 'Family and Work Experience Archive' (Essex), 'Home Life after Leaving School', No. 25.

[15] Springhall, *Youth, Empire and Society*, pp. 44–5; Anon., *Boys' Life Brigade* (1900); John Lewis Paton, *J. Brown Paton: A Biography* (1914), 321–4,329, 422–4; J. Marchant, *J. B. Paton, M A, DD: Educational and Social Pioneer* (1909), ch. 6–9.

[16] Paton, *John Brown Paton*, p. 308.

[17] *Boys' Life Brigade*, pp. 3, 4.

[18] Springhall, *Youth, Empire and Society*, pp. 71–80.

be recruited, largely through clubs associated with University
Settlement Houses and Public School Missions.[19] In common
with the CLB the cadets portrayed themselves as offering a
substitute public-school environment in which the boy would
'learn the duty and dignity of obedience . . . get a sense of
corporate life and civic duty [and] learn to honour the power of
endurance and effort'. These virtues were contrasted by
Octavia Hill, the housing reformer and champion of the cadet
principle, with the 'ill educated, dirty, quarrelsome, drunken,
improvident, unrefined, possibly dishonest, possibly vicious'
environment from which the cadets were to be recruited.[20]

Once the problem of 'boy labour' found its way into middle-
class consciousness, recreation and religion were deemed to be
insufficient for coping with this new and alarming aspect of
the youth question. At the same time as reformers, investigators, and social administrators were beginning to appreciate
its complexity, a new uniformed group appeared which sought
to mobilize boys aged between 11 and 18 with a programme of
outdoor activities and a strong sense of patriotism and moral
purpose.

The story of the Scouts is too familiar to require further
repetition, except in so far as some acknowledgement of the
movement is worthwhile in order to complete this description
of the range of voluntary youth provision in the period.[21]
Whereas the late nineteenth-century organizations had seen
themselves as combatting indiscipline, irreligion, immorality,
and social neglect of their members, the Scout movement
looked to encourage certain positive values necessary for
national and imperial security. It is not quite true to say that
by 1914, 'Ideologies of national purpose, often couched in

---

[19] W. L. Newcombe, *Army Cadet Force*, (1949); Eagar, *Making Men*
pp. 315–16;, J. R. Pimlott, *Toynbee Hall: Fifty Years of Social Progress, 1884–
1934* (1935), 78.

[20] Octavia Hill, quoted in Springhall, *Youth, Empire and Society*, p. 77.

[21] See e.g. ibid., ch. 3; and Springhall's essay in J. A. Mangan and J. Walvin,
(eds.), *Manliness and Morality . . .* 1987); E. E. Reynolds, *The Scout Movement*
(1950); W. Harcourt with Olave, Lady Baden-Powell, *Baden-Powell: Two Lives
of a Hero* (1964); H. Collis, F. Hurll, and R. Hazlewood, *B.P.'s Scouts: An
Official History of the Boy Scouts Association* (1961); M. Rosenthal, *Baden-
Powell and the Boy Scouts. A Character Training Factory* (1986); A. Warren,
'Sir Robert Baden-Powell, the Scout Movement and Citizen Training in Great
Britain, 1900–1920', *English Historical Review* (Ap. 1986), pp. 376–98.

Social Darwinist terms of racial survival, had supplanted earlier religious and moral justifications, though the latter were still very much a part of public rhetoric.'[22] If Scouting was about imperialism and militarism, it was also about 'citizenship'—that repository of a variety of moral precepts.[23] In this respect, as the discussion on continuation schools and citizenship will show, the ideological stance of the movement reflected the larger external debate among educationalists, philosophers, social scientists, and politicians.[24] The basic text was *Scouting for Boys*, although the clue to its meaning was in the subtitle: *A Handbook for Instruction in Good Citizenship*. In choosing the full title, Baden-Powell was responding to the already well-established interest in civics manifested in class-room instruction, the influence of philosophical idealism in educational circles, the propaganda of the Moral Instruction League and to his association with R. B. Haldane, the War Minister, who was also a professional philosopher and a leading educational theorist.[25]

In his search for the most effective approach to the training of boys, Baden-Powell made an extensive study of past and present methods.[26] What emerged was a scheme that sought the development of 'character', partly through the expectation of certain standards of behaviour (a kind of *esprit de corps*), and partly through doing (activities). The importance of the latter was conveyed in the opening chapters dealing with 'camping, camp life, tracking, woodcraft, or, knowledge of animals and nature, saving life, or how to deal with accidents', which were followed by chapters with advice and exhortation: 'Endurance

[22] J. R. Gillis, *Youth and History* (1974), 144.
[23] Hendrick, 'Boy Labour Problem', ch. 5; Warren, 'Sir Robert Baden-Powell' *passim*; K. Orr, 'Moral Training in the Boy Scout Movement', *Melbourne Studies in Education, 1963* (1964), 283–320.
[24] See below, ch. 8.
[25] Warren, 'Sir Robert Baden-Powell', pp. 380–2; F. H. Hilliard, 'The Moral Instruction League, 1897–1919', *Durham Research Review* 3, (1961), 53–63; A. Vincent and R. Plant, *Philosophy, Politics and Citizenship; The Life and Thought of the British Idealists* (1984), ch. 8; P. Gordon and J. White, *Philosophers as Educational Reformers: The Influence of Idealism on British Educational Thought and Practice*. (1979). Apparently Haldane encouraged Baden-Powell to leave the Army and form the Scouts: G. R. Searle, *The Quest for National Efficiency* (1971), 66.
[26] Hendrick, 'Boy Labour Problem', pp. 268–9; Harcourt, *Baden-Powell* pp. 254–5 and Springhall, *Youth, Empire and Society*, pp. 53–4, 59.

for Scouts, or how to be strong', 'Chivalry of the Knights' and, finally, 'Patriotism, or our Duties as Citizens'. The boys were to be given a certain amount of trust in their activities so that they might have the opportunity to make themselves moral, which in turn could help them become good and valuable members of the community.[27] The Scout Law was, after all, 'a statement of a moral condition'.[28] Consequently, the emphasis on 'doing' fitted in with the Idealist view that proper citizenship required purposeful, moral actions. It is this sentiment, as much as any exaggerated nationalism, which explains Baden-Powell's famous objection to the passivity of the working-class football crowd, when he compared football to Roman circuses.[29]

The Scout movement was obviously a conservative organization, conformist and profoundly respectful of properly designated authority. This is manifestly evident in the often quoted passage from a 'Scout's duty as a Citizen' which warned:

A house divided against itself cannot stand . . . Remember, whether rich or poor . . . you are all Britons in the first place . . . If you are divided among yourselves you are doing harm to your country. You must sink your differences . . . We have got, each one of us, to take our place as we find it in this world and make the best of it, and pull together with the others around us . . . Don't think of yourself, but think of your country and your employers. Self-sacrifice pays all round.[30]

Despite the crudity of this message, it was extremely popular as a rallying cry because, in calling for shared community values, it so neatly combined Liberal and Conservative fears about the threat from urban democracy.[31] Loyalty, service, and duty were exactly the values which the 'boy labour' reformers sought to impress upon young workers, and as many of the reformers were also active, or had been active in one or more of

[27] Reynolds, *Scout Movement*, p. 156, quoting Baden-Powell.
[28] R. H. Kiernan, *Baden-Powell*, (1939), 218.
[29] R. Baden-Powell, *Scouting for Boys: A Handbook for Instruction in Good Citizenship* (1910 edn.), 19, 292. See also Harcourt, *Baden-Powell*, p. 251 and Reynolds, *Scout Movement*, pp. 9, 27.
[30] Baden-Powell, *Scouting for Boys*, pp. 272–3.
[31] See below, ch. 8 'Citizenship'.

the youth groups, they were sympathetic to the objectives of the Scout movement. This is not to say that they thought the movement could solve the boy labour problem, or the youth problem in general, but its ideas and its personnel would be useful in sustaining scientific collectivism. There is surely a certain irony in the fact that such a conservative movement should have been enlisted in the service of an essentially liberal aspiration.

2. THE CLUB MOVEMENT

2.1 The origins

The official history of the movement sees it as the outgrowth of 'homes and refuges for the destitute and institutes opened in the evenings with a mainly educational purpose in view'.[32] The institutes which began to open in London in the late 1850s appear to have recruited from among the lower-middle class, though Waldo McGillicuddy Eagar, a young Edwardian club worker (later to be a leading figure in the National Association of Boys' Clubs) claimed that 'as anxiety about the working classes was intensified, some Youths' Institutes reached down from the middle classes to the poor, and increasingly diluted their formal educational programmes with recreational activities'.[33] This was partly due to the unattractiveness of education classes and partly to the pervasive influence of the public-school obsession with games. Whatever the cause, many institutes began to drop the word from their title, and turned themselves into clubs. The distinction between the recreational and the educational establishments was apparent when the Revd Daniel Elsdale opened what has been called the first proper boys' club in the poorer area of his Kennington parish in 1872, and the following year a 'Youth's Institute' in the more middle-class district.[34]

If the origins of clubs are entangled in the intricate web of mid-Victorian religious philanthropy, the lines of development near the end of the century are much easier to discern. The

[32] Dawes, *Cry from the Streets*, p. 26.
[33] Eagar, *Making Men*, p. 169.
[34] Ibid., 170–8.

main sources for the movement as it developed between 1880 and the early 1900s, were University Settlement Houses, Public School Missions, the 'Independents', and the motley collection of local parish clubs and others, many of which were affiliated to larger parent organizations, such as the Girls'· Friendly Society, BB, YMCA, the Wesley Guild of Youth, and the Army Cadets. While the religious influence continued to be a factor, the new movement was not simply an extension of the evangelical impulse; it involved that impulse, but more besides. The clubs were interested in what was termed 'wholesome recreation' and in keeping boys and girls 'off the streets', and they expressed their concern through a social rather than a religious ethos, placing far less emphasis on Church and Bible, preferring instead to emphasize the 'making of men' (albeit Christian men).[35]

The question arises, however, as to why clubs rapidly expanded nationally throughout the 1880s and 1890s. The immediate answer requires us to remind ourselves of the principles governing the Settlement Movement, since the club spirit was essentially that of the settlement. It is well known that the movement was part of a complex colonizing process which began in the early 1880s in the East End of London, whereby members of the upper classes lived among the poor, providing them with a variety of educational, recreational, and welfare services.[36] The intention of the 'residents' was to familiarize themselves with sections of the working class, to develop a sense of contact, both physical and spiritual, between rich and poor. The movement owed its existence in part to an amalgam of anxieties specific to the London crisis of the 1860s, in particular to what Gareth Stedman Jones has called 'The Deformation of the Gift', that is, the emergence of a gulf between the classes which had not only destroyed the 'gift relationship' involving elements of 'prestige, subordination and obligation', but was also fundamentally responsible

[35] C. E. B. Russell and L. M. Rigby, *Working Lads' Clubs* (1908), 22.
[36] For general histories of the movement see A. Briggs and A. Macartney, *Toynbee Hall, The First Hundred Years* (1984), ch. 3–4; Pimlott, *Toynbee Hall* H. Barnett, *Canon Barnett: His Life, Work and Friends* (1919 edns.); B. Simon, *Education and the Labour Movement, 1870–1920* (1965), 78–85; Vincent and Plant, *British Idealists*, ch. 7.

for the 'demoralization' of the poor.[37] In 1883 Canon Barnett, Warden of Toynbee Hall, the first settlement house, expressed the movement's philosophy:

Inquiries into social conditions lead generally to one conclusion. They show that little can be done *for*, which is not done *with* the people. It is the poverty of their own life which makes the poor content to inhabit 'unthinkable' houses . . . which makes so many careless of cleanliness, listless about the unhealthy condition of their workshops, and heedless of anything beyond the enjoyment of a moment's excitement . . . Such poverty of life can best be removed by contact with those who possess the means of higher life. Friendship is the channel by which the knowledge—the joys—the faith—the hope which belong to one class may pass to all classes.[38]

Contact between the classes was vital if political and social harmony were to prevail; as Barnett continued:

It is distance that makes friendship between classes almost impossible, and therefore, residence among the poor is suggested as a simple way in which Oxford men may serve their generation. By sharing their fuller lives and riper thoughts with the poor they will destroy the worst evil of poverty. They will also learn the thought of the majority—the opinion of the English nation—and they will do something to weld Classes into Society.[39]

Here Barnett is opening up a whole store of perceptions, aims, and criticisms which marked out important features of the class relationship in the period (and which were also relevant to age relations), such as the alleged pauperization of self-respect among the poor; their grasping of excitement; and the superiority of middle-class culture which made contact between the classes so crucial. The same kind of critique has already been described in relation to the adolescent 'personality' and to the role played by habits and principles in working-class life. Similarly, the significance of friendship as a means of exercising influence was appreciated by youth workers, as it would be after 1910 in the working out of the

[37] G. Stedman Jones, *Outcast London* (1971), 252–71.
[38] Barnett, *Canon Barnett* vol. i, p. 307.
[39] Ibid., 307–8. See also M. D. Stocks, *Fifty Years in Every Street: The Story of the Manchester University Settlement* (1945; 2nd edn. 1956), 7. On the need for social classes to mix see e.g. Paterson, *Across the Bridges*, pp. 258–71 and H. Bosanquet, *Rich and Poor* (1908 edn.), 142.

juvenile labour exchange, vocational guidance and after-care schemes.

If the crisis of the 1860s provided the original impetus for the settlements, the events of the 1880s made colonization even more necessary.[40] As the first report of Oxford House, run by Keble Anglicans, declared in thought similar to that of Barnett:

Colonisation by the well-to-do seems indeed the true solution . . . for the problem is, how to make the masses realise their spiritual and social solidarity with the rest of the capital and of the kingdom: how to revive their sense of citizenship, with its privileges which they have lost, and its responsibilities which they have forgotten. Among these privileges should be education, rational amusement and social intercourse; and these can best be supplied by local Clubs, with their various guilds, classes and societies. Among the duties . . . which require to be revived, thrift and prudence are pre-eminent; and thrift and prudence can only be taught by men who will associate with the people and thus induce them to face the elementary laws of economy.[41]

The clubs could attempt the task, and indeed their origins include the desire on the part of settlement workers to preach the virtues of citizenship, just as Scouting did more than twenty years later.

In many respects the Public School Missions, widely regarded as 'civilizing' and 'Christianizing' the community, paralleled the settlements, with an ostentatious display of social conscience and religious conviction.[42] Eton, Harrow, Winchester, Marlborough, Rugby, Clifton, Haileybury, Shrewsbury, Wellington, and Charterhouse established clubs as part of their mission work in London, Swindon, Birming-

[40] On religion and secularism see H. McLeod, *Class and Religion in the Late Victorian City* (1974), 67–8, and ch. 3 and 4, and pp. 111 and 125, n. 68, for a contradiction of Stedman Jones, *Outcast London*, that 'fear' rather than 'empathy' was the main ingredient of middle-class consciousness of poverty, in particular as it was expressed by Toynbee Hall. On the franchise and working-class politics, see D. Read, *England, 1868–1914* (1979), 309–39, and Eagar, *Making Men*, pp. 32, 431. For the impact of Henry George's *Progress and Poverty* on Barnett, Eagar, *Making Men*, pp. 32, 183, and for the impact of *The Bitter Cry*, see Barnett, *Canon Barnett*, pp. 309–10.

[41] Quoted in Eagar, *Making Men*, pp. 194–5.

[42] J. Britten, *Catholic Clubs* (1891), 23, and Percival, *Youth Will Be Led*, pp. 99–100.

ham, Liverpool, Bristol, and Portsmouth.[43] The idea of the School Mission had first been conceived by Edward Thring, headmaster of Uppingham, but it was Eton which opened the first club in 1880, followed by Harrow in 1883. The early mood of the schools' social commitment was best expressed by Montague Butler, headmaster of Harrow, when, holding a copy of the revelatory *The Bitter Cry of Outcast London* in his hand while delivering a sermon in Oxford, he called out:

God grant that it may not startle only to be read and pondered by thoughtful brains as well as by feeling hearts . . . God grant that *here* in this great home of eager thought and enlightened action and generous friendship the bitter cry of outcast London may never be intrusive or uninteresting but that year by year her choicest sons may be arrested by it.[44]

By the 1890s, however, it seems that the wave of public-school interest in clubs had passed, and there developed 'an intensification of the snobbery which had always been latent in them, and of the mere athleticism which caricatured the *mens sana in corpore sano* tag'.[45] Nevertheless, among the middle class, there were few institutions so revered as the schools, and their influence in clubs was held to be of great consequence as reformers regularly called for public-school men to come forward to work in the clubs.[46] In 1908 Russell wrote of how the club movement sought to emulate the schools, 'the special pride of the country'. The significance of this, he said,

may be appreciated when we reflect that if our rulers in the nineteenth century were educated at Eton, our rulers of the twentieth century are being educated in the elementary schools. If it is largely the public- school spirit which has made England great in the past, any means by which a similar spirit may be fostered in the boys who leave the elementary schools at the very age when the sons of the

[43] Eagar, *Making Men*, pp. 205–25 and Dawes, *Cry from the Streets*, pp. 42–7. Several of these clubs also organized Cadet companies, indicating the overlap between different groups within the youth movement. See C. Atlee, *As it Happened* (1954), 19, 23.

[44] Quoted in Eagar, *Making Men*, p. 211.

[45] Ibid. 224.

[46] Revd H. S. Pelham, *The Training of the Working Boy* (1914), 113–14, and W. J. Braithwaite, 'Boys' Clubs' in E. J. Urwick (ed.), *Studies of Boy Life in Our Cities* (1904), 199.

monied classes are entering on the most valuable years of their school career, is of incalculable importance.[47]

2.2. Aims

In his classic manual, *Working Lads' Clubs*, Russell argued that the principal aim of clubs was 'to provide youths of the poorer classes with an opportunity of becoming happier, healthier, and better citizens than they are likely to become if they spend their leisure in loafing about the streets'.[48] If working-class youths were to achieve their 'fullest possible development', then attendance at the club was essential. But there were differences as to how best the opportunity could be given to the young people. Some clubs pursued their aim by focusing on recreation, physical exercise, and outdoor games; some were more concerned with general academic education; others with religious instruction; while many tried to offer varied programmes. Whatever the differences between them, however, those who were not attached to religious organizations saw sport and recreation as the 'first reasons' for their existence.[49]

These reasons secured agreement among club workers because they offered an immediate, convenient, and popular response to what was universally seen as the major problem: how to keep adolescents, especially the young ones, 'off the streets'. We have seen how 'the street' and 'the city' played important roles in middle-class demonology, so it is easy to understand why youth workers sought to provide counter-attractions to them, believing as they did that 'there is nothing worth doing to be done there'.[50] But it would be a superficial reading of club ideology to view the movement simply in terms of its 'rescue' work, for though this may have been so in the early days, it was never the sole aim which would imply a passivity hardly reconcilable with the ambitions of the

[47] Russell and Rigby, *Working Lads' Clubs*, p. 267.
[48] Ibid. 22–3.
[49] Ibid.
[50] V. Brooke-Hunt, *Clubs for Boys and Young Men* (1897), 5; see also E. Cadbury, M. Cecile Matheson, and G. Shann, *Women's Work and Wages* (1906), 272; Braithwaite, p. 231; Dawes, *Cry from the Streets*, p. 85; T. H. W. Pelham, *Boys Clubs* (1890), 3; E. M. S. Pilkington, *An Eton Playing Field* (1896), 63; P. Neuman, *The Boys' Club* (1900), 10–11; F. Wills, *Church Polytechnics for Young Men and Lads* (1888), 3–7.

founders of clubs, or with that of the missions and settlement houses. While rescue was the initial objective, it was soon surpassed by the desire to reclaim and re-educate. After all, club life was intended to serve as a practical course in citizenship.

Clubs, Russell wrote, had three main interests: recreation, education, and religion. Boys, he said, needed 'excitement', and if they could not get it by legitimate ways then they would 'seek it in mischief and vice'.[51] The answer to this problem lay in healthy recreation, which meant games, swimming, gymnastics, boxing, indoor games, and, in certain clubs, cycling and country walks.[52] The notion of education was to be interpreted in the widest sense of the word to include physical, moral, and mental training. Religion was also to be given a broad interpretation. Some of the older clubs were narrowly evangelical, but Russell wanted to see religion used 'to comprehend all the impalpable influences which give a club a grip on its boys and tend to awaken their higher nature or further their spiritual development'. [53] 'Real religion', he said, was concerned with 'the quest of the Highest, the practical doing of good, the helping of the weaker, and the unselfish work done for others'.[54] Whatever the rhetoric behind these sentiments, they reflected precepts of duty and service, and were antipathetic to notions of merely keeping boys off the streets.

Another aim, often hinted at, but rarely stated explicitly, was to counter the threat of early sexual and marital relationships—to help the young people 'when they are having a very hard time, physically and often morally'.[55] It was generally agreed that 'One great good of the lads' club is to fill their lives with interests and excitements, so as to prevent premature

---

[51] Russell and Rigby, *Working Lads' Clubs* (1932 edn.), pp. 14–15.

[52] Pelham, *Training of the Working Boy*, pp. 126–7.

[53] Russell and Rigby, *Working Lads' Clubs* (1932 edn.), p. 15; and C. E. B. Russell, *Social Problems of the North* (1913), 72.

[54] Russell and Rigby, *Working Lads' Clubs* (1908 edn.), pp. 205–6. The majority of club workers would probably have agreed with the Catholic writer who wanted religion to be present, but not too obviously so, for 'in striving for too much, we may easily lose all'. Britten, *Catholic Clubs*, p. 13; see also Neuman, *Boy's Club*, p. 17. Those clubs operating under the auspices of a parish church or under the influence of Pelham's handbook were likely to be more religious: Pelham, *Boys Clubs*, pp. 11, 16.

[55] Butler, *Social Conditions in Oxford* (1912) 180. For various aspects see

love-making, the connections, and even the marriages'.[56] Girls
were alleged to have tendencies towards 'flirtation', and were
usually seen as a threat to the healthy development of the
boy.[57] At best they were regarded as a distraction, if not a
danger; the assumption being that as they did not smoke or
play outdoor games, 'they devote themselves . . . to inducing
lads to leave humming-tops and marbles, and cleave only to
them'.[58]

Maude Stanley, for example, a founder of girls' clubs, voiced
the wider social anxiety about the role of girls in the alleged
deterioration of the race and the threat of over-population
among the working class. Furthermore social surveys had shown
that early marriage, by unskilled workers could lead to poverty
and destitution. Reformers believed that one way of preventing
these marriages was to provide clubs with attractive and
organized recreational facilities in the hope that 'the girl who
has her clubs will not need the idle companionship of lads'.[59]
Unsurprisingly, as girls were always portrayed as sweethearts,
and as future wives and mothers, Russell could write:

It is largely a waste of work and energy to train the boys if the girls are
left uncared for and untaught. Far more than is suspected are
inefficient wives responsible for the misery of many back-street
homes, and it is perhaps more than a coincidence that some of the
Lancashire towns with the worst repute for their high rate of infant
mortality have no girls' club within their areas.[60]

E. J. Bristow, *Vice and Vigilance: Purity Movements in Britain since 1700*
(1977), 125–53; J. Weeks, *Sex, Politics and Society* (1981), 48–52; D. Gorham,
'The "Maiden Tribute to Modern Babylon" Re-examined: Child Prostitution
and the Idea of Childhood in Late-Victorian England', *Victorian Studies* 21–3
(Spring 1978); J. R. Gillis, *Youth and History* (1974), 113–14, 158–9;
P. Thompson, *The Edwardians*, (1977), 75–80. See also Slaughter, Clouston
and Hall for views of psychologists; and for a sample of contemporary
pamphlets, see *Pamphlets on Personal Morals*: 'Danger Signals'; 'Self-
Mastery'; 'The Great Secret; 'A Private Letter to a Boy', (Bod. 26521 f. 24).

[56] M. A. Lewis, *A Club for Boys. Why Not Open One?* (1905), 8.
[57] L. Montagu, 'The Girl in the Background', in Urwick (ed.), *Boy Life*,
p. 251.
[58] Wills, *Church Polytechnics*, p. 7.
[59] M. Stanley, *Clubs for Working Girls*, (1904), 216–17, and F. Freeman,
Religious and Social Work among Girls (1901), 93.
[60] Russell, *Social Problems*, p. 72 and Stanley, *Clubs for Working Girls*,
p. 4.

The extent to which contemporaries really believed that clubs affected the infant mortality rate is difficult to gauge, though in club circles such a proposition may well have been tenable. However, it was certainly the case that girls (like their mothers) were seen as 'helpers' and 'guides' to men and to families, and the significance of the club was that it could show them how to overcome their 'understandable selfishness' and reveal 'the beauty of unselfish devotion to others'.[61] All this helps to explain why founders and managers were usually opposed to a mixed membership.[62]

Generally speaking, the movement strove to develop discipline, obedience, self-control, and self-respect, which were the essentials of 'character'. Most founders and managers felt that discipline was the first step on the road to all kinds of mental, moral, and physical improvement. Thus it was looked on as 'the all important matter'.[63] Maude Stanley was only expressing a truism, as far as respectable society was concerned, when she advised that in starting a club 'discipline and order are the first requisites'.[64] Members were required to realize that 'rules have to be obeyed and that obedience is a necessary virtue'.[65] Russell devoted a whole chapter to the topic, where he argued in favour of both the narrow, imposed variety and the more important 'constructive self-discipline'.[66] This emphasis on discipline, has to be seen in the context of the specific nature of the social critique of youth, and of working-class life in general, which focused on notions of chaos, irrationality, spontaneity, and so on. Discipline was important, indeed essential, because in the widest sense of the word, it could open up a more ordered world. There had to be some 'element of order or discipline to contrast ... with the undisciplined nature of the streets'.[67] But it was not just a question of the physical environment; discipline was also

[61] Stanley, *Clubs for Working Girls*, pp. 143–5 and Montagu, 'Girl in Background', pp. 246–7.
[62] Lewis, *A Club for Boys*, p. 8.
[63] Pelham, *Working Boy*, p. 131.
[64] Stanley, *Clubs for Working Girls*, p. 15.
[65] Pelham, *Working Boy*, p. 131.
[66] Russell and Rigby, *Working Lads' Clubs* (1932 edn.), p. 74 and Neuman, *Boys' Club*, pp. 135–41.
[67] Braithwaite, 'Boys' Clubs', p. 176.

integral to the control of the mental environment of individuals; it was part and parcel of self-respect, self-control and perseverance, as well as the ability to shape the nature of one's own existence.

And yet the process whereby the dutiful, rational, moral citizen could be developed was complex. He or she could not be expected to emerge simply as the result of exposure to the properly approved values, though such exposure was crucial, hence the importance of suitable club workers, in particular those with a public-school background. Of equal, if not greater, importance, however, was the personal contact bonded by friendship which all youth groups advocated between members and personnel. As William Smith had understood, contact,—friendship,—influence,—were the means by which not only could the youth be rescued and disciplined, but also civilized. In the words of the Head Missioner of the Birmingham Street Children's Union: 'personal influence, the reaction of character on character, is the only effective force in social or religious reformation'.[68] Similarly, T. H. Pelham, the evangelical pioneer of youth work, and author of the very first club manual, urged on his readers the value of friendship, stressing that 'Personal influence is one of the first conditions of success'.[69] But it was E. J. Urwick who most aptly summarized the approach to youth work:

The right man can produce almost as much impression on a boy in a month as he could on a man in a year, but he must first understand him . . . He must know . . . not only the influences to which he may be made to respond, but those to which his nature is now day by day responding—the complex environment which . . . is the unconscious education of his body and mind and will.[70]

'Making men', then, was an active process, the emphasis was on 'the making', the success of which depended on establishing a relationship that could bring about, through influence and example, a change in the boys' character. Eagar claimed that the friendship was 'uncalculating', but, given the social and

[68] Pelham, *Working Boy*, p. 113; Montague, 'The Girl in the Background', p. 248; Barnett, *Canon Barnett*, vol. ii, pp. 73–4.
[69] Quoted in Eagar, *Making Men*, p. 241; Russell and Rigby, *Working Lads' Clubs*, (1908 edn.), p. 71; Freeman, *Boy Life and Labour*, F. Freeman, *Social Work Among Girls*, pp. 120–37 on importance of 'Visiting'.
[70] Quoted in Eagar, *Making Men*, p. 340.

political environment of the youth organizations, this is most unlikely.[71]

The organized youth movement can easily be identified as emerging from out of the economic and social crises commonly associated with the late Victorian period. On the one hand these groups, which in some respects mark the bridge between the old and the new philanthropy, were the first to focus their attention directly on urban working-class (and in some instances lower-middle-class) youth, rather than on children *and* adolescents, or women *and* girls. In this respect they are the forerunners of the juvenile labour exchanges with their affiliated services of vocational guidance and after-care. On the other hand, unlike their predecessors, they were not advocates of single causes, such as temperance or even religious instruction, but instead sought to attract members with a varied programme which consciously mixed recreation with education, welfare, and sometimes church attendance, for a variety of reasons all of which rested on the specificity of youth in relation to age and to class.

Boy labour reformers disapproved neither of the youth movement in general, nor of its goal, which was the building of Christian character, driven by civic responsibility in search of class harmony. By the early 1900s, however, the youth question was being redefined. Many of those involved had reached the conclusion that the philanthropic provision of youth services was inadequate by itself for the task of tackling the economic, social, and what were coming to be regarded as educational problems concerning working-class adolescents. Several factors had brought about this new attitude. First, the settlement house policy of 'neighbourliness' was trenchantly criticized by young radicals such as George Lansbury and C. F. G. Masterman who saw such movements either as laboratories for ambitious young men or as having lost their initial enthusiasm.[72] Barnett's hope of 'humanizing' the working man

[71] Ibid.
[72] K. S. Inglis, *Churches and the Working Classes in Victorian England* (1963), ch. 4, esp. pp. 172–3.

through friendship and influence alone, though still not completely redundant, looked somewhat antiquated by 1900. Even so, that wave of philanthropically inspired work among boys and girls which began in the 1880s had exhausted itself a decade or more later, and despite the opening of new clubs and the formation of the Scouts, youth work no longer inspired the same missionary zeal. Secondly, it is well known that the impact of the rediscovery of poverty in the 1880s helped to bring about a much more complex analysis of poverty and its causes, which in turn looked toward the State to begin to solve the problem. Once youth was seen to figure in that problem, it became illogical to suppose that it could be kept separate from the collectivist response. Thirdly, and more precisely, social scientists and youth workers themselves were increasingly aware of and worried by the 'boy labour' topic. The range of essentially economic issues revealed by the ensuing debate was such that it was almost impossible to conceive of the solution being affected by either brigade or club.

Given this to be so, under the influence of the new analyses (of poverty and of the youth labour-market), it was appreciated that the critical features of the youth question were not only those relating to church attendance, unorganized leisure, absence of *esprit de corps* and, at the extreme end of the spectrum of anxiety, juvenile delinquency. No one denied the importance of these factors, but it was now felt that others would have to be included. Where the late Victorian perception of youth emphasized their social identity—religion, leisure, discipline, character—the Edwardian perception, while accepting the significance of the social (and elaborating upon it), in addition gave working-class youth an economic identity which was important in itself, and as a conditioning factor in the development of the citizen.

The change in attitude was perhaps most clearly evident in *Studies of Boy Life in Our Cities*, where Urwick and his collaborators saw the boy neither 'as an amusing playmate nor as a vagrant from the ecclesiastical fold, but as the product of a still imperfect educational system and the embryo of the citizen who would decide the destiny of a still incohate democracy'.[73] In his concluding essay, Urwick wrote: The club

---

[73] Eagar, *Making Men*, p. 386.

can catch him, but cannot discipline him, the Boys' Brigade can discipline him to a small extent, but cannot catch or keep him when he most needs it; the voluntary evening school can do neither. Nothing short of a compulsory system in which both physical and mental training are combined, can hope to do both successfully.'[74] This criticism was in part a reflection of the call made by the *Report of the Committee on Physical Deterioration* for greater physical and mental education for adolescents, but it also pointed to the three main criticisms of clubs which were reiterated years later by Freeman: that they could only really provide amusement; that their positive educational value was small; and that they failed to reach the mass of boys.[75]

None the less, it should be stressed that in the changed climate of the early twentieth century, there was no question of abandoning the youth organizations: that would have meant jettisoning the principle of voluntary action. Moreover, several of the leading reformers, who were to become important administrators in local and national government agencies, were also prominent in the youth movement and had no wish to weaken it: Jackson, Russell, Paterson, and Norman Chamberlain. (And Baden-Powell had been asked to become the first chairman of the Juvenile Organizations Committee, established by the Home Secretary, Herbert Samuel in 1916.)[76] There was, then, no intention of repudiating all the work of the clubs, brigades, and the Scouts. It was true that in the 1880s youth work had meant philanthropy and religion, whereas in

---

[74] Urwick (ed.), *Boy Life*, p. 290. See also Braithwaite, 'Boys' Clubs', p. 207 and Russell, *Social Problems*, p. 71.

[75] Freeman, *Boy Life and Labour*, pp. 128–31.

[76] Other well-known figures involved at one time or another in the youth movement included Clement Atlee, R. H. Tawney, W. J. Braithwaite, A. H. Norris, and Basil Hendriques. Under the influence of wartime concern over juvenile delinquency, the Home Secretary, Herbert Samuel called a conference of leading figures in the youth movement, out of which came the Juvenile Organizations Committee (1916), with Russell as Chairman. The JOC had a fitful existence until 1939. Eagar, *Making Men*, pp. 397–9, and V. Bailey, *Delinquency and Citizenship: Reclaiming the Young Offender, 1914–1948* (1987), 11. The important educational role of the clubs was recognized by HMI, J. Dover Wilson, when he looked to them to work with the proposed compulsory part-time day continuation schools. PRO. Ed, 46/15/a. Paper 9, p. 21. For the influence of club work on 'reclaiming' delinquents in the inter-war period, see Bailey, *Delinquency and Citizenship*, passim.

the 1900s it was felt to be the responsibility of local education authorities, juvenile employment committees, after-care committees and part-time day continuation classes in liberal and vocational studies. However, not only were these statutory bodies to work with the voluntary sector, but much of the day-to-day running of the new 'services' would continue to rely on volunteers from the youth groups, for their time and expertise were essential if the new schemes were to be viable. In the area of youth policy, as in many other areas of welfare, the philanthropic tradition was incorporated into the social service state which was emerging from the Liberal reform programme.

7. Rites of Passage: Origins of the Youth Employment Service

The means by which school-leavers made the transition from school to full-time wage-earning have been described, as have the criticisms of reformers who dubbed it 'haphazard'.[1] Once it became obvious that youth organizations could not solve the 'boy labour problem', either socially or economically, the question arose as to what needed to be done. The idea of a youth employment service, however, did not figure prominently as a solution to the problem, probably because social scientists did not begin to examine the possibilities of labour exchanges until after 1905.[2] The fact that very little concerted thought had been given to organizing the juvenile labour-market does not mean that no action had been taken at the local level by schools, skilled employment committees, and several or more local education authorities.[3] In many respects, between them these bodies, especially the Apprenticeship and Skilled Employment Association (ASEA), pioneered the basic elements of the service as it was to develop, namely, vocational guidance, registration and placement, and after-care. Furthermore, in forging a connection between juvenile employment and education, they helped to portray the transition as essentially an educational rather than a trade process. This had two important consequences. First, it kept the school-leaver within the realms of dependence, emphasizing the need for guidance and employment advice; and, secondly, it led to the eruption of a lively dispute between the Board of Education and the Board of Trade over which department should have final authority for adolescent workers in the administration of the Labour Exchanges Act 1909. However, before describing the dispute and the practices of the two main schemes to emerge

---

[1] See ch. 3, sec.2, and ch. 4 s. 1.
[2] J. Harris, *Unemployment and Politics: A Study in English Social Policy, 1886–1914* (1972), 199–200.
[3] See ch. 3, s. 2.

out of the compromise, it will be useful to look more closely at the work of the ASEA which, in its legacy to the service, was the most influential of all the voluntary agencies.

1. THE APPRENTICESHIP AND SKILLED EMPLOYMENT ASSOCIATION

Apprenticeship and skilled employment committees of one sort or another had existed in London since the 1860s and 1870s when the Jewish Board of Guardians decided to organize apprenticeship schemes for their own young workers. Several years later this example led to the establishment of an Association for Befriending Boys, followed in 1906 by the Lads' Employment Committee, though neither was exclusively concerned with formal apprenticeships.[4] There is some confusion as to the exact origins of the first Apprenticeship and Skilled Employment Committee, but it probably derived from the activities of the Charity Organization Society (COS) in assisting women and girls to find skilled occupations. A number of COS district branches soon began to form themselves into separate committees for this purpose, and in 1902 a Central Industrial Bureau was opened which, under pressure from increased applications from boys as well as girls, addressed itself to both sexes. Within a few years it had evolved into the ASEA, and by 1909 there were seventeen affiliated committees in London and ten in the provinces.[5]

---

[4] For Jewish youth work see S. Bunt, *Jewish Youth Work in Britain* (1975), 17–19, and V. D. Lipman, *A Century of Social Service, 1859–1959: The Jewish Board of Guardians* (1959), 67–9, 119–123. For others see A. Greenwood, *Juvenile Labour Exchanges and After-Care* (1911), 42–4.

[5] The story of the Association's roots can be pieced together from J. Parsons, 'The Work of an Apprenticeship and Skilled Employment Committee', *Toynbee Record* (Mar. 1907), 74–5; H. Heginbotham, *Youth Employment Service* (1951), 2; Anon., *Charity Organisation Review* (July 1905), 45; H. Bourdillon, 'Apprenticeship Work and How to Carry it On', *Charity Organisation Review* (Apr. 1905), 207; J. Parsons, 'Skilled Employment Committees', *Charity Organisation Review* (July 1907), 23; O. J. Dunlop and R. D. Denman, *English Apprenticeship and Child Labour* (1912), 327; F. Keeling, *The Labour Exchange in Relation to Boy and Girl Labour* (1910), 14; Greenwood, *Juvenile Labour Exchanges*, pp. 41–2; E. Jebb, 'Apprenticeship and Skilled Employment Committees', in M. E. Sadler (ed.), *Continuation Schools in England and Elsewhere* (1907), 454–71; the *Poor Law Commission*, vol. IX, Cd. 5068, (1910), xlix, appendix no. lxiii, p. 913; H. Bosanquet, *Social Work in London* (1914; 1970 edn.), 259–61: M. Rooff, *A Hundred Years of Family Welfare* (1972), 86–7. Among the cities with affiliated committees were Liverpool, Hove, Birmingham, Hastings, Oxford, Glasgow, Cambridge and Edinburgh.

The main objectives of the ASEA were to prevent elementary school-leavers from 'drifting into unskilled occupations,
and later on into unemployment'; and to promote industrial
training through 'apprenticeships and other methods', usually
trade schools and technical education classes. In addition, and
just as important, it sought to co-ordinate and supplement
information from local committees concerning industrial
intelligence and vacancies through meetings, conferences, and
literature.[6] The critical work, however, was performed by the
local committees with their voluntary membership, whose
aims included recruiting applications from juveniles for assistance in obtaining apprenticed positions, compiling a register of
suitable vacancies and employers, keeping themselves informed about the condition of local trades, and supervising the
observation of indenture regulations by both apprentices and
employers. But by far the most important duties were to offer
vocational guidance to prospective apprentices, to negotiate
with employers on their behalf, and to encourage 'thrift among
the parents' so that they could save towards the cost of the
premiums.[7]

From their earliest days the local groups relied upon the co-
operation of schools and education authorities, and to a lesser
extent club workers, to supply them with the necessary
information concerning pupils who were about to leave school.
The London County Council (LCC), for example, drew the
attention of head teachers to the existence of the ASEA, and by
1909 the Council was trying to establish a formal liaison
between local branches and its own reconstituted Children's
Care Committees.[8] The usual procedure was for sympathetic
teachers to provide branches in their areas with lists of school-
leavers each of whom was then interviewed at home with his
or her parents by a 'visitor' who discussed the general
employment situation with them, urging the importance of
continued education and inviting the parents to make a formal
application to the committee for assistance. If the visitor was

[6] Greenwood, *Juvenile Labour Exchanges*, pp. 40–1, quoting Annual Report
for 1909, p. 5; ASEA, *Trades for London Boys and How To Enter Them* (1908),
p. v; *Poor Law Commission*, Appendix lxiii.
[7] Anon., *Charity Organisation Review*, pp. 45–6 and Parsons, 'Work of an
Apprenticeship', p. 80.
[8] *Poor Law Commission*, Appendix lxiii, pp. 913–14; and Keeling, *Labour
Exchange*, pp. 16–17.

unsuccessful, influences were brought to bear from other quarters, such as the clergy, the district visitor, or some other agency with knowledge of the family. It seemed, however, that an increasing number of juveniles, with the permission of their parents, were being referred directly to the ASEA committees by teachers, club managers, clergymen, and welfare workers. Many were also referred by elder brothers and sisters or friends who had already been placed.[9]

When parents applied for assistance they were asked to provide general information about the family, including occupations, earnings, rent, and size of accommodation. At the same time, teachers were asked to make out a special report card on the child, itemizing health, academic standard, character, ability, and what they considered would be a suitable employment.[10] The next step was to enter all the details on a single form to which were attached any other relevant papers. These were then filed and added to with frequent reports, letters, and documents. The final phase in the procedure involved giving parents advice about prospective job opportunities for their children, and this was considered to be the most difficult part of the work as it meant balancing all the different factors in an attempt to situate the best applicant in the best position. Once parental approval had been obtained, the committee entered into negotiations with employer and parents and on reaching a satisfactory agreement, the young person might be taken on a month's trial.[11]

While the ASEA emphasized vocational guidance and suitable placement, it was equally concerned with after-care

[9] Parsons, 'Work of an Apprenticeship', pp. 75–6; Jebb, 'Apprenticeship and Skilled Employment Committees', pp. 456–7; Bourdillon, 'Apprenticeship Work' p. 208–9; Anon, 'Work on a Skilled Employment Committee', *Oxford House Magazine* 11/8 (Oct. 1910), 32–7; Greenwood, *Juvenile Labour Exchanges*, p. 40. Details of the home visits by members of the Oxford committee, known as the Council for Industrial Advancement (CIA), are available in Butler Papers, 'CIA, 1908–15. Mis. Papers'. Box 4. Contains details on file cards of visits and reports of visitors to homes of young people during 1909–10. 330 homes were visited; usually only parents were interviewed. For comments on girls' families, see 'CIA 1905–8, "The Girls Book"', Box 3.

[10] Butler Papers, 'CIA, A–E. 1909–12 "Boys Employment Committee. Teachers' forms"', Boxes 6, 7.

[11] Parsons, 'Work of an Apprentice', pp. 76–8; details on local employers in Butler Papers, 'Boy and Girl Labour, 1909–11', Box 5.

supervision, usually until the youth was aged 17 or 18. Each committee appointed a member who acted as a 'guardian' whose main responsibilities were to supervise the working of the indentures, to make monthly visits to the home, and to be 'on friendly terms' with parents and child. After-care was considered necessary in order to ease the employer-employee relationship and because it added 'the personal touch which is the breadth of life to this and every form of charitable effort'.[12]

When the committee system of the ASEA is considered as a whole, it is apparent that members were consciously operating an employment policy based upon casework, the practice most conspicuously associated with the COS, which, given the origins of the Association, is by no means unexpected. The renowned original intention of the COS was to organize charity, but it soon found itself investigating individual cases, and as a result developed a casework methodology, the fundamentals of which were home-visiting, comprehensive and in-depth interviewing, written records, committee discussions, emphasis on 'character' as well as circumstances, preservation of family respectability, and, generally applicable, a 'carefully specified procedure'.[13] Personal contact and visits to the homes of the poor and the sick were part of a long-established visiting tradition, but the COS fused this with casework to produce a quite distinctive practice.[14] And after the 1880s the renewed emphasis throughout philanthropic work on the 'personal' relationship between the classes gave these contacts a special significance in terms of influencing the 'character' of parents and their adolescent children.

In theory, the committees were to provide opportunities for skilled and apprenticed employment, though members

---

[12] Parsons, 'Work of an Apprentice', p. 78.

[13] Ibid. C. L. Mowat, *The Charity Organisation, 1869–1913: Its Ideas and Work* (1961), 29–30, 39; A. F. Young and E. T. Ashton, *British Social Work in the Nineteenth Century* (1956), 102–3; K. Woodroofe, *From Charity to Social Work in England and the United States* (1962), 42, 44, 47; J. Fido, 'The Charity Organisation Society and Social Casework in London, 1869–1900', in A. P. Donajgrodzki (ed.), *Social Control in Nineteenth Century Britain* (1977), 217.

[14] On visiting, see F. K. Prochaska, *Women and Philanthropy in 19th Century England* (1980), 47–137; A. Summers, 'A Home from Home; Women's Philanthropic Work in the Nineteenth Century', in S. Burman (ed.), *Fit Work for Women* (1979), 33–63.

admitted that formal apprenticeship, at least, was not always possible, partly because it appeared to many observers that machines had eradicated a number of handicrafts, turning the worker into a 'machine-tending artisan', and partly because 'skill' was a relative concept, demanding different degrees of training.[15] Consequently, the 'visitors' and 'guardians' usually settled for any occupation that required 'some training which offered a prospect of continuous employment, and which fulfils the other desirable conditions'.[16] Even so, the machine factor remained an important consideration, in particular what was seen as the growing practice of instructing boys in a single process. Thus while the committees hoped their work would act as an antidote to the apparent tendency 'to reduce workpeople to the mental condition of animated machines', they also sought to encourage an all-round improvement in efficiency and a training designed to develop 'the habit of regular industry . . . a healthy growth in mind and body', the inculcation of thrift, and the ever popular 'discipline'.[17]

Clearly, more than simple apprenticeship is at issue here. The clue to the ambitions of the ASEA is to be found in the plea that the training of youths was to be 'a continuance of their education', and an aspect of the committees' work that 'should ever be borne in mind'.[18] This reiterated the belief, common among all those concerned with the youth question, that 'adolescence' should be regarded as a period of education, supervision, control, and guidance. It was also an attempt, in certain respects a successful attempt (at least in terms of creating a social image), to project the early years of full-time wage-earning as an 'apprenticeship' to an approved form of adulthood. However, these reformers found, just as others would find within the framework of the national labour exchange system after 1910, that the economic reality of the free market in labour was always the more influential factor.

Although widely admired, the ASEA was by no means

---

[15] H. W. Jevons, 'Industrial Prospects for Boys and Girls', *Charity Organisation Review*, 20/117 (Sept. 1906), 125–39, and Keeling, *Labour Exchange*, p. 14.

[16] Parsons, 'Work of an Apprentice', p. 77.

[17] Ibid., pp. 80–81, and his 'Skilled Employment Committees', p. 19.

[18] Parsons, 'Work of an Apprentice', p. 80.

without its critics, and considerable doubt was expressed as to whether it offered a practical answer to the problem of boy labour. The small scale of its activities was always mentioned: it was estimated that of the 30,000 boys who annually left London elementary schools, not more than 2% came under its influence and that of similar organizations.[19] Other major weaknesses were said to be the emphasis on skilled employment, of either the apprenticed or respectable kind, and the individualist approach to the problem. The committees could find 'a nice place for a nice boy', wrote Bray, but the problem remained untouched, in part because apprenticeship alone was no solution.[20] And Dearle claimed that in addition to the small scale of their work and the inexperience of their members, the committees also suffered from a difficulty in gaining the support of employers, especially in persuading them to grant the young worker time off for further education. Too much attention, he added, was given to obtaining indentures and too little to the quality of the training.[21]

The most trenchant criticisms came from Urwick, who argued that the ASEA simply did not understand the workings of the labour-market. The fact was, he said, the market wanted boy labour for occupations 'for which there is a relatively low demand for adult labour'. So boys flocked to take up these jobs which were harmful to their long-term interests and, therefore, philanthropists felt moved to interfere by 'choking off' the juvenile supply and by turning juvenile labourers into skilled workers.[22] In Urwick's view, those who sought to turn every boy into an apprentice wished to construct an 'ideal market' where the demand was for skilled labour. This ignored, or misunderstood, the regular complaint of employers about the lack of good workmen, which did not mean they required

---

[19] R. A. Bray, *Boy Labour and Apprenticeship* (1911), 91; Dunlop and Denman, *English Apprenticeship*, p. 327; N. B. Dearle, *Industrial Training* (1914), 461. During 1909, for example, the London committees dealt with 2,751 applicants but placed only 948: 'Editorial Notes', *Charity Organisation Review* (May 1914), 231. In Oxford, the committee received 119 applications over an eighteen-month period, but placed only 39. *Butler Papers* 'Report of the Council for 1908–19', Box 4.

[20] Bray, *Boy Labour*, pp. 228, 189.

[21] Dearle, *Industrial Training*, pp. 461–2.

[22] E. J. Urwick, 'Apprenticeship and Skilled Employment: A Criticism', *Toynbee Record* (May 1907), 103–4.

'skilled' workers, who were always available; what they
required were efficient workers. The real need was for 'efficient
labourers and factory workers by the million and for "efficient"
skilled workers by the thousand'.[23] In the present situation,
the ASEA could never be a remedy for the 'general wasteful-
ness of industry'; instead, its proper role was in helping
employers to get the right kind of boy, and boys to find the
right kind of employer and to ensure that training was
effective, both in terms of the workshop and of continued
education. The fundamental answer to the 'boy labour problem', however, lay in state action to prohibit employers from
exploiting juvenile labour, just as the State had acted in the
past in 'the case of children and women'. Urwick maintained
that the hopes for a sound economy rested on state interfer-
ence, more than on 'the exaggerated hopes' of the various
skilled employment committees.[24]

Notwithstanding these criticisms there are five reasons
which explain why the ASEA was important in the origins of
the juvenile labour exchange system. First, it developed the
concept of integrated and comprehensive provision; secondly,
in making a connection between school and wage-earning, it
successfully rendered the transition as a social and educational
process; thirdly, it made vocational guidance and after-care
appear to be essential features of any youth employment
scheme; fourthly, it showed that the service could offer
significant opportunities for exercising a personal influence
over the adolescent and his family. Finally, and of some
significance, not only did many of the personnel continue to
serve in the state system on a voluntary basis after 1909, no
doubt bringing their ideas with them, but also the casework
procedures became the basic methodological practice of the
service.

2.   THE LABOUR EXCHANGES LEGISLATION

The Labour Exchanges Act 1909 was part of the response by
the Liberal Government to the problem of unemployment and

---

[23] Ibid. 104–5 and his second article of the same title, *Toynbee Record* (June
1907), p. 117.
[24] Ibid. 118–19.

underemployment. But the state labour exchanges established by the new legislation were by no means the first attempt to assist workers in finding jobs, though most of the previous efforts had been confined to specific trades or occupations.[25] In 1885 a new type of exchange had opened in Egham, Surrey, known as the Egham Free Registry, which was designed to make contact between employers and workers. A similar exchange opened in 1880 in Ipswich, and in 1891 the Borough of Chelsea launched the first municipal exchange. By the end of 1892 there were seventeen private registries and thirty-one under the control of local authorities in England and Wales.[26] In 1905 the Unemployed Workman Act gave statutory force to a scheme inaugurated the previous year by Walter Lang, the President of the Local Government Board, under which a Central Executive Committee founded a Central Employment Exchange.[27] The Committee soon became the Central (Unemployed) Body (CUB), with one of its functions being to 'establish, take over, and assist Labour Exchanges or Employment Registers and collect information'.[28] By 1907, the CUB, acting on a plan initiated by W. H. Beveridge, was busy opening exchanges in every London borough, each of which made special provision for women and juveniles, and provided vocational guidance for school-leavers through working in co-operation with the ASEA and the Education Department of the LCC.[29] This shows that from the earliest days of government interest in organizing the labour-market, Beveridge at least saw juvenile labour as a separate category which would require the formulation of a joint approach by the exchanges and local education authorities.

In 1908, Beveridge, who by now was an acknowledged expert on unemployment and its remedies, joined the Board of Trade as an unestablished civil servant and prepared his first brief for the president, Winston Churchill. In his paper, Beveridge repeated what he had been saying for some time, namely, that

[25] Harris, *Unemployment and Politics*, p. 279. In this and the next section I am endebted to the account provided by José Harris.
[26] Ibid. 279–80, and Heginbotham, *Youth Employment Service*, p. 8.
[27] Ibid. 8.
[28] Ibid. 9 and Harris, *Unemployment and Politics*, pp. 201–2.
[29] J. Harris, *William Beveridge: A Biography* (1977), 127 and her *Unemployment and Political*, pp. 201–2.

there was no general breakdown of the labour-market, instead
there was an overstocking of individual trades which was due
to 'inadequate labour information and local hindrances to
labour mobility'.[30] He believed there was not one problem of
unemployment, but several, some of which were simply part of
modern industry, while others could be cured by state
intervention.[31] Beveridge also held the view that throughout
'modern industry' there was a lack of mobility, a lack of
communication, and 'wasteful duplication of the labour force'.
In his opinion the system of production had not developed an
equally modern system of labour organization, and the result
was widespread unemployment. He identified the several
causes of unemployment as poor organization of industry,
seasonal and cyclical fluctuations in the demand for labour,
structural decline of certain industries or trades, personal
deficiencies and, to a certain extent, 'blind-alley' situations.[32]

Though Beveridge was rather ambivalent about the role of
the 'blind alley', his recognition of the imaginary nature of
many of the faults attributed to the juvenile labour-market has
been established. He nevertheless shared with other critics a
concern about the untrained, unregulated, and unsupervised
adolescent work-force, and found it impossible to separate
completely the behaviour of these young workers from the
larger problem of unemployment. The use of labour exchanges
to encourage vocational guidance and industrial training
would, he argued, have three consequences: it would reduce
risks of individual 'maladjustment', which often meant waste
of abilities and even unemployment; it would adjust the flow
of labour between trades; and it would discourage 'blind-alley'
occupations, which he saw as not only demoralizing, but also
as likely to lead to 'a fresh point of stress in industry—the
transition to a new occupation at manhood'.[33] While denying

---

[30] Harris, *Beveridge*, pp. 146, 149. For the development of his views, see his
'Labour Bureaux', *Economic Journal* 16/63 (Sept. 1906), 436–9; 'Labour
Exchanges and the Unemployed', *Economic Journal* 17/65 (Mar. 1907), 66–81,
and 'The Problem of the Unemployed', *Sociological Papers* 3 (1906), 323–41.

[31] Harris, *Beveridge*, p. 141.

[32] W. H. Beveridge, *Unemployment: A Problem of Industry* (1909; 1917
edn.), ch. 3, 7. Though his views on blind-alley situations were a little
inconsistent: see his pp. 212–13.

[33] Ibid. 212.

the importance of industrial training as the 'principal' remedy for unemployment, he looked to technical education to raise the general level of skill 'from which men start', as well as to divert juvenile labour (which he described as 'adaptable') into new and growing trades.[34] If each of these requirements were to be implemented, it was, he said, necessary to have at least an organized labour-market, though much more would be needed.[35]

Churchill gave his approval to the idea of labour exchanges and, in a cabinet paper drafted by Beveridge, he circulated the details of the proposed system in January 1909.[36] In the section entitled 'Juvenile Employment', Beveridge pressed the view that the exchange should be more than a place of registration and placement: it should be 'both a market-place and a centre of guidance and supervision in the choice of 'careers'. Accordingly, he suggested separate facilities at each exchange for dealing with juveniles; notices with information about the exchanges were to be displayed in schools; lists of prospective school-leavers to be sent to the local exchange with details of their 'ability, tastes and desires'; and each school-leaver to be told to call at the exchange for an interview. 'In this way boys and girls would get ample opportunity of guidance as to their choice of careers, and those who were going to be apprenticed or learn skilled trades might have all their arrangements made while still at school.' Beveridge also recommended the establishment of 'special juvenile advisory committees' at the exchanges with representatives from education authorities; or, alternatively, the exchanges could co-operate with the ASEA and similar agencies. Whenever special committees were formed, they were to be 'in connection with the schools' and their duties were to include supervising conditions of labour, making recommendations as to continuation and technical education classes, forming 'a public opinion' against 'blind-alley' occupations, organizing apprenticeships, and caring for juveniles with special disabilities.[37]

These details make it clear that Beveridge regarded young

---

[34] Ibid. 213. For 'adaptability', see below, ch. 8, s. 3.1.
[35] Beveridge, *Unemployment*.
[36] Harris, *Beveridge*, p. 151.
[37] PRO CAB 37/97/17, 'Memorandum on Labour Exchanges' (Jan. 1909), 10.

workers as constituting a separate source of labour supply
which required specialized provision and that he agreed with
the ASEA and the 'boy labour' reformers in wishing to see the
transition from school to work treated as an educational
matter (though not necessarily one controlled by the Board of
Education). The thinking of Beveridge on the subject was
governed by one principal consideration: how to make the
labour-market more efficient. He (among others) perceived
adolescent labour as an obstacle to efficiency not only because
it lacked knowledge of employment opportunities and the
ability to distinguish between the merits of different
occupations, but also because its inherent 'adaptability' was
'wasted' (always a key notion in National Efficiency circles) by
the 'haphazard' nature of the transition which left too many
youths in dead-end jobs and failed to enrol them in any form of
further education.[38]

The Labour Exchanges Bill passed its second reading without
a division on 16 June 1909, and the new exchanges opened their
doors in February 1910.[39] But the Act made no specific
reference to special provision for young workers.[40] However, it
was well known that Beveridge, together with Churchill and
other important officials such as Llewellyn Smith and George
Askwith, were intent on setting up a scheme for juveniles.[41]
The question had been raised in the Commons during the
debates on the Bill, when Churchill indicated that the Board of
Trade hoped for co-operation between labour exchanges and
local education authorities (LEAs) in the sharing of information,
and that in certain instances Juvenile Advisory Committees
(JACs) could be established. Where this did not happen it
would be possible for part of the membership of the Exchange
Advisory Committees (provided for in section 2, subsection v

[38] Harris, *Unemployment and Politics*, p. 285.
[39] For details of the early exchanges see C. F. Rey, 'The National System of
Labour Exchanges', in *Proceedings of the National Conference on the
Prevention of Destitution* (1911), 394–402, and the *Board of Trade Gazette*, 18/
2, (Feb. 1910), 67.
[40] The Act is easily accessible in appendix E of Beveridge, *Unemployment*
(1917 edn.).
[41] Harris, *Beveridge*, p. 160. Both reports of the Poor Law Commission had
also called for special provision for juveniles; *Majority*, pp. 631 and *Minority*,
pp. 1190–1, as had Cyril Jackson in his *Special Report on Boy Labour in
London and Certain other Towns*, Cd. 4632 (1909), xliv, p. 31.

of the Act) to be co-opted to assist with the local education employment bureaux which were being started in Scotland and in parts of England. Churchill was emphatic in saying that 'boy labour' would be dealt with in conjunction with education authorities 'because we have no intention of allowing the commercial side to override the educational side in regard to young people'.[42] Whether this meant that market forces were not going to be allowed unrestrained activity is unclear; there was definitely no legal mechanism to inhibit them. The more immediate problem, however, was which of the two Boards (trade or education) should have overall authority for the juvenile side of the exchanges and Churchill may well have sensed that a controversy was brewing.[43]

3. THE DISPUTE BETWEEN THE BOARD OF EDUCATION AND THE BOARD OF TRADE

The rival claims of the two departments never became a contentious matter among the 'boy labour' group of reformers, though the majority appear to have favoured the Board of Trade. The general view was that the exchanges, through their JACs should work in co-operation with LEAs, schools, and voluntary agencies such as the ASEA.[44] The important issue for reformers was the creation of a national, comprehensive system offering guidance, placement, and after-care. No doubt many of them agreed with Beveridge in regarding the local authorities as unsuited by themselves to cope with the administration of the service.[45] However, despite the repeated calls for co-operation between the different interests, nothing could be done to allay the criticisms of certain members of the

[42] *Hansard*, (1909), C. 501–2 and vi (1909), C. 1039–40.

[43] Harris, *Beveridge*, pp. 160–3.

[44] Greenwood, *Juvenile Labour Exchanges*, pp. 13–14, 48–52; Keeling, *Labour Exchange*, pp. 9–11, 34, 56–9, 61, 65. Keeling noted that even the ASEA shared his view, p. 56. See also Bray, *Boy Labour*, pp. 222–24; G. W. Knowles, *Junior Labour Exchanges: A Plea for Closer Co-operation between Labour Exchanges and Education Authorities* (1910), 9–22; J. Myers, 'The Juvenile Side of the National Labour Exchange', *School Child* (May 1910), 10–11, (Sept. 1910), 5–6; Dunlop and Denman, *English Apprenticeship*, pp. 343–4 (Denman was the first chairman of the London JAC); C. Jackson, *Unemployment and Trade Unions* (1910), 66–7; Dearle, *Industrial Training*, pp. 506–11.

[45] Harris, *Beveridge*, p. 161.

Board of Education, sections of the educational press, notably the *School Government Chronicle* (organ of the LEAs), and several local Directors of Education.[46] José Harris has gone as far as to describe the dispute as 'a major conflict of principle' between the two boards.[47] Certainly Sir Robert Morant, the powerful Permanent Secretary at the Board of Education, argued strongly that organizing a juvenile employment service was part of the education process and as such should be in the hands of his department.[48] Similarly, E. K. Chambers, who was an official at the board, was determined to secure for education committees the sole right of both advising and placing juveniles.[49] Morant, Chambers and others were aware that for ten years or more several LEAs including Sheffield, Nottingham, Wigan, Liverpool, Carlisle, Finchley, Bolton, Cambridge, and Edinburgh had been experimenting with their own employment schemes.[50] It was no doubt with this in mind that an editorial in the *Chronicle* explained how the provision of vocational guidance had grown gradually and represented the interaction of official and voluntary organizations, the intricacies of which were not appreciated by the Board of Trade.[51]

One of the most vociferous voices in the dispute was that of Mrs Ogilvie Gordon, chairwoman of the Education Committee of the National Union of Women Workers, and an old campaigner on behalf of vocational guidance for young people. In 1904, at a meeting in Glasgow, she had proposed the establishment of a national system of 'Educational Information and Employment Bureaux' to be run by the local

[46] However, Denman wrote to Sidney Buxton, President of the Board of Trade, saying that the Board of Education was not 'over popular' with the LEAs, many of whom, he thought, probably wanted the Board of Trade scheme. Denman Papers, Box 3. Letter dated 24 Nov. 1911.
[47] Harris, *Beveridge*, p. 160. See also *School Government Chronicle*, (hereafter *Chronicle*) 3 Dec. 1910, p. 470 for list of educational organizations opposed to the Act as it stood.
[48] Harris, *Beveridge*, p. 161.
[49] S. Tallents, *Man and Boy* (1943), 186.
[50] *Chronicle*, 9 Jan. 1909, pp. 26–7; 30 July 1910, pp. 90–1; 13 Aug. 1910, p. 135; Heginbotham, *Youth Employment Service*, p. 6; Mrs Ogilvie Gordon, 'Juvenile Employment Bureaux', *Contemporary Review* 546 (June 1911), 725; M. N. Keynes, *The Problem of Boy Labour in Cambridge* (1911), 20; Keeling, *Labour Exchange*, pp. 24–34.
[51] *Chronicle*, 30 July 1910, pp. 90–1.

authorities.[52] Although she made little initial impact in England, her scheme gained influential support in Scotland where it was adopted by the Scottish Education Department which agreed to give School Boards 'choice of employment' powers under the Education (Scotland) Act 1908.[53] Mrs Gordon's particular interest in the educational aspects of vocational guidance is evident from her remark in a letter to Morant that the bureau was to help to 'humanise the roughest elements among our young population'.[54] This was by no means an uncommon aim among reformers and administrators, and she was no doubt aware that Morant was one of those who were most anxious to find a way of humanizing, not simply young people, but the entire labour-force.[55] Likewise Churchill, who would have agreed with her sentiment when she told him that without the Board of Education, the Board of Trade was 'powerless' to make 'a better worker, a better man, or a better citizen of the young worker.'[56] Obviously vocational guidance, registration, and placement of school-leavers involved more than just the organization of the labour-market; they were seen as essential to the incorporation of working-class adolescents into what influential social theorists were calling 'the community'.[57]

The draft regulations which Beveridge had written in December 1909, were published in February 1910, to coincide with the opening of the exchanges.[58] The rules began by clarifying the 'special advisory committees' for juveniles and

[52] The scheme is reprinted in her *A Handbook for Employments* (1908), 12–19. See also her paper to the *National Conference on the Prevention of Destitution* (1911), 255–7, and the *Chronicle*, 14 Nov. 1911, pp. 43–4.

[53] Heginbotham, *Youth Employment Service*, pp. 3–6, and *Chronicle*, 14 Nov. 1911, p. 44.

[54] PRO. Ed 24/246. Gordon to Sir Robert Morant, 20 Mar. 1908.

[55] For Morant's views on the labour force and mass democracy see below, ch. 8, s. 4.

[56] PRO. Ed 24/246. Gordon to Walter Runciman, 8 May 1909. See also Harris, *Beveridge*, p. 162.

[57] See below, ch. 8, s. 3.2.

[58] 'Special Rules with regard to the registration of Juvenile Applicants in England and Wales made in pursuance of regulation no. IX of the Central regulations for Labour Exchanges managed by the Board of Trade', in appendix C of Greenwood, *Juvenile Labour Exchanges*, pp. 91–3. These regulations may have been the result of discussions between the two Boards after the passing of the Exchanges Act. See *Board of Education, Annual Report*, 1909–10 (1911), xvi. 37–8, and Heginbotham, *Youth Employment Service*, p. 5.

spelt out in some detail the procedures for registering them at the exchanges. Secondly, the Board of Trade was allowed to form JACs in co-operation with LEAs in such areas as it thought 'expedient'. The membership was to include appropriate volunteers who had knowledge of 'education and of other conditions affecting young persons', and who were in a position to advise the exchanges. Thirdly, the committees were allowed to take steps 'either by themselves or in co-operation with any other bodies or persons, to give information, advice, and assistance to boys and girls and their parents with respect to the choice of employment and other matters bearing thereon.' In other words, the Board of Trade could more or less control the Service, co-operating with other agencies when and where it thought necessary, although those LEAs which had or might have in the future statutory powers for dealing with juveniles were permitted to submit schemes for the exercise of these powers, provided they could obtain the permission of both Boards.[59]

The Board of Education was far from happy with the rules and throughout the spring and summer the dispute rumbled on.[60] In August 1910 the Board finally introduced its own legislation in the form of the Education (Choice of Employment) Bill, which empowered LEAs to create and finance their own juvenile employment services.[61] Immediately prior to the passing of the Act, Beveridge and Llewellyn Smith attended several conferences with Education Board officials which resulted in the publication of a joint memorandum intended to clarify the position in a spirit of co-operation. The memorandum specified that the employment of young people should be primarily considered 'from the point of view of their

[59] 'Special Rules', see n. 58 above. The reference to LEA schemes might have been in deference to the popularity of Mrs Gordon's draft scheme of 1904. See Heginbotham, *Youth Employment Service*, p. 18.

[60] *Chronicle*, 2 July 1910, pp. 12–14, report of deputation of LEAs to see president of Board of Trade; Mrs Gordon addressed the National Association of Head Teachers, *Chronicle*, 25 Aug. 1910, p. 488; see also *Board of Education Circular*, no. 743, 'Labour Exchanges and School Records', 24 May 1910, and *Board of Education, Annual Report*, 1909–10, xvi. p. 37, and Harris, *Beveridge*, p. 162. The various stages of the dispute can be followed in the *Chronicle*, 2 July 1910, pp. 12–14; 25 May 1910, p. 488; 4 June 1910, p. 518; 25 June 1910, p. 588; 9 July 1910, pp. 31–2; and Harris, *Beveridge*, p. 163.

[61] The Act is reprinted in Greenwood, *Juvenile Labour Exchanges*, pp. 85–6.

educational interests and permanent careers rather than from that of their immediate earning capacities', and consequently LEAs were urged to undertake their new responsibilities and to exercise them 'in the fullest co-operation with the national system of Labour exchanges'. Those areas where the Board of Trade already operated JACs, or were about to do so, were to be excluded from the LEA schemes. If, however, local authorities had not exercised their powers by the end of 1911, then further JACs could be established. [62]

The responsibilities of the two departments were to be as follows: the education authorities who operated a service under the 1910 Act had to confine themselves to 'interviewing, advising, registering and selecting juvenile applicants', while the labour exchanges would 'register vacancies, place juveniles with employers and oversee their progress during the early years of employment'.[63] In practice this distinction was almost impossible to maintain, especially as the exchanges and the education employment committees often failed to provide each other with the necessary information. The 'uneasy partnership' continued with some modifications throughout the 1920s and 1930s, and by 1945, 104 out of 315 LEAs were still running their own schemes.[64]

4. THE ADMINISTRATION OF THE ACTS

The fact that responsibility for the juvenile labour exchange system was divided forced LEAs to choose between either

[62] PRO Ed 24/248, 'Memorandum with regard to Co-operation between Labour Exchanges and Local Education Authorities Exercising their Powers under the Education (Choice of Employment) Act, 1910', 3 Jan. 1911. Mrs Gordon criticized the time limit, saying it would take many months for LEAs to prepare their plans: *Chronicle*, 25 Nov. 1911, p. 433–4. During 1911 JACs were established in Ashton-under-Lyne, Birmingham, Blackburn, Bristol, Bury, Carlisle, Devonport, Dewsbury, Exeter, Halifax, Huddersfield, Ipswich, Leeds, London, Middlesbrough, Northampton, Norwich, Nottingham, Plymouth, Rochdale, Southampton and Sunderland. Details in *Hansard*, xxiv (1911), C. 1561. Choice of Employment schemes were approved in Birmingham, Liverpool, Bournemouth, Burton-on-Trent, Cardiff, Wallasey, Gloucester, York and Hornsey: *Board of Education, Annual Report 1910–11*, (1912–13), p. 61.
[63] 'Memorandum with regard to Co-operation . . .'; see also *Report of the Committee on the Juvenile Employment Service* (1945), 5.
[64] *Report on Juvenile Employment Service*, pp. 5–7.

administering their own scheme (with Board of Education approval), or accepting the Board of Trade JAC. The largest authority, the LCC, opted for the JAC structure, while the second largest authority, Birmingham, decided to create its own individual scheme. There is no way of knowing how representative these specific approaches were of the national system as it developed, but an examination of their administrative organization will show that whatever the theoretical differences between them, there was little to choose in terms of their objectives and procedures.

In August 1910, the LCC decided to establish the Board of Trade JAC, to be worked in co-operation with its education department. The JAC was the central body for a number of local juvenile advisory committees and its chief function was to organize them in connection with each labour exchange in the area. The JAC membership comprised six members of the education committee, two employers, two trade unionists, two representatives from the ASEA, two persons otherwise interested in juvenile welfare, and a chairman. In general its powers included giving information, advice, and assistance to adolescents and their parents on choice of employment and related matters; filtering available young workers into openings on the basis of a detailed knowledge of each applicant and each vacancy; acting as a centre for enquiries from other youth agencies, such as clubs, Scouts and apprenticeship committees; and organizing propaganda for the creation of 'responsible' opinion among parents, juveniles, employers, and the public as to the 'evil' effects of the disorganized methods of recruitment into the youth labour-market.[65]

In order to implement its duties, the JAC relied upon local committees, each of which had a much larger membership than the parent body: ten nominees from the LCC education department, two headteachers, four employers, four workers,

---

[65] R. D. Denman, 'Working of the London Juvenile Advisory Committee', in *Proceedings of the National Conference on the Prevention of Destitution* (1911) 238–9; Bray, 'The Functions of the Juvenile Advisory Committee', in *Proceedings of the National Conference on the Prevention of Destitution* (1912), 226, 229–31. By 1912 Bray was chairman of the London JAC.

[66] Denman, 'London JAC', pp. 238–9. Local membership tended to be recruited from SCCs, teachers and representatives from MAYBS, ASEA, clubs, and Friendly Societies. By 1912 there were 18 local JACs in London. See also Bray, 'Function of the JAC', p. 226.

and ten persons nominated by the central JAC for their interest in adolescent welfare.[66] The main function of these committees was to carry out JAC policy, but this involved detailed work in organizing both the industrial and the welfare aspects of the developing service, and dovetailing much of the administration with that of education authorities. The comprehensive nature of the local groups is evident from a list of their duties, which were to focus the efforts of different agencies dealing with juvenile employment; to organize methods of collecting information about the character, education, and home life of school-leavers, usually with the assistance of teachers and school care committees (SCCs) (which were under the control of the education offices); to form subcommittees or rotas to attend the labour exchange for the purpose of interviewing applicants and parents; and to organize a system of 'after-care' in co-operation with SCCs, clubs, and other similar organizations.[67] The London committees concentrated their attention on school-leavers (rather than all those in the 14–17 age-group), which meant involving voluntary agencies, emphasizing home visits, and consolidating the structure of the SCCs. Consequently, from its earliest days the service had a strong welfare orientation.[68]

Before looking at the day-to-day working of the system in London and Birmingham, it is worth pausing to describe the role of the school care committees, for in both cities they were the vital link in the attempt to make the transition an educational rather than an industrial process. Moreover, as will be argued below, they provided the continuity between the older philanthropic tradition and the labour exchange system as an example of collectivist social policy.

The London SCCs originated in part from the Relief Committees established in 1899 by the School Board, and continued by the LCC until they were renamed in 1907 when the Council put into effect section (1a) of the Education (Provision of Meals) Act 1906, which called for the establishment of Canteen Committees.[69] However, they soon came to

[67] Denman, 'London JAC', p. 246.
[68] Ibid., p. 242.
[69] M. Frere, *Children's Care Committees* (1909), 8; M. Davies, *School Care Committees. A Guide to their Work* (1909), p. 3. See also Ronald G. Walton, *Women in Social Work* (1975), p. 64 and n. 12, p. 270; Bosanquet, *Social Work*

deal with a whole range of children's welfare in addition to
health and feeding, which included helping school-leavers, in
conjunction with the ASEA, to find suitable employment.[70] In
1909 the LCC completely reorganized its school welfare
programme and formed a central co-ordinating body with a
number of Children's Care (School) Committees on the basis of
one for every elementary school. Besides their duties relating
to general welfare, these committees (SCCs) were specifically
instructed 'to advise and help parents in connection with the
after-employment of children, referring suitable cases to the
local apprenticeship committees, and generally to befriend
with useful advice and guidance'.[71] This not only involved the
SCCs in vocational guidance and after-care in a formal sense
prior to the creation of juvenile labour exchanges, but also it
provided an influential role for the ASEA, certainly for its
practice.[72] For instance, as SCCs were formed, so each would
appoint a number of 'Friendly Visitors' to interview the school-
leavers and their parents at home and to collect all relevant
information from teachers as to academic ability and
character. The completed report cards were then passed on to
the SCC for discussion, after which the details would be
forwarded to either the association of SCCs (covering a wider
area than a single school), the ASEA, or to some other agency,
such as the Girls' Friendly Society, the Metropolitan Society
for Befriending Young Servants or the Recreational Evening
Schools Association.[73] A vacancy might already have been
found if the visitor or the committee had made direct contact
with an employer. If the youth was left to find his or her own
employment, the visitor was to persuade the parents to forgo
the relatively high initial earnings of blind-alley jobs in favour
of one with a more permanent future.[74]

Once the London JAC was established, the SCCs were
instructed by the LCC to co-operate with the local com-

in London, pp. 255–7, who claims the committees originated in COS work,
and Rooff, *Family Welfare*, p. 102. The first organizer, Miss. H. T. Morton, was
seconded from the COS.

[70] Frere, *Children's Care Committees*, pp. 38, 40.
[71] Davies, *School Care Committees*, pp. 3, 6–7; *Chronicle*, 27 Mar. 1910,
pp. 281–2.
[72] D. Pepler, *The Care Committee, the Child and the Parent* (1914), 41, 59.
[73] Davies, *School Care Committees*, pp. 70, 75–6.
[74] Ibid., 70.

mittees, having as their principal duty the reporting of the economic, social, and educational condition of the school-leavers, while the local JACs were to supervise the conditions of employment, ensuring that they were as favourable as possible for the young people, and that 'round' children were put into 'round holes'.[75] Without the existence of the SCCs the JAC would have been forced to create its own committee system at the level of the school; as it was, the SCCs brought with them a network of contacts, an established structure, and a large number of volunteers, amounting to some 5,000 by 1914.[76]

The bringing together of school-leavers and vacancies began with the adolescent being interviewed at school, after which a form was completed by the headteacher and a member of the SCC, just as the 'Friendly Visitors' had done prior to 1910. But now the details relating to academic, social, personal, and occupational aptitude were forwarded to the juvenile section of the local labour exchange where vacancies had been notified by employers. On receipt of the form, and with parental consent, the exchange registered the boy or girl. After parents agreed to use the exchange (and not all of them did agree), they were summoned with their child to an interview by a selection of the members of the local JAC, which had a list of vacancies, and the young person was sent to one of these. Once the school-leaver was placed, the after-care supervision was entirely in the hands of the SCCs, and other associated bodies, who made periodic reports to the local JAC, and as with the earlier form of care committee, a 'visitor' was named who had the duty of keeping in touch with the young workers until they were 17 or 18.[77]

Although the day-to-day arrangements in Birmingham were similar to those in London, a brief account of the details is useful because Birmingham was the first and the largest

[75] Pepler, *Care Committee*, pp. 64–6.

[76] Ibid., 50–1, 55, 57, 59.

[77] Denman, 'London JAC', pp. 242–4; Bray, 'Function of JAC', pp. 226–8; M. E. Marshall, 'Labour Exchanges and Juvenile Employment', *Women's Industrial News* (July 1911), 91. There were some doubts expressed as to their success, see M. Davies, 'The Work and Organisation of a Care Committee', *Proceedings of the National Conference on the Prevention of Destitution*, 308. For example of Reports, see City of Oxford Education Committee. Juvenile Employment Committee. Report Card in Butler Papers, 'Employment', Box. 9, 1913–22.

provincial area to operate a scheme independently of the Board
of Trade. Moreover, it was very much a conscious decision
inspired by the welfare work of Norman Chamberlain, its
leading social reformer, and his co-worker Edward Birchall.
Chamberlain was the chairman of the JAC, established by the
Board of Trade, but he made it clear that he wanted to see 'a
separate department of the city's government, in which the
education authority and the Ministry of Labour would co-
operate in order to cover all sides of juvenile welfare'.[78] With
the passing of the 1910 Choice of Employment Act, the
education committee decided to exercise its powers and
petition for the closing of the JAC (which had not yet begun its
work) so that it could open what was termed a Juvenile
Employment Bureau and Care Committee System.[79] In July,
1911, a Central Care Committee (CCC) was appointed, with
members drawn from the Women's Settlement, the Sunday
School Union, the Children's Service Union, Church of
England Sunday Schools, the CLB, the BB, the Boy Scouts, the
Street Children's Union, the Church of England Men's Society,
and the Trades Council.[80] The duties of the CCC, which was
to work 'in close touch' with the Central Juvenile Employment
Exchange, were to arrange for the vocational guidance of
prospective school-leavers and to liaise with exchange officials
in registering juveniles and in selecting applicants for inter-
views.[81]

[78] W. McG. Eagar, *Making Men: The History of Boys' Clubs and Related
Movements in Great Britain* (1953), pp. 308–9. See also *Chronicle*, 25 Dec.
1910, p. 525.
  [79] *Chronicle*, 24 Dec. 1910, pp. 525–6; Greenwood, *Juvenile Labour
Exchange* p. 31. Full report given in Birmingham Education, *Report of the
Special Sub-Committee on the Institution of a Juvenile Employment Bureau
and Care Committee in Birmingham*, (1910), (approved by the Board of
Education, July 1911). See also C. Sandler, 'Working-Class Adolescents in
Birmingham: A Study in Social Reform, 1900–1914', Oxford University D.Phil.
thesis, (1987), 244–76.
  [80] Birmingham CCC, *1st Annual Report*, pp. 7, 12. This was the usual sort
of membership: for London see Davies, 'Work of a Care Committee', pp. 309–
10 and for Oldham, see *Chronicle*, 26 Apr. 1913.
  [81] The CCC combined the duties of both the London JAC and CCC. It also
co-operated with the local authority's medical officer in supervising the health
of young workers. *Report of Special Sub-Committee* p. 20, and *1st Annual
Report*, p. 22. It also circulated leaflets and guides with such titles as
Birmingham Trades for Women and Girls (1914) and *Report on Birmingham
Trades* (1913).

The second foundational feature of the Birmingham scheme was the creation of a Juvenile Employment Exchange and Bureau under the direction of the Board of Trade, but housed on education premises (an important fact for those who wished to preserve the 'educational' nature of the transition), together with 'the continuous co-operation and interchange of views', which was to be the basis of a real partnership between exchange officials and the LEA.[82] It was intended that the bureau should receive applications from both juveniles and employers, but no applicant could be put in touch with an employer without the exchange first contacting the CCC. The education authorities, probably under the influence of Chamberlain, obviously recognized that the gathering of information concerning industrial conditions needed to be linked to the exchanges, as did the mechanism of registration.[83]

At the local level there were to be branch juvenile exchanges and wherever possible branch care committees, and the duties of both corresponded to those of their London counterparts. This is evident from detailed instructions given to the SCC members which show how the educational aspects of the scheme were regarded as crucial. Members were to influence the 'industrial history and character' of the young people by taking account 'of the needs of individual cases' and of the general conditions of industry, and by encouraging 'the wider use of educational institutions' during the adolescent years. Members were also to influence parents because their co-operation and support was seen as 'absolutely essential' in the long run.[84] Similarly, in their daily practice, as in London, each SCC nominated a 'responsible helper' who first met the headteacher to discuss those juveniles who were about to leave school, and then interviewed the young people themselves and their parents. Once the Juvenile Employment Bureau had registered and placed the adolescent, the 'helper' resumed responsibility by attempting to keep 'in effective touch' with either him or her and with the home. On the basis of the school reports, each youth was graded A, B or C, depending on how

[82] *Report of Special Sub-Committee* p. 20.
[83] Ibid. 19–20, 24–5.
[84] Ibid. 32.

much after-care was thought necessary.[85] There was no attempt to supervise all juveniles (aged between 14 and 17) who numbered about 36,000 in 1910; instead, the intention was to make contact with the school-leavers, of whom there were approximately 9,000, with each 'helper' responsible for ten or less.[86] By 1914 this target had been achieved, with over 2,000 helpers attending to 8,472 cases through 91 care committees.[87]

5. HOW SUCCESSFUL WAS THE SERVICE?

By 1914, there were over 400 Board of Trade exchanges in the United Kingdom dealing with juveniles; in 44 districts the Board had also authorized JACs, and in 58 districts the LEAs were running their own schemes.[88] The number of placements and registrations rose so that in 1913, 74,535 boys and 54,206 girls aged between 14 and 17 filled labour exchange vacancies and the number registering was 137,668 and 115,171 respectively.[89] As the total number of *filled* vacancies for all ages was 652,306, this means that juveniles accounted for about 20% of all those finding employment through the exchanges.[90] When only school-leavers are considered the percentage naturally falls: of the filled vacancies, 24% of boys and 30.4% of girls, numbering together 42,000, were in this category.[91] Given that approximately 500,000 children left school each year, the figure of 42,000 represents about 8% of all school- leavers who found their first full-time job through the juvenile exchange system, though a far greater number registered.[92] But not

[85] Ibid. 32–3; A. Freeman, *Boy Life and Labour: The Manufacture of Inefficiency* (1914), 131, 225; CCC, *1st Annual Report*, pp. 10–11.
[86] *Report of Special Sub-Committee*, pp. 10, 16 (figure of 9,000 was an estimate).
[87] CCC, 3rd Annual Report, p. 6.
[88] F. Keeling, *Child Labour in the United Kingdom* (1914), ix–x.
[89] *17th Annual Abstract of Statistics, 1913* (1914–16), Cd. lxi, 7733, p. 16.
[90] Ibid. 17.
[91] *Board of Trade, Labour Gazette* 22/2, (Feb. 1914), 45.
[92] There was always a difference between the number who registered and those actually placed. In Birmingham, the number of school-leavers using the exchange system between Mar. 1913 and Oct. 1914, was approximately 24%. A very approximate figure for all juveniles (14–17) using the exchanges during the same period would be 16% CCC, *1st Annual Report*, pp. 29–31; *3rd Annual Report*, p. 31; *Report of Special Sub-Committee*, p. 9. In London the

much more than a vague impression of the early impact of the service is provided by these figures, for without an extensive number of regional studies, it is difficult to estimate either the local variations in the success rate or the extent to which different areas established SCC systems alongside the employment bureaux.

Leaving aside the question of how many juveniles used the exchanges, how far was the service successful in channelling school-leavers away from so-called 'blind-alley' occupations? The education lobby, in arguing for control of the service often alleged that the Board of Trade exchanges sent young people to any kind of job in order to show a high ratio of filled vacancies.[93] In Birmingham, the largest number of placements for juveniles during the first eighteen months of the scheme were as messengers and porters, workers in drilling, milling, engineering, and brass foundries, business clerks, and labourers in warehouses.[94] In Oxford, out of 312 boys, 119 became errand lads, while 110 girls out of 223 became domestic servants.[95] The JAC in Leeds admitted that it had not been able to counter the numbers going into dead-end jobs, and a similar admission was made by the Plymouth authorities.[96]

These local impressions are confirmed by the national returns which show that between 1911 and 1914, the major occupational group to which boys were sent was conveyance of goods, men, and messages, followed by metals and commercial employment; (for girls, the major employers were dress, outdoor domestic work, and food, tobacco, drink, and

exchanges were dealing with nearly 48,000 juvenile applicants out of a total juvenile population of over 200,000, which indicates a figure of about 25%. Denman, 'London JAC', p. 242 and Bray 'Functions of JAC', p. 229. In Leeds the JAC report claimed that 1 in 8 school-leavers obtained their employment through the JAC: *Chronicle*, 2 Nov. 1912, p. 357. In Oxford the Juvenile Employment Committee reported that between 22 and 28% of school-leavers found work through the exchange. City of Oxford Education Committee, Juvenile Employment Committee, *Annual Reports, 1913–15*.

[93] *Chronicle*, 2 July 1910, pp. 14–15; 4 June 1910, p. 518; 25 June 1910, p. 588.
[94] CCC, *1st Annual Report*, pp. 31–2. The CCC admitted that the impact of the scheme was 'intangible'. See Sandler, 'Working-Class Adolescents', pp. 267–72.
[95] Juvenile Employment Committee, *2nd Annual Report*, pp. 7–8.
[96] *Chronicle*, 2 Nov. 1910, p. 357, and 4 Jan. 1913, p. 8.

lodging).[97] Few of these occupations offered any opportunity for either 'skilled' or (where boys were concerned) respectable employment as understood by the ASEA and other reformers. The fact that family circumstances gave the school-leaver little option but to take the first available work, and the highest paid, was appreciated by exchange officials. But even had they sought to do otherwise, they felt obliged to fill the 'blind-alley' vacancies if only because employers would always manage to find workers for this type of employment however much the exchanges tried to frustrate them. It therefore seemed better that the JACs and SCCs co-operate in order that they would at least be in a position to provide after-care supervision.[98] In this way, it was hoped that the 'care' features of the service could counter the allegedly demoralizing effects of the employment.

To some extent there was a contradiction between the declared aim of the service, which was to organize the transition from school to full-time wage-earning in a thoughtful and informed manner so that the adolescents went into respectable occupations with long-term prospects, and the policy actually pursued. Whether Churchill and Beveridge really believed that the exchanges could successfully redirect young people away from 'uneducative' labour is doubtful. It is much more likely that they shared the wish of Arthur Greenwood who looked to the after-care workers to:

bring into active play all the possible forces, schools and clubs, etc., to neutralise and overcome the pernicious influences of 'blind alley' employment, to insure that, however uneducative and useless a juvenile's job may be from the point of view of the future, he shall not on that account emerge from it unfitted for any other kind of labour.[99]

At one moment Beveridge can be found looking to the exchanges for the 'discouragement' of 'blind-alley' work, but he also warned against starting out with 'the idea of rigidly prescribing all but the best employments ... So long as "blind-

[97] *17th Annual Abstract of Statistics*, pp. 16–17. See also A. Greenwood and J. Kettlewell, 'Some Statistics of Juvenile Employment and Unemployment', *Journal of the Royal Statistical Society* 75 (June 1912), table 4.

[98] Denman, 'London JAC', p. 239.

[99] Greenwood, *Juvenile Labour Exchanges*, pp. 73–4.

alley" openings . . . are not absolutely illegal . . . the choice of them can only be discouraged generally by bringing them [boys] into direct competition with better openings at a general exchange.' He concluded, rather lamely, that the youth who becomes a van-boy via the service 'would at least learn that other occupations existed'.[100] This was Beveridge expressing the 'expert' view that working-class parents and school-leavers were ignorant about the range of job opportunities. But while young people were being sent to 'blind-alley' and other unskilled vacancies, the exchanges could do little to alter the condition of the juvenile labour-market since 'wider knowledge of possibilities and prospects' could not offset demand.[101] If the success of the service is measured against an economic criterion, it appears to have been partial, at least in its early years. If, however, the service is seen as a social institution, with aims which were, to a large extent, independent of market organization, then it is possible to see it as much more successful and of far greater significance.

6. CONTINUITY AND CHANGE

In her authoritative study, José Harris tells us that where unemployment was concerned, Liberal policy dealt with 'only an ice-berg tip' of the problem as it had been defined by Booth, Llewellyn Smith, Beveridge, and the Webbs. Very little was done about juvenile labour, she says, with no attempt being made to raise the school-leaving age or to make further technical education compulsory until the age of 17.[102] It is true that technical education remained not much more than a debating topic, although the Education Act 1918, did make 14 the universal minimum leaving age and, far more controversial, it began to introduce compulsory part-time day continuation classes.[103] Both of these measures had been under discussion for a number of years, and but for the war there is every reason to believe they would have been enacted earlier. All the same, the failure of the labour exchange legislation to affect the

[100] Beveridge, *Unemployment*, pp. 212–13.
[101] Ibid., 212.
[102] Harris, *Unemployment and Politics*, pp. 349–50.
[103] See below, ch. 8.

reorganization of the juvenile labour-market, at least in the short term, can hardly be denied. And any attempt to make it more effective would have been virtually impossible in political terms. The problem for Liberal politicans was a fundamental one: how to combat the economic and social consequences of juvenile labour without interfering with, and effectively undermining, one of the principles of political economy, namely, the free market in labour. It would be a mistake, however, to dismiss this aspect of the Liberal reform programme as being of no legislative or historical significance, at least in so far as the preceding details have revealed that the different schemes were the result of much thought and argument on the part of a number of interest groups, each of which cared about the transition process, believing it to be critical for the economic and moral welfare of working-class youth. To this extent, in establishing the service, certain governmental and educational authorities were signalling with all the pomp and circumstance of legislation that youth did constitute a separate and, in important respects, an immature source of labour which required special treatment.

Before describing some of the ways in which the service changed age relations, the continuity of the older methodological practices (mainly through elaboration) needs to be emphasized. Contemporaries noted the continuation of the voluntary tradition within the developing framework of Edwardian collectivism, and probably nowhere was this more obvious than in the realm of child and adolescent welfare.[104] The emergence of the SCCs and the ASEA, for example, has been shown to have arisen from the work of the COS, and to have copied its basic committee structure, together with its use of a few paid organizers supervising a large number of volunteers. JACs and juvenile employment committees also made use of COS methodology and volunteers, who brought with them experience of working with young people. But COS influence was at its most profound in passing on to the service the principle of casework, for this embodied a number of middle-class assumptions about individualism, character, and

---

[104] R. C. Davison, 'The Voluntary Social Worker and the State', *Economic Review*, 22/3, (July 1912), 264–71; Pepler, *Care Committee*, said that the development of SCCs and JACs raised the question of the role of the volunteer.

family responsibilities. Despite a new relationship between philanthropy and the state being forged, and with it a new role for the voluntary social worker, there remained the old focus on family, home, and character. Indeed, voluntary helpers were seen by many observers to be indispensable intermediaries between the state and the home precisely because as 'friendly visitors' they were able to respond to individuals.[105]

All this meant that the tradition of 'visiting' remained inherent in the new welfare provision for young people. As one settlement worker remarked, while the after-care committees provided 'many more opportunities for direct personal service than there had been in the past', the exchange system brought the home visitors and the club managers into the 'industrial side' and, therefore, united the social and industrial welfare of adolescents.[106] But it should be kept in mind that the home visit, for reasons of either vocational guidance or after-care, was intended to do more than simply attend to the school-leaver, who was urged to 'put your shoulder to the wheel' in order 'to reduce to a minimum the number of inefficient citizens'.[107] The procedure was also designed to exert an influence on the parents. In 'Suggestions for Helpers', Birmingham care workers were advised to make parents feel that their visit was the result of a desire to be 'really helpful and friendly'. Elsewhere, it was stressed that no one wished to interfere with the 'responsible and competent parent', but where they were not so, 'action is needed either to reinforce the consciousness or replace the incompetency'. Voluntary efforts, by themselves, did 'not cover nearly the whole ground'.[108] In other words, legislation offered the opportunity to begin a new programme of education for the working-class family.

The incorporation of visiting and casework into the adminis-tration of the juvenile exchange system not only reflected the continuation of both the practices and the perspectives of the

---

[105] Pepler, ibid., and Davison, 'Voluntary Social Worker', pp. 266–8.
[106] B. Baron, *The Growing Generation: A Study of Working Boys and Girls in Our Cities* (1911), 75–6.
[107] *Greenwood Papers, Mis. notes. pre 1914:* his article in *Huddersfield Examiner*, 4 Feb. 1911. See also *Chronicle*, 1 Mar. 1913, p. 192.
[108] Leaflet produced by Birmingham Education Committee. See also *Report of Special Sub-Committee*, p. 7.

reforming middle class, but also, and ultimately this was of greater importance, it altered the nature of the age relationship, certainly in the degree to which volunteers were in contact with young workers. This is partly evident in the innovatory character of the legislation. It was, after all, the first comprehensive Welfare Act directly intended for adolescents (14–17), although previous legislation had specified hours and conditions of labour for children and young persons, and young adolescents were included in several of the clauses in the Children Act 1908. Broadly speaking the interest of the State in vocational guidance, registration and placement, and after-care, marks the beginning of its concern with wage-earning youth, which was to develop over the next twenty years with the formation of the Juvenile Organizations Committee in 1916, the various measures to ameliorate juvenile unemployment between the wars, and the inauguration in 1939 of The 'Youth Service', each of which was a response to economic and social pressures, and all of which refined and extended the image of youth. Furthermore, it was the role of the adolescent as worker which first introduced the State into this area of collectivism, proof of the importance with which the juvenile labour-market was regarded in relation to the social problem.

But in what ways did the creation of the exchange system, and those elements of continuity and change, actually affect the image of youth? In the most obvious sense the establishment of special facilities for young workers emphasized their distinctiveness and their separateness; it also suggested that by virtue of their ignorance and incompetence they needed to rely upon 'professionals' for assistance in choosing and finding an occupation. In effect, the service portrayed the adolescent as essentially a dependent person. The capacity of the young worker for rational, thoughtful, and informed actions was brought into question by the new identity that was bestowed upon the transition process. The legislation turned the transition into a public activity, performed to certain rules, clothed in the rhetoric of advice, guidance, and protection which, it was claimed, could only be given by 'experts' and selected voluntary 'helpers'. The procedures of the system made it seem overwhelmingly complex: the visits, the record cards of teachers and helpers, the correspondence with

employers, the labour exchange forms, the committee structure, and their numerous meetings. This input of detail, with
the emphasis on the need for guidance and care made the
transition appear to be a period of effort, anxiety, and danger;
and such a representation was convenient at a time when
social scientists, and others, were 'discovering' adolescence as
a stage of life characterized by 'storm and stress'.

The purpose of the labour exchanges, as Churchill said, was
to curtail the 'haphazard and unorganized state of our industrial life'.[109] The principal aim of the Juvenile 'Rules' was to
continue 'the supervision of the boy or girl, when placed, with
a view to his or her further education, both technical and
humanistic' and to bring to bear on the life of the adolescents
'all the influences making for industrial efficiency, for
enlightened citizenship and self-realisation'.[110] It is beyond
doubt that the service was meant to be a social institution
with aims in addition to those of an economic nature. As
Dearle wrote in summarizing what he called 'The Needs of the
Future': the 'supreme necessity' was not merely to 'establish
certain regulations and forms of control', but to 'encourage and
develop good industrial and social habits'.[111] Reformers
continually blurred the occupational role of wage-earning
youth by fusing economics with 'character', and in presenting
youth as 'raw material' for the future.[112] Perhaps the prevailing
attitude towards adolescents was most plainly and simply
described by the objectives of the Birmingham CCC: 'To bridge
the gulf between the disciplined life of the school and the
comparative freedom of the industrial world; to ensure that
care of the young shall not cease with the end of school life;
and to provide the means for the guidance of young persons
through the difficulties and perils of adolescence.'[113]

All in all, the juvenile labour exchange legislation served to
institutionalize the transition from school to full-time
employment, and in so doing provided it with priests and

---

[109] *Hansard*, VI, (1909), C. 1039.
[110] Beveridge, *Unemployment*, p. 212; Keeling, *Labour Exchanges*, p. 9;
Greenwood, *Juvenile Labour Exchanges*, pp. 13–14.
[111] Dearle, *Industrial Training*, p. 526.
[112] Tawney, 'Economics of Boy Labour', p. 536.
[113] Helper's Card in *1st Annual Report*.

rituals; the transition became a *rite de passage* and, therefore, brought this aspect of the adolescent's life into a formal arena where it was subject to critical scrutiny. Prior to the legislation, the transition was obviously in the hands of the young people themselves, and of their parents, relations, and friends. The significance of the service lies in the attempt to take the process away from them and place it under the control of national and local welfare élites. Of course, it might be objected that while the description given here is theoretically accurate, in practice the exchange officers and 'helpers' were never able effectively to guide, supervise, influence, and control the school-leavers (and their parents) who continued to deviate from an 'ideal' behaviour pattern.[114] The strength of a social institutional ideal, however, is not that it always attains its stated objectives, but that it establishes itself as the desirable norm.

[114] On ideal adolescent behaviour, see J. R. Gillis, *Youth and History* (1974), 114–83, and his 'Evolution of Juvenile Delinquency in Edwardian England, 1890–1914', *Past and Present* 67 (May 1975), 96–126.

8. Day Continuation Schools: Creating the Adaptable and Efficient Citizen

Part of the impetus behind the establishment of the Youth Employment Service was the perceived failure of the home, philanthropy, and the workshop to train, supervise, and guide adolescent workers through their 'critical years'. In the minds of reformers, however, the service was only one of two policies designed to bring working-class youth under the purview of state agencies and their officials. More deeply felt, more tendentiously extolled, and more verbose were the arguments in favour of what was really to be a new form of further education: the compulsory part-time day continuation school. While there was a continuing interest in 'technical' instruction (though the term itself was both confused and confusing), it was the concept of a very generalized 'continued' education for adolescents which held the centre stage of the education debate during the Edwardian period and, together with the raising of the school-leaving age, throughout the First World War.[1] Despite its popularity in certain quarters, however, the idea of compulsory part-time day classes met with strenuous opposition from politicians, employers, and from sections of

[1] The debate on technical education was more specific in its content than the movement for part-time day continuation schools, although there was an overlap of issues in areas such as 'vocational' studies and 'trade' teaching. However, this chapter concentrates on the questions raised about the nature and purpose of the proposed schools and, therefore, tends to ignore the separate campaign for differentiated technical instruction suitable for the various grades in industry. The standard texts on the history of technical education are M. Argles, *South Kensington to Robbins* (1964); S. F. Cotgrove, *Technical Education and Social Change* (1958); P. W. Musgrave, 'The Definition of Technical Education, 1860–1919', and 'Constant Factors in the demand for Technical Education, 1860–1960', in P. W. Musgrave (ed.), *Sociology, History and Education* (1970). For a discussion of technical education in relation to skill see C. More, *Skill and the English Working Class, 1870–1914* (1980), ch. 10.

the labour movement. Undaunted, the 1918 Education Act made provision for local authorities to begin to open such schools for all 14–16 year-olds not otherwise engaged in full-time secondary education. But within a few years, before the majority of LEAs could submit their schemes for departmental approval, a combination of factors forced the closure of the half-dozen or so schools which had opened.

So, it might be asked, why is it important to examine in detail what, after all, merits little more than a few paragraphs in conventional histories of education?[2] There are three reasons. It was the first time that there had been a debate on the viability and the desirability of having an element of compulsory further education, which in theory was to enrol all adolescents, though in practice it applied mainly to those from the working class. Furthermore, while the nature of the curriculum was shrouded in generalizations, it was clearly intended to offer more than a narrow technical expertise. Rather the intention was to offer a mixture of liberal and vocational courses designed to produce the 'humane' but 'efficient' citizen. The proposal, then, was momentous in its implications for the juvenile labour-market and for industrial training. Secondly, the discussion on why the schools were needed and what they could achieve reveals significant features of both the age and the class relationships. By examining the arguments of the reformers, in looking at their aspirations and ambitions, it is possible to see something of these relationships as they were evolving. Thirdly, and following on, the debate helped to formulate a new image of young workers and to project it, not only well beyond the immediate confines of the reformers and their circles, but also well beyond the realms of education into the public domain.

---

[2] The exceptions are B. Simon, *Education and the Labour Movement, 1870–1920* (1965), 351–7; G. Sherington, *English Education: Social Change and War, 1911–1920* (1981); D. Thoms, 'The Emergence and Failure of the Day Continuation School Experiment', *History of Education* 4/1 (Spring 1975), 36–50; B. Doherty, 'Compulsory Day Continuation Education: An Examination of the 1918 Experiment', *The Vocational Aspect* 18/39 (Spring 1966), 41–56; H. Hendrick, ' "A Race of Intelligent Unskilled Labourers": The Adolescent Worker and the Debate on Compulsory Part-Time Day Continuation Schools, 1900–1922', *History of Education* 4/2 (1980), 159–73.

1. NARRATIVE OF EVENTS

The term 'continuation school' was derived from the wording
of the Education Code of 1862 which defined the Evening
School as one providing 'not secondary, but continued
elementary instruction'. This limitation was removed by the
Education Act of 1890, but the description remained un-
changed until the 1918 Act.³ The passing of the 1902
Education Act placed all types of public education, elementary,
secondary, and technical, under one control, the Board of
Education. At the local level control was taken away from the
School Boards and put into the hands of local councils who
were to serve as LEAs in their own areas. This reorganization
gave an overview of the education system which had not
previously been possible. It specifically made visible the gap in
post-elementary provision, one to which the subsequent
enquiries addressed themselves.⁴

Many of the reformers were keenly aware that their proposal
would entail an extension of state activity and the curtailment
of the voluntary principle. Such a development required a
strong defence, and the point to which they referred time and
time again was that 'modern conditions' made it imperative
that education be structured into a coherent national system,
with special attention being paid to working-class youth, not
merely to trade classes for apprentices, but to the mass of
young workers. Nowhere was the call for a new attitude more
clear than in the inquiry conducted at Manchester University
by Michael Sadler and his associates and published in 1907.
Sadler began by reminding readers that throughout the nineteenth century the 'authority of the state' had gradually made
itself felt in relation to education, resulting in the 1870 Act.
Now, he wrote, seeing that during the 'critical years of
adolescence' not more than one out of every three elementary

³ E. Waterfall, *The Day Continuation School in England* (1923), 32; *Report
of the Consultative Committee on Attendance, Compulsory or Otherwise, at
Continuation Schools*, Cd. 4758 (1909), xvii. 77.
⁴ The enquiries were those of M. E. Sadler (ed.), *Continuation Schools in
England and Elsewhere: Their Place in the Educational System of an
Industrial and Commercial State* (1907); the *Report and Evidence of the
Consultative Committee on Continuation Schools*, 2 vols.; and the *Depart-
ment Committee on Juvenile Education in Relation to Employment after the
War, Final Report*, i, Cd. 8512, (1917–18), p. xi (hereafter the *Lewis Report*).

school-leavers received any kind of educational care, there 'is reason for thinking that once more the national minimum should be raised'.[5]

Adolescence was seen as 'critical' because it was during this stage of life 'when stimulating instruction, technical training and well-directed guidance in matters of conduct and personal hygiene are often most needed and, if wisely given, most helpful towards healthy living and self- control'.[6] Those who worked among young people were said to lament 'the spoiling of promise and the waste of power which they see caused by lack of tendance and of invigorating discipline.'[7] Moreover, economic factors, such as the 'blind alley', seemed to be making matters worse. But, as Sadler shrewdly and significantly observed, it was not merely economic change that gave rise to social and political anxieties, for there were 'psychological causes of unrest' which were 'more subtle and not less powerful'.[8] Sadler was sensitive to what he called 'the great stir of thought' which had disturbed 'the traditional ways of looking at things', and had affected all classes. Society was being moved by 'the tremendous force of the intellectual and economic movements which are carrying us forward not solely to new dangers but also to new opportunities of good'. There was a new desire for 'reality' and for 'self-expression', and while they held within them dangers, they also held the possibility of 'veracity and strenuous life'. He felt able to offer comfort: 'It is no unreasoning or ill-judged confidence which relies upon the force of the truth and wisdom of the old order to hold their own and indeed to extend and deepen their influence under conditions which, after all, will for the most part be only superficially new'.[9] Although he may have underestimated the depth of the changes, his confidence reflected a widespread

---

[5] Sadler (ed.), *Continuation Schools*, pp. xi–xii; *Consultative Committee on Continuation Schools, Report*, p. 129; *Lewis Report*, pp. 3, 224. Sadler had been Director of 'Special Inquiries and Reports' in the Department of Education between 1895 and 1903, after which he became Professor of Education at Manchester University. For biographical details see L. Grier, *Achievement in Education* (1952).

[6] Sadler (ed.), *Continuation Schools*, p. xii.

[7] Ibid.

[8] Ibid., p. xiv.

[9] Ibid., p. xv.

fundamental optimism among social scientists with respect to the reform of working-class youth.

Sadler was no doubt thinking of the climate of opinion in which his inquiry was conducted, in particular the movement for 'National Efficiency' which questioned not only the principle of voluntaryism, but also the apparently redundant individualism of late nineteenth-century Liberalism.[10] While the continuation school proposal was never a major feature in the programme of those who sought to reconstruct British society, as an issue education was considered to be of vital importance. The various critics accused Britain of neglecting its 'brains', wasting the results of its elementary schools, and of failing to offer facilities for proper training (technical, vocational and liberal) to appropriate students.[11] The key themes of the movement were: racial fitness; the elimination of all kinds of waste, in particular resources of human ability; experts and 'knowledge', especially scientific knowledge; and a form of collectivism, or state-directed public policy, in preference to what one journalist called 'the idea of personal liberty'.[12] In effect, those who argued in terms of national efficiency (and they cut across party boundaries) were pressing for a 'National Minimum' in social, economic, and educational affairs.[13] And Sadler knew that he would strike a responsive note with his claim that the voluntary evening classes were 'wasteful of human material which might

[10] G. R. Searle, *The Quest for National Efficiency* (1971), ch. 1.

[11] Ibid., pp. 72–80; see also C. Magnus (ed.), *National Education: A Symposium* (1901); R. B. Haldane, *Education and Empire* (1902); C. Money, *Things that Matter* (1912); M. E. Sadler, 'The Unrest in Secondary Education in Germany and Elsewhere', *Special Reports on Educational Subjects*, ix, (1902). Sadler was a member of the Co-Efficients, a dining group started by the Webbs: see B. B. Gilbert, *The Evolution of National Insurance in Great Britain: The Origins of the Welfare State* (1966), 80, and B. Semmel, *Imperialism and Social Reform* (1960), 72–82. On the impact of National Efficiency see L. Fleet, 'Some Margins of Continued Education. Some Limitations of the Concept of Universal Compulsion with Special Regard to the School Leaving Age and Educational Minority', Bristol University Ph.D thesis (1977), 79–93.

[12] Quoted in Searle, *Quest for National Efficiency*, p. 63.

[13] The 'National Minimum' was associated with the Webbs and the New Liberals: see M. Freeden, *The New Liberalism: An Ideology of Social Reform* (1978), *passim*; Searle, *Quest for National Efficiency*, pp. 63, 248; Gilbert, *Evolution of National Insurance*, ch. 2; and E. J. T. Brennan, *Education for National Efficiency: The Contribution of Sidney and Beatrice Webb* (1975).

by timely care be made more serviceable to the State'.[14] The
question which had to be decided was 'whether we in England
gain more through stimulating and rewarding the energy of the
vigorous few by our voluntary system . . . than is lost through
our failure to raise the general average of trained and disciplined efficiency by means of compulsory attendance for all'. [15]
Then, donning his philosophical idealist heritage, Sadler
quoted Aristotle to remind his readers that the purpose of the
State was to enhance life for its citizens: 'the State was *formed*
to make life possible, and *exists* to make life good'.[16]

Sadler's inquiry joined many other calls for a comprehensive
extension of day-time continued education: government committees, teachers' organizations, the Workers' Educational
Association (WEA), the Labour Party, and the Liberal-inspired
Education Reform Council all asserted their approval.[17] Nor
was the issue ignored by the House of Commons where
between 1908 and 1914 a number of Bills were presented
without sucess.[18] However, despite all the interest at official
level and among reformers and commentators, on the eve of
the First World War many were pessimistic about the chances
of a compulsory system ever reaching the statute book. Two of
the best-known figures, Sir Philip Magnus, the Conservative
MP and propagandist for technical education, and R. B. Haldane,
the Liberal politician and educational philosopher, lamented
the lack of public interest and despaired for the future.[19]

[14] Sadler (ed.), *Continuation Schools*, p. 68. On 'Waste' see Searle, *Quest for
National Efficiency*, ch. 3, and Freeden, *New Liberalism*, pp. 128–34.
[15] Sadler (ed.), *Continuation Schools*, p. 70.
[16] Ibid. 71. For his Philosophical Idealism see P. Gordon and J. White,
*Philosophers as Educational Reformers: The Influence of Idealism on British
Educational Thought and Practice* (1979), *passim*.
[17] Sadler (ed.), *Continuation Schools*, pp. 724–7; Fleet, 'Some Margins of
Continued Education', p. 42; Sherington, *English Education*, p. 32; R. Barker,
Education and Politics, 1900–1951: A Study of the Labour Party (1972), 24.
Many of these submissions to the Board of Education are in PRO. ED 46/15A,
1904–1918. See also *Consultative Committee on Continuation Schools*,
pp. 16, 215–35. Other calls for part-time day schools came from the reports of
the *Poor Law Commission: Majority Report*, pp. 408, 411; *Minority Report*,
pp. 1191–2, and in C. Jackson's *Special Report*, pp. 29–31.
[18] For accounts of these Bills, see Fleet, 'Some Margins of Continued
Education', pp. 42–67; Sadler (ed.), *Continuation Schools*, pp. 718–23, and
Sherington, *English Education*, pp. 14–15.
[19] Sherington, *English Education*, p. 38, and *Times Educational Supplement (TES)*, 1 April 1913, p. 6.

The 1914–18 War radicalized informed opinion on educational matters. The pre-war debate was motivated by concern over the 'boy labour problem' in its social and economic contexts. The onset of war, however, not only brought forward other anxieties relating to working-class youth, in particular the rising rate of juvenile crime, but also, and not unrelated, exaggerated fears about the consequences of high wages and precocious independence. Of even greater consequence, the participation of adolescents in society was of special interest in the latter part of the War when 'reconstruction' promised both efficiency and a liberal, social democracy in which everyone had a part to play. This helps to account for the publication of different schemes by Labour, Liberal, and professional organizations.[20]

In 1916, H. A. L. Fisher, the Vice-Chancellor of Sheffield University, was appointed President of the Board of Education, with the promise that 'money would be found for ambitious educational measures'.[21] The brief given to Fisher was not simply to prepare the way for a measure of egalitarian reform, but to introduce some order into the whole area of adolescent education which, given the increase in juvenile delinquency, and mounting industrial unrest, was felt to be a social issue of some significance.[22] Fisher no doubt knew in advance the recommendations of the *Lewis Report*: a uniform school-leaving age of 14, the abolition of exemptions, and day continuation classes for all those aged between 14 and 18, all of which measures were embodied in his Bill. The intention behind the reforms was made clear in the famous words: '[the conception of the juvenile] as primarily a little wage-earner' was to give way to the conception of him 'as primarily the workman and citizen in training'.[23] During its passage through

---

[20] For wartime developments, see *Lewis Report, passim*; Waterfall, *Day Continuation School*, pp. 45–8; *Board of Education Annual Reports*, 1915–17; Workers' Education Association, *Report of National Conference on Educational Reconstruction* (1917); Education Reform Council, *Educational Reconstruction* (1917); Simon, *Education and the Labour Movement*, ch.10.

[21] D. Ogg, *Herbert Fisher, 1865–1940. A Short Biography* 1947), 62.

[22] On rising juvenile crime, see *Lewis Report*, p. 5; V. Bailey, *Delinquency and Citizenship* (1987), 7 and tables 1(a), 1(b), 2, and 3, pp. 311–15; and C. Russell, *The Problem of Juvenile Crime* (1917), Barnett House Papers, No. 1.

[23] *Lewis Report*, pp. 5, 8.

the House of Commons, however, an amendment was introduced by spokesmen for groups of employers, and reluctantly accepted by Fisher, which postponed for seven years the continuation class clauses for those aged between 16 and 18.[24] Even so, by the end of the War, the part-time day continuation school looked set to become a permanent feature of the British educational system.

Within four years of the passing of the Education Act, the few schools which had been established closed their doors, with the single exception of Rugby. What, then, had gone wrong? The reasons for the failure of the experiment have been discussed in detail elsewhere and so need be only briefly described here.[25] The principal obstacles to its success were: the economic climate in which the Geddes Report emphasized the low priority of education when financial restraint was inevitable; the less than enthusiastic response from numerous LEAs in submitting their schemes (they were allowed to proceed at their own pace without a universal appointed day); the beginning of opposition from the National Union of Teachers and the labour movement in favour of 'Secondary Education for All' and a school-leaving age of 15; and, perhaps most significantly, the opposition of large sections of industry, including the Federation of British Industries.[26]

---

[24] An account of the passage is given in Simon, *Education and the Labour Movement*, pp. 350–7; Fleet, 'Some Margins of Continued Education', H. A. L. Fisher, *An Unfinished Autobiography* (1948), 108. For WEA opposition see Sherington, *English Education*, pp. 111–12, 114, Waterfall, *Day Continuation School*, pp. 54–6, and almost any issue of the *TES* during 1917–18. Parents and pupils who failed to attend could be fined. Employers could be prosecuted.

[25] Sherington, *English Education*, pp. 158–63; Thoms, 'Emergence and Failure', *passim*; Doherty, 'Compulsory Day Continuation Education', *passim*.

[26] Thoms, 'Emergence and Failure', pp. 46–7; Doherty, 'Compulsory Day Continuation Education', pp. 52–3; Sherington, *English Education*, pp. 53 and 161; Waterfall, *Day Continuation School*, p.57; W. J. Wray and R. W. Ferguson, *A Day Continuation School at Work* (1920; 1926 edn.), pp. 11–12; Simon, *Education and the Labour Movement*, pp. 355–7; H. C. Dent, *Part-Time Education in Great Britain* (1949), 30–1; *TES*, 25 Oct. 1917, p. 14; 22 Feb. 1918, and 1 May 1919, p. 211; Fisher, *Unpunished Autobiography*, pp. 107, 111; Federation of British Industries, *Memorandum on Education* (Jan. 1918), 2–4; J. Dover Wilson, *Milestones on the Dover Road* (1969), 91; and L. Brooks, 'The London Compulsory Day Continuation Schools', London University MA dissertation (1923), 32.

2. THE CURRICULUM

The greater part of the debate on part-time day continuation schools centred around what it was claimed they could achieve. There were, it seemed, endless opportunities for physical education, the building of 'character', the production of efficient and 'adaptable' workers and, as was most consistently argued, for the creation of 'citizens'. At the same time, the curriculum through which all this was to be achieved remained remarkably unexplored and neglected; and in many respects this in itself was a comment on the nature of the reformers' aims and aspirations. However, it is possible to identify a few fairly distinct elements upon which there was general agreement. No one doubted that some form of physical education should be part of the programme; nor was there any dissent from the view that girls were to be taught domestic economy and similar subjects in addition to trade and academic courses; and, thirdly, the terms 'vocational' and 'liberal' should be generously interpreted, rather than be seen as mutually exclusive.[27]

The most difficult aspect of the discussion on the curriculum, such as it was, revolved around the problem of deciding the relationship between vocational and liberal subjects. An influential voice in the debate was that of Georg Kerschensteiner, Director of Education in Munich, 'the Mecca of all school reformers', who was famous for his opposition to 'general' continued courses, preferring instead the 'vocational' but in an integrated curriculum designed to train young workers as citizens.[28] Modern society, he said, no longer

[27] *Report of the Physical Deterioration Committee*, Cd. 2175, (1904), xxxii, p. 91 and paras. 230, 372 and 380; Sadler, (ed.), *Continuation Schools*, pp. 102–4,710; *Poor Law Commission, Minority Report*, p. 1213; *Poor Law Commission*, ix, Cd.5068 (1910), xlix, p. 184 (evidence of S. Webb) and p. 317 (evidence of Bray); *Consultative Committee on Continuation Schools*, Report, pp. 34, 203–4, 237; *Lewis Report*, pp. 17, 40–41; R. A. Bray, *Boy Labour and Apprenticeship* (1911), 219; Revd S. J. Gibb, *The Boy and his Work* (1911), 142; A. Freeman, *Boy Life and Labour: The Manufacture of Inefficiency* (1914), 221; H. Dyer, *Education and National Life* (1912), p. 103 and his *Education and Industrial Training of Boys and Girls* (1913), 94–6. He also thought trade classes for girls should be provided where necesary. C. Webb, 'The Need for Compulsory Continuation Schools: A Plea on Behalf of Girls', *University Review* (June 1906), quoted in Sadler (ed.),*Continuation Schools*, pp. 702–4.
[28] *Consultative Committee on Continuation Schools, Report*, ch. 10;

required either the nineteenth-century intellectual or the 'perfect individual' of German classicism, but rather the citizen who was a member of a community, and whose education had turned him into a 'social being'.[29] By 1914 Kerschensteiner was probably one of the most quoted of educationalists. He had written several very influential books, of which *Education for Citizenship, The Idea of the Industrial School,* and *The Schools and the Nation* were translated into English, and had lectured in Scotland and Chicago.[30] In an account of the continuation school movement, written in the 1920s, he was credited, together with Sadler and Stanley Hall, as being the man who made 'the issue clear: either organize the adolescent life of the nation on liberal lines or reap the consequences in a citizen body less stable, less progressive, less sound in mind and body than it might be'.[31]

The widespread influence of Kerschensteiner ensured that reformers referred to him for guidance on the matter. The basis of his educational philosophy lay in the belief that 'practical instruction' should be central to any curriculum for only then could 'mental and moral training' occur which, together with a sense of *esprit de corps* created within each school, would help to cultivate the spirit of 'civic responsibility'. By 'practical', Kerschensteiner had in mind drawing, modelling, knowledge of materials and tools, and so on, as required by particular trades, which was to be accompanied by practical civic training, such as a degree of self-government in the school and

J. H. Whitehouse (ed.), *Problems of Boy Life* (1912), 196–205; R. H. Best and C. K. Ogden, *The Problem of the Day Continuation School and Its Successful Solution in Germany: A Consecutive Policy* (1914), 7; Dyer, *Education and National Life*, pp. 83–90. For the life and work of Kerschensteiner, see D. Simons, *Georg Kerschensteiner: His Thought and its Relevance Today.* (1966). Surprisingly, Sherington makes only a passing reference to him, *English Education*, p. 6.

[29] Simons, *Georg Kerschensteiner*, p. 28.
[30] For his influence in Chicago, see P. A. Sola, 'Vocational Guidance: Integrating School and Society in Chicago, 1912–16', *Vocational Aspect of Education* 28/71 (Autumn 1976), 118.
[31] Waterfall, *Day Continuation School*, pp. 10–11, 139; see also *School Government Chronicle*, 3 Aug. 1916, p. 216 and 11 Jan. 1913, p. 45; *House of Commons Debates*, 16 April 1913 (51), cols. 1968–9; and, for Haldane's enthusiasm, Fleet, 'Some Margins of Continued Education', pp. 115–16.

organizing social activities, together with theoretical instruction in civics and hygiene.[32] In Munich, as one observer reported, each apprentice was made 'industrially efficient'; and 'with this end in view' it was 'not sufficient' to receive instructions merely in the technical side of the trade, for the young worker to become 'a worthy citizen', he should know something 'of his duties and responsibilities to the State'.[33] It is significant that Kerschensteiner insisted on the practical and the theoretical being part of the same syllabus, with the former leading on to an appreciation of the latter: it meant that 'civic virtues' had to be practised in order for them to become meaningful. In his opinion, the theory of civics, in whatever form it was taught, was useless without a real social context, which for him meant the practice of 'work', in all its senses. This explains why he considered the argument over the merits of vocational versus liberal education as an 'unnecessary dispute' because 'on the way to the ideal man stands the useful man, he who realises his own task and the task of his country . . . [and, therefore,] Vocational education is the door to the education of the man'.[34]

Popular opinion among those British 'boy labour' reformers who considered the curriculum seems to have favoured basing the organization of the classes on the Munich model in which trades either had their own schools, or groups of trades had their own curriculum. There was, however, meant to be a distinction between the subjects taken by senior students, aged between 16 and 18, and those taken by juniors aged between 14 and 16, just as there was between those employed in skilled trades and those who were in unskilled occupations. One recommendation was for the older pupils to be divided into four occupational groups: engineering; commerce; domestic

[32] Kerschensteiner in his introduction to Best and Ogden, *Problem of the Day Continuation School*, p. xiv; *Consultative Committee on Continuation Schools, Report*, p. 153; Simons, *Georg Kerschensteiner*, pp. 48–52. See also G. Kerschensteiner, *Schools and the Nation* (1914), ch. 2 and 3, and *Education for Citizenship* (Eng. trans. 1912), 71–72.

[33] C. Stockton, 'The Continuation Schools of Munich', in Sadler (ed.), *Continuation Schools*, p. 536.

[34] Kerschensteiner, *Schools and the Nation*, pp. 34–5, 47; see also Simons, *Georg Kerschensteiner*, pp. 31–9.

work; and industries for which no vocational instruction was necessary.[35] Tawney, Sadler, Bray, Gibb, Best and Ogden, and Dyer, among others, all argued for trade-based courses with an emphasis on practical instruction. A boy attending a wood-work trade school, for example, would continue his ordinary education, as well as being taught drawing, mensuration, and science, 'all specially adapted to the requirements of the trade', and lastly, 'in the school workshop he will acquire skill in the general use of woodwork tools'.[36] With boys in unskilled employment, the intention was not so much to impart skills, 'as to retain [them] at an impressionable age and to mould and discipline their character', and in such cases specialization or technical training would be out of place.[37] In principle at least, no one disagreed with Kerschensteiner when he said that the education given should not be 'a mere trade or industrial training in the narrower sense of these words', but should involve 'everything which leads to a wider outlook and a broader life'.[38] Such schools, claimed Bray, rather hopefully, would then be in a position to train 'the man in the interests of the community and in the interests of the trade.'[39]

Despite these intentions there is some evidence, however, drawn from proposed schemes submitted by LEAs (but never implemented), which suggests that in practice the allegedly integrated curriculum emphasized 'liberal' studies for the 14- to 16-year-olds who were to be the first age-group to attend under compulsion. Even in those schemes which included vocational courses, the instruction consisted of historical, economic, and sociological aspects, rather than a particular form of vocation.[40] Furthermore, there was sustained opposi-

---

[35] PRO. Ed. 46/15/a, paper 2, p. 7. See also recommendations of *Lewis Report*, pp. 40–41 and *Consultative Committee on Continuation Schools, Report*, pp. 114–15.

[36] Bray, *Boy Labour*, pp. 218–19; Tawney, evidence to *Poor Law Commission*, p. 340, Q. 96654; Gibb, *Boy and his Work*, pp. 141–2; Dyer, *National Life*, pp. 83, 86–90; and Best and Ogden, *Problem of the Day Continuation School*, p. 60.

[37] *Consultative Committee on Continuation Schools, Report*, pp. 114–15 and 189–90.

[38] Best and Ogden, *Problem of the Day Continuation School*, p. 62.

[39] Bray, *Boy Labour*, pp. 220–1; see also Best and Ogden, *Problem of the Day Continuation School*, p. 62, and Dyer, *National Life*, pp. 19–20.

[40] Waterfall, *Day Continuation School*, pp. 69–71, 85–6, 164.

tion to vocational courses from labour interests, teachers' unions, local authority directors of education, and from the WEA.[41] No wonder Selby-Brigge, successor to Morant at the Board of Education, remarked in 1917 that the controversy over the curriculum was an 'endless one'.[42] Introducing his Bill, Fisher voiced the opinion of liberal educationalists when he told the House that the schools would 'continue the general education' of the elementary level, and would give 'in addition vocational bias, the force of which will be graduated according to the age and occupation of the pupil'.[43] But this could not disguise the fact that however much influential educationalists, notably those associated with the Education Reform Council, might refer to combining vocational and general subjects (in whatever mix for whatever age of pupil), and might intellectually appreciate the relevance of vocational training, they lacked an effective political policy for reconciling both types of syllabus. More significantly, they lacked the personal conviction necessary to argue for the 'balanced' curriculum for the younger pupils. Instead, they were left with their deeply-rooted faith in 'humanism' which was to be derived from citizenship, and this encouraged them to think in terms of the whole person, rather than training for specific trades.[44]

[41] WEA, *Educational Reconstruction*, p. 25, resolution, 2; Fisher, p. 111; Sherington, *English Education*, pp. 118, 145, who quotes from a government committee that technical education remained 'a debatable country'; The Incorporated Association of Head Masters, *Educational Policy* (1917), 10; *TES*, 28 Dec. 1916, pp. 259–60.

[42] Quoted in Sherington, *English Education*, p. 81. For a discussion of the curriculum in schools, see R. J. W. Selleck, *The New Education* (1968).

[43] Fisher, introduction to his Bill in House of Commons, *Hansard* (August 1917).

[44] Sherington, *English Education*, p. 12; Fisher, *Unfinished Autobiography*, p. 100. The Board of Education was dominated by classicists and literary figures. Fisher himself was an important historian, and three of his officials were literary scholars: J. W. Mackail, E. K. Chambers, and J. Dover Wilson. The only scientist was Frank Pullinger, head of the technical section, but he worked under Chambers. The emphasis on Humanism came from the Education Reform Council, whose membership included Sadler, Percy Nunn and A. N. Whitehead. On this see Sherington, *English Education*, p. 62, quoting *TES*, 30 Nov. 1916, p. 221; Simon, *Education and the Labour Movement*, pp. 349–50; and Gordon and White, *Philosophers as Educational Reformers*, *passim*. In 1903 Sadler had emphasized the need for a liberal education up to age 16 as the best preparation for technical training. Quoted in Musgrave (ed.), *Sociology, History and Education*, p. 149. See also H. Silver, 'The Liberal and the Vocational', in his *Education as History* (1983), 151–72.

The idea of 'humanism' had been raised in the report of the Consultative Committee when it warned: 'That the schools should humanise their pupils is an indispensable condition to their being able to impart true economic efficiency.'[45] It was, however, J. Dover Wilson, at the time an HMI, who wrote in detail of the need for a type of education which was 'adapted to the needs of citizens in an industrial democracy' and this, he maintained, required not technical classes but 'informed humanism'.[46] The origins of this view probably came from within the Board of Education under Morant who, together with his assistants, desired to bridge the gap between education and industry so as to create a 'balanced culture for the masses' with the schools providing pupils with 'meaning for the work they did with their hands'.[47] Echoing this anxiety over the future of democracy at the end of the First World War, another government inspector wrote of the need to keep working-class youth 'in touch with "the forces of civilisation" ', for it was necessary always to keep in mind that 'we are training a whole social class'.[48]

And what, thought reformers, could be more effective in pursuit of this goal than to inculcate in young workers the values of citizenship—a popular doctrine which drew support from all political perspectives? There was, then, unanimous agreement that the overriding function of the continuation schools was to prepare their pupils for 'the efficient discharge of the duties of citizenship', but it was also understood that in order to make this viable, young people had to be taught to 'increase their adaptability and skill in bread-winning occupations'[49]

[45] *Consultative Committee on Continuation Schools*, p. 144.
[46] J. Dover Wilson, *Humanism in the Continuation School* (1921), 6. This was originally written in 1919, see PRO Ed.46/15/A, Memo C, No. 2, May 1919.
[47] Dover Wilson, *Milestones*, pp. 67, 88; Sherington, *English Education*, pp. 14–15.
[48] PRO. Ed. 46/15/a. Paper 2. Memo by HMI, Owen. pp. 1–2. In predicting that 'the next government' would make provision for continuation schools, readers were reminded that 'the aims . . . will be largely disciplinary and social, certainly not merely instructional, and this makes it specially desirable that the rougher element should be got into them': *Journal of Education* (Apr. 1914), 243–4.
[49] *Consultative Committee on Continuation Schools*, p. 30, and Sadler (ed.), *Continuation Schools*, p. 690.

3. THE SEARCH FOR THE 'ADAPTABLE' WORKER

The notion of 'adaptability' was always attractive to various groups of reformers because it appeared to promise so much. The transitive verb meant 'to make suitable' and when translated into human terms this indicated a solution to a number of perceived difficulties in the juvenile labour-market: at the very least it offered a safeguard against redundancy through technological change; it provided a necessary companion for 'intelligence', one of the qualities demanded by 'modern' industrial conditions; and it seemed to imply a degree of social contentment, integration, and stability, which were important, if only in so far as they could serve as protection against the ravages of unemployment and, in extreme cases, unemployability.

But what did contemporaries mean when they used the word? Although precise definitions are hard to come by, it is clear that they looked to some kind of ideal worker, that is, someone who was trustworthy, interested, intelligent, literate and numerate, full of initiative, and capable of mental and physical agility. E. J. Urwick, in a pioneering essay, told his readers that 'in the present conditions of industry', the 'supreme essentials' for both skilled and unskilled labour were 'intelligence and adaptability'. This was not to deny the importance of technical education for the prospective trades-man, but he would be 'unsafe' unless this was supplemented by a training which allowed him 'to adapt himself to new conditions'. And for the unskilled, the urgent requirement was a general education which would develop 'intelligence, quick-ness of brain, and power of adaptation'. Urwick quoted an employer: 'I want ordinary men who have learned to use their brains.' This, said Urwick, leading his readers, reflected the essence of modern labour, namely, that it was 'mental'. While machines could do the work of muscle, 'the labourer is needed to guide the machines, and to take his place as an intelligent factor in the complex system of modern industry.' [50]

The aim of the schools, said Sidney Webb, was not to turn every man into a skilled worker at an apprenticed trade, but into

[50] E. J. Urwick (ed.), *Studies of Boy Life in Our Cities* (1904), 280–2.

a man of trained hand, eye, and brain; disciplined and good mannered; of sound muscle and fully developed lungs; with a general knowledge of common tools and simple machines; able to read a plan and make a drawing to scale; ready to undertake any kind of unspecialised work; and competent, even if he does unskilled work, to do it 'with his head'.[51]

Similarly, Freeman argued, in relation to unskilled labour, that 'uneducative' employment was unavoidable and, therefore, it was necessary that 'the intelligence and character of the adolescent be trained outside the workshop': 'We cannot train for a trade, but we can enable the worker to do his duties as thoroughly as possible'; such training would give a 'familiarity' with 'ordinary tools' and 'simple machines', a grounding in 'mechanics' and 'competent draughtsmanship'. He then added: 'What is required of the low-skilled worker is that he shall be energetic, intelligent, careful, resourceful, trustworthy and adaptable.'[52] Intelligence was also a critical factor for Bray who interpreted adaptability as 'a trained intelligence'. Where skilled labour was concerned, he said, employers wanted this quality as well as 'trustworthiness' and 'a highly specialised manual dexterity'. The skilled man was one who had acquired 'a general use of the tools employed in his trade' (even though this was not necessarily of use to his employer) which would give him 'adaptability'. In the case of unskilled labour, Bray criticized the assumption that it required no training and made no demand on 'skill': this was 'a grave mistake'. Such labour also required intelligence, together with 'manual training and practice'. At present, he argued, the unskilled were engaged with machinery and they were 'almost always inadequate and unsatisfactory'. But all kinds of labour 'had to be capable of readily adapting themselves to new conditions, and not become petrified in a rigid and inflexible mould'. Young workers needed to develop the 'ability to grapple with unfamiliar conditions, and the habit of applying one's mind and one's knowledge to what one has to do'.[53]

So, adaptability had two meanings. First, it referred to the ability of a worker to move about within a workshop—

---

[51] *Poor Law Commission*, evidence, p. 184.
[52] Freeman, *Boy Life and Labour*, pp. 218–19.
[53] Bray, *Boy Labour*, pp. 210–17. He was quoting from a London County Council report on Higher Education.

hopefully from process to process—a mobility bestowed by 'knowledge' of different processes which in turn involved familiarity with the tools of the trade and the necessary skill to use them. In many respects reformers viewed the term simply as the obverse of specialization. Secondly, it referred to mental qualities: dexterity, attitudes, intelligence, flexibility, initiative, and so on. This was a crucial consideration, especially for the unskilled, because it was seen to be their only asset. But it was by no means to be confined to labourers since the emphasis on being adaptable was an implicit recognition of the importance of the mental factor inherent in all forms of labour, and one which was deemed to be of increasing relevance under 'modern conditions'.

If this is what was meant by adaptability, why was it such a popular idea among those who discussed industrial training within the framework of compulsory part-time day continuation schools? The answer, as far as 'boy labour' reformers were concerned, lay in their perceptions of the condition of the juvenile labour-market, which meant 'the apprenticeship question', the influence of machinery, and the relation of 'boy labour' to the problem of unemployment. This is an enormous area to consider briefly because it touches on the central issue of what is sometimes called 'the second industrial revolution' and, more precisely, on the relationship between labour and technological change. Some consideration, however, is essential in order to clarify the aspirations of reformers.

It has been shown that one of the basic criticisms of 'boy labour' was the 'decay' or 'decline' of 'old-style' apprenticeship under the impact of excessive specialization of process which resulted in a 'dilution' of apprenticeship proper. There is some difficulty, however, in establishing the reality of apprenticeship during the Edwardian period because historians disagree about the meaning and extent of 'de-skilling'.[54] Some reformers have been accused of either exaggerating or misunderstanding contemporary developments.[55] Although it is conceded that a 'decline' occurred in a few trades, reformers are said to

[54] See More, *Skill and Working Class, passim*; W. Knox, 'Apprenticeship and De-Skilling in Britain, 1850–1914', *International Review of Social History*, pt. 2 (1986), 166–84; More, 'Skill and the Survival of Apprenticeship', in S. Wood (ed.), *The Degradation Work?* (1982); and Wood, *passim*.
[55] More, *Skill and Working Class*, pp. 46–50.

have been confused by terminology and to have failed to distinguish between 'deskilling of individual jobs and industrial changes which led to the number of jobs in certain industries or occupations declining either relatively or absolutely, but not to the nature of the job themselves changing'.[56] Other writers have concluded differently, especially with reference to engineering, building, ship-building, and printing.[57]

Whatever the disagreements, it seems reasonable to say that the period *circa* 1890–1914 witnessed 'an unprecedented advance of machine technique and of mechanisation generally and automatism in particular'.[58] There occurred a 'new era of accuracy and precision in engineering . . . the spread of the interchangeable system . . . increasing subdivision of productive processes and specialization of both plant and labour'. Machine technique entered the boot and shoe trade, certain processes connected with the erection of the hull of a ship and type-setting. An entirely new development was the spread of the automatic machine, for example, the turret-lathe and the Norththrop automatic loom. In general, the division of labour principle was 'making some revolutionary progress in certain pursuits', especially in engineering where the craft of the turner was completely changing and in the production of boots.[59] In addition to changes in existing trades, such as engineering and boot and shoe manufacture, new trades were developing from the 1880s: sewing-machines, cycles, and motor and electrical manufacture.[60] The chief characteristics of this second phase of industrialization have been described as

the introduction of new semi-automatic machines . . . the increasing use of unskilled and semi-skilled labour in trades hitherto the exclusive preserve of the skilled man . . . the adaptation of a rudimentary system of standardised and interchangeable parts . . . the

[56] Ibid., 47–8.
[57] Knox, 'Apprenticeship and De-Skilling', *passim*; A. L. Levine, 'Industrial Change and its Effects upon Labour, 1900–1914', London University Ph.D thesis (1954); and J. Hinton, *The First Shop Stewards' Movement* (1973).
[58] Levine, 'Industrial Change', pp. 2–3.
[59] Ibid., 3, 5. See also Knox, 'Apprenticeship and De-Skilling', p.175 for technical change in building and printing.
[60] Levine, 'Industrial Change', pp. 5, 10. See also E. H. Hunt, *British Labour History, 1815–1914* (1981), 30.

predominance of factory over the workshop as the unit of production . . . the introduction of aspects of Taylorism, particularly the premium-bonus system'.[61]

The undeniable fact was that these changes had 'a widely varied impact on skilled workers'.[62] Every day, wrote one social investigator, the 'old methods which require manual skill and long practice are being superseded by the progress of mechanical invention. "Skill" in the old sense, is no longer what is wanted.'[63] Several observers even suggested (wrongly) that 'skilled' and 'unskilled' no longer had a definite meaning and, therefore, the important distinction was between 'good' and 'bad' occupations.[64] However extreme this view, there was some truth in the assertion that 'the changes in methods of production are rapid', and this posed a threat to the employment prospects of both skilled and unskilled labour.[65] Moreover, the greater use of semi-skilled labour, either in new processes or in those previously monopolized by apprenticed tradesmen, not only threatened to undermine job security but also helped to create a new and indeterminate category of 'skill'. Traditional terms denoting job status, such as 'labourer', 'apprentice', 'tradesman', and 'mate', were no longer amenable to straightforward definitions.[66]

The 'unprecedented advance of machine technique' (in common with other developments in production) seemed to be altering the nature of 'work' itself as it made more complex and numerous demands on labour. With this in mind, in advocating the 'New Apprenticeship', Bray warned of the dangers of 'monotony' in the workshop which, he said, was hostile to industrial wisdom:

Unless there is a well-trained intelligence to begin with, the continual performance of a single task will reduce the man to the level of a machine . . . the employer does not want a mere machine . . . He wants a machine with intelligence; he must therefore have a man. But

[61] Knox, 'Apprenticeship and De-Skilling', p. 174.
[62] Ibid.
[63] C. B. Hawkins, *Norwich: A Social Study* (1910), 205.
[64] Anon, 'The Boy in Industry', *Toynbee Record* (1905), 155.
[65] Ibid., 156.
[66] G. Routh, *Occupation and Pay in Great Britain, 1906–1979* (1968; 1980 edn.), 4–11, 32–7. By 1911, nearly 40% of the work-force was classed as semi-skilled, while the proportion of unskilled was just under 10% .

the intelligence must rest on a broad basis of education or the machine element will prove too much for it.[67]

And Sadler made a similar observation:

In many of its new developments . . . modern machine-industry does not . . . necessarily degrade the operative into a machine. On the contrary, one of its chief characteristics is to sieve out the workers into grades according to the degree in which they possess the required kinds of ability and alertness. An automatic machine does not want mere automata to look after it. It sifts the workers according to their capacity of skilfully watchful service. There is a greater demand than ever for men possessing good judgment, trustworthiness of character and the power of dealing intelligently and thoughtfully with new conditions.[68]

'One of our most pressing problems', he concluded, 'is how to deal with the human waste which has come through the discarding of the services of workers unable to adjust to the new requirements'.[69] Sadler was expressing the widely-shared belief among reformers that, given the prevalence of machinery, the labour demand of the present, and even more so of the future, was for 'skilled and versatile *minds*'.[70] The importance of such 'educated' minds lay, of course, in their presumed ability to cope with a variety of industrial processes, including the total environment of modern production.

In contributing towards the creation of the properly trained worker, adaptability was also thought to be an indispensable element in the struggle to reduce unemployment, (what Sadler called 'human waste'), though its direct impact was the subject of some discussion. On the one hand, there were those who argued for a simple causal relationship between education and security in the labour-market. The author of a social study of Norwich reasoned that as 'Unemployment is partly a problem of education', so 'a half-trained or untrained man cannot adapt

[67] Bray, *Boy Labour*, pp. 211–13; see also Millis, 'Trade Schools' in Sadler, (ed.), *Continuation Schools*, p. 414.
[68] Sadler, (ed.), *Continuation Schools*, p. 707.
[69] Ibid., 707–8.
[70] Urwick (ed.), *Boy Life*, p. 283 and his article 'Apprenticeshsip and Skilled Employment: A Criticism', *Toynbee Record* (June 1907), p. 117. See also C. Jackson, *Special Report*, p. 149; N. B. Dearle, *Industrial Training* (1914), 373, and 530; and Mills, 'Trade Schools', pp. 402–3.

himself easily and rapidly to the endless changes of production under modern conditions.'[71] J. H. Whitehouse, the Liberal MP, proclaimed that 'in view of the relation of unemployment to adolescent and child labour', an improved system of education was 'a matter of urgent necessity'.[72] Bray also thought that with the onset of adaptability, the problem of unemployment 'would be comparatively easy of solution'.[73]

Sadler, however, was more cautious. Education, in itself, he said, was 'no panacea', but it could help the young person to avoid unskilled labour.[74] Sidney Webb and Beveridge were equally careful in expressing their views. Webb denied the value of adaptability alone in preventing unemployment, for there was no straightforward correlation between education and an individual's ability to find regular work.[75] In the analysis provided by Beveridge, education could keep the intelligence 'alive and growing', but it could not affect either the causes of industrial fluctuation or prevent casual labour. However, adolescents were by definition 'adaptable' and this asset, he said, needed to be developed. Young people could be 'moulded to the demand' from employers and this was crucial because in the long term, the 'character of the demand . . . is ultimately governed by the possibilities of supply.' In other words, as the supply changed its character, so the demand would also change and unemployment could be reduced, in particular that caused by 'lack of mobility and adaptability under circumstances making these qualities essential'.[76]

But there was another very significant aspect of adaptability which indicates the continual blurring, by almost everyone concerned, of economic and social (moral) issues. In the minds of reformers, being 'adaptable' suggested both individual fulfilment and a sense of community loyalty and, therefore, social and occupational cohesion. In effect, the concept implied a commitment on the part of the employee to *work* as a moral good in

[71] Hawkins, *Norwich*, p. 193.
[72] *Hansard*, xvi, 2200–235 (20 Apr. 1910), and his *Problems of Boy Life*, p. 2.
[73] Bray, *Boy Labour*, p. 217.
[74] *Poor Law Commission*, evidence (Sadler), pp. 213, 219.
[75] Ibid., Q. 93184.
[76] W. H. Beveridge, *Unemployment: A Problem of Industry* (1909; 1917 edn.), 115–16, 131.

its own right, irrespective of wages, conditions, or personal (selfish) satisfaction. Instead, the satisfaction was to be derived from being prepared for labour and in the performance of tasks, conscious of their relation to a greater whole. The adaptable worker would partner machines without being alienated, while simultaneously displaying interest, application, and initiative, in addition to possessing an all-round competence. Adolescents were to be taught that they had a duty to serve the community and these ideas were to be bound together within the framework of 'citizenship'. In a lecture given before the British Association, C. T. Millis, the educationalist and principal of the Borough Polytechnic Institute, said 'We need good citizens, but good citizens must be good workers.'[77] There was no necessary connection between these two categories; their relationship was entirely founded on ethical and political considerations.

4. THE SEARCH FOR THE 'CITIZEN'

One of the most popular demands of 'boy labour' and other sympathetic reformers, or perhaps it should be described as an aspiration, for that is what it was, referred to the creation of 'a satisfactory race of citizens'.[78] The idea of citizenship itself had a special status during the late Victorian and Edwardian periods as politicians, philosophers, educationalists, and social scientists were continually calling for a revival of the concept, by which they had in mind a form of social organization stressing harmony, duty, service, self-realization, rationality, and morally good behaviour. Throughout the latter part of the nineteenth century 'citizenship' had been part of the civilizing process; so it was not without reason that T. H. S. Escott, writing in 1897, described 'Social Citizenship' as 'a Moral growth of Victorian England', probably best exemplified by the Settlement Movement, beginning in the 1880s, with its emphasis on 'civic idealism'.[79] But, as a concept determining a

---

[77] Millis, 'Trade Schools', p. 426.
[78] Mrs Ogilvie Gordon, 'The Social Organisation of Adolescence', *Proceedings of the National Conference on the Prevention of Destitution* (1911–12), 253–64.
[79] Quoted in H. Meller, *Leisure and the Changing City, 1870–1914* (1976),

political and educational programme, it remained rather vague, standing as it did for all manner of virtues before a spectrum of interests. In the context of the debate on continuation schools it can best be understood through an examination of two of its principal features, namely, political stability, which of necessity included social harmony, and what has been called the 'civic ideal', which meant service to the community.

First, the philosophical source from which citizenship emerged needs to be recognized, as does the relationship which existed between the philosophy and New Liberalism. It is well known that the belief in citizenship was derived from the writings of T. H. Green, the Oxford Idealist philosopher, who more than any other figure made the connection between philosophy and educational theory and practice.[80] The substance of the meaning of citizenship was that the extension of the suffrage in 1867 should be accompanied by 'a spiritual advance imposing new duties as well as new rights'.[81] This became an even more important matter with the extension of the franchise in 1884–5, and when the votes for women campaign intensified after 1905.[82] Accordingly, for many public figures writing in the 1890s and early 1900s, the character of citizenship and the common understanding and experience of it, all of which was bound up with the imperatives of progress, became urgent political and social issues.

9. Of course, Humanism had a much longer history in British cultural and educational thought. See e.g. references to Newman, Ruskin, Huxley, and Arnold, in S. J. Curtis and M. E. A. Boultwood, *A Short History of Educational Ideas* (1953), 425–62. On the revival of interest in 'citizen training', see A. Warren, 'Sir Robert Baden-Powell, the Scout Movement and Citizen Training in Great Britain, 1900–1920', *English Historical Review* (Apr. 1986), 376–98, and F. H. Hilliard, 'The Moral Instruction League, 1897–1919', *Durham Research Review* 3, (1961), 53–63. See also M. E. Sadler, *Moral Instruction and Training in Schools: Report of an International Enquiry*, (1908).

[80] Gordon and White, *Philosophers as Educational Reformers*, p. 3 and M. Richter, *The Politics of Conscience: T. H. Green and his Age* (1964), ch. 2. Sadler, for example, confessed that 'T. H. Green taught me to think about Moral Obligation', letter dated 27 Nov. 1934 in *Sadler Papers*, C. 550. Misc. 315–16.
[81] Richter, *Political Conscience*, p. 344 and Green in frontpiece to A. Vincent and R. Plant, *Philosophy, Politics and Citizenship: The Life and Thought of the British Idealists* (1984) 1.
[82] D. Read, *England, 1868–1914* (1979), 309–12, 502–4.

The roots of British Philosophical Idealism were to be found in the philosophy of Hegel, as well as in that of Kant, Fichte, Plato and Aristotle. This body of thought, sometimes called Neo-Hegelism, which had been introduced into Britain by Benjamin Jowett, Green's tutor at Balliol, rejected the dominant philosophical view, derived from the Enlightenment, which was 'empiricist, individualistic, utilitarian', and chose instead to see reality as 'an organic interconnected whole, no part of which was independent of the rest'.[83] To the Idealists, man was essentially 'a social creature' and one very much bound up with the State. Consequently, and this was of critical significance for all those who were concerned about the various aspects of the youth question, 'His education, which is the means whereby he becomes a citizen, is thus one of the State's foremost concerns.'[84] The process of 'becoming' involved the development of the 'character' of pupils, since only in this way could they be properly prepared for their 'shared social and political' life.

If citizenship embraced the reconciliation of rights and duties within a democracy, in general terms, as Vincent and Plant suggest, the concept also 'implied a noble purpose', orientated as it was toward 'community life'; it represented 'the consciousness of the ends of life and their origin and unity in the community as a whole'.[85] The specific values of citizenship voiced the social significance of 'the common good', 'service', 'character', 'rationality', 'self-realisation', and 'morality'. These were the terms that gave substance to the concept, and in so doing represented 'a co-ordination and subordination of individual actions towards some common good'.[86]

But what was it about the concept of citizenship that made it so popular in political discussion and why were 'boy labour' reformers so eager to introduce working-class adolescents to its supposed virtues? The espousal of citizenship in particular, and philosophical Idealism in general, coincided with the growth of New Liberalism, a radical political creed which was

---

[83] Gordon and White, *Philosophers as Educational Reformers*, p. 4.
[84] Ibid., 3.
[85] Vincent and Plant, *British Idealists*, p. 80.
[86] Ibid., 26.

virtually synonymous with economic and social reform and, therefore, it is not easy to separate the theory and practice of the former from that of the latter.[87] It is especially difficult given that several of the most important Idealists were also actively contributing to the reinterpretation of Liberal principles.[88] But whether Idealism helped Liberalism and the 'New' Liberals to speak and act on the basis of a more dynamic and conceptually successful social theory, or whether, to quote Michael Freeden, 'Rather than Idealism giving birth to a new version of liberalism, it was liberalism that was able to assimilate certain aspects of Idealism to its mainstream and thus bestow new meaning upon Idealist tenets', is not a problem of immediate relevance here.[89] We should, however, appreciate the close relationship that existed between the philosophical beliefs and the political doctrine, which not only manifested itself in the convergence of interests with respect to social problems and class politics, but also provided the proposed reform in education (and other attempts to 'educate' young workers, such as the club movement) with a certain authority. On the other hand, the nature of the relationship was always contested, and ultimately it failed to produce a lasting system of part-time day continuation schools.

Secondly, and this was most important in terms of associating adolescents with the community, many of the ideas and precepts embodied in citizenship, such as duty, service, neighbourliness, social stability, self-realization, and contentment with one's societal position, were politically convenient to reformers who stressed the significance of providing instruction for the moral development of young people. The provision of instruction was crucial for the improvement of the environment, which in turn was a necessary precondition for the emergence of 'character'.[90] Philosophical Idealism, then, was well suited to be called upon as testimony in support of what, after all the huffing and puffing was basically a political

[87] Freeden, *New Liberalism, passim*; Vincent and Plant, *British Idealists*, ch. 5; and M. Bentley, *The Climax of Liberal Politics* (1987), 76–83.
[88] For example, Acland, Grey, Samuel, Hobhouse, Hobson, Beveridge, Morant, Braithwaite, and Haldane.
[89] Freeden, *New Liberalism*, p. 18, and Vincent and Plant, *British Idealists*, pp. 43–4.
[90] Freeden, *New Liberalism*, pp. 170–1.

programme. The rhetoric of Idealism, as proclaimed by, for
example, Sadler, Urwick, and Haldane, gave intellectual
credence to their views on the importance of educating for the
new democratic age, as they perceived it, especially after 1918.
With its ethical imperatives, Idealism was perfectly suited to
debate the 'boy labour' problem which was usually seen, in one
way or another, as a problem of 'character' and, therefore,
notions of duty, service, subordination, and so on, were eagerly
and easily incorporated as desirable features in the making of
the new image of youth. Of course, individual reformers did
not need to be committed Philosophical Idealists in order to
adhere to the new image; old-fashioned ageism reached the
same conclusion and had more or less the same remedies for
the 'problem'. But once again, Idealism provided the theoretical justification for a (political) critique based upon
combined ageist and class prejudices.

Of the two principal features of citizenship, political stability, including social harmony, was by far the most comprehensive and provided the fundamental *raison d'être*. In the final
analysis, all questions concerning harmonious relations in
society were derived from issues relating to social class.
T. H. Green had hoped to see a dialogue between opposing
interests in a society where self-sacrifice would overcome self-
interest, and where citizenship rather than class consciousness
would determine priorities. In fact he

tried to inaugurate a new concept of citizenship which would link
men of different social classes. The concept was based upon the
notion that there was a good common to members of all classes, a goal
the existence of which could be established from German Idealist
metaphysics and which could be made visible in actual measures of
educational reform and social welfare.[91]

The 'antagonism of interest', which Green knew existed, could
'only be met by moral ideas appropriate . . . to the citizen
stage . . . the reconciliation must come through a higher gospel
of rights—the gospel of duty'.[92] By the end of the nineteenth
century it was fairly obvious that the dialogue was not

[91] Quoted in frontpiece to Vincent and Plant, *British Idealists*, see also A.
MacIntyre, *A Short History of Ethics* (1966), 244–8.
[92] Richter, *Politics of Conscience*, p. 355.

materializing, as the social and political events of the 1880s had made clear, and the employers' counter-attack on trade unions in the 1890s gave little hope for any kind of reconciliation. By the early 1900s, the birth of the Labour Party, despite being closely involved with Liberalism, signalled a new phase in class politics, and between 1910 and 1918 the continued growth of the party together with a rapid increase in trade-union membership, syndicalism, deteriorating industrial relations, social unrest, and the influence of the Russian Revolution, were all factors pointing in an ominous direction. The nervous mood was captured by the Conservative *Morning Post* which reminded its readers that the modern franchise was concentrating more power into the hands of the working class. 'Can we afford', it asked, 'to leave our National and Imperial interests to the control of an ignorant and illiterate and unprogressive democracy?'[93]

It seemed to many reformers that certain 'interests' were threatening the survival and growth of the 'common good'. This feeling was unambiguously expressed by J. H. Muirhead, a Professor of Idealist Philosophy and secretary of the Ethical Society, who, while acknowledging the long history of 'class differences', nevertheless warned that 'Class conflicts waged in the name of fundamentally different and irreconcilable social and ethical standards are a new thing.'[94] Consequently, although reformers saw 'adaptability' as a *sine qua non* of citizenship, many were equally insistent on the more overtly

[93] *Morning Post*, 6 Mar. 1914 in PRO. Ed. 46/15a.

[94] J. H. Muirhead, 'Philosophy in Social Reform', in *Converging Views of Social Reform* (June 1912). see also Gordon and White, *Philosophers as Educational Reformers*, p. 115. Consider, for example, hostility of Hobhouse, Hobson, Beveridge, and Masterman to trade unions and to the Labour group. See also Henry Jones arguing that Labour 'stands for the interests of one class'. Labour appealed to the working man, he said, 'on a class basis, not as citizens.' Quoted in Vincent and Plant, *British Idealists*, pp. 78–9. For a more detailed discussion see Freeden, *New Liberalism*, pp. 15–8. Where Liberals identified with masses, Labour identified itself with classes. Nevertheless, certain Socialists claimed to have the same ethics as Liberals, see Ramsey MacDonald in his reply to Henry Jones, in Vincent and Plant, *British Idealists*, p. 79. As far as citizenship was concerned, George Lansbury thought it should teach young people that: 'The State was a sort of co-operative society of which they were all members, they should be prevented from getting the notion, that the State was some big thing outside and apart from themselves': Quoted in Fleet, 'Some Margins of Continued Education', p. 129.

political aspects of what was usually paraded as a moral concept, even though the intensification of class politics from the 1880s onwards more or less completely subordinated the purely moral principles. Sadler had articulated the political sentiment in his Manchester inquiry when he remarked on how education was but one aspect of 'a many sided problem', and as such it necessitated both the development of individuality and personal conviction and 'a sense of national duty and obligation towards the State', which could only come through 'better and more systematic training for the duties of citizenship and for home-making and family claims'.[95] The critical factor in the 'many sided problem' was felt to be the question of 'Rights and Duties within the State', and their relation to the wider issues arising out of an increasingly democratic society, notably that of the 'sectional interest' of the labour movement, which was always of profound concern to the New Liberals who regarded it as undermining political stability and social harmony.[96] The task of education was to reinvigorate citizenship in order that pupils might act morally and embrace 'duty'.

Many of those who talked and wrote about the concept pined for the ideal situation which had existed in ancient Greece where

the meaning of citizenship was plain. Nothing stood between you and your fellows in the community. Citizenship was obviously and visibly a life, your whole life, with common dangers, common responsibilities, common enjoyments, and common ambitions . . . In modern life it is very much harder to see our way . . . [it] has almost ceased to be a controlling conception for us.[97]

Education no longer meant, 'as it should, the victory over the idols of class'; instead everything was judged 'by the standard of a class or clique'.[98] Urwick shared this view, arguing that too narrow an interpretation of citizenship prevailed: 'the sense of duty is not realised, and the all-pervading duties of

[95] Sadler (ed.), *Continuation Schools*, pp. 711–12.
[96] Vincent and Plant, *British Idealists*, pp. 77–79.
[97] B. Bosanquet, 'The Duties of Citizenship', in B. Bosanquet (ed.), *Aspects of the Social Problem* (1895). For 'Greece' in Idealist philosophy, see MacIntyre, *History of Ethics*, p. 244.
[98] Bosanquet, 'Duties of Citizenship', pp. 6–7.

citizenship are lost sight of in the wilderness of interests of both individuals and groups'.[99] Similarly, James Bryce, chairman of the Royal Commission on Secondary Education, also looked on sectional interests as a danger to the common good because 'civilized societies', he said, were progressing towards popular government and, given this direction, 'each member of a free community must be capable of citizenship' which involved 'Intelligence, Self-Control, Conscience'. The true citizen must be 'able to understand the interests of the community, must be able to subordinate his own will to the general will, must feel his responsibility to the community and be prepared to serve it by voting, working, or (if need be) fighting'.[100] The most difficult requisite to produce was 'Conscience' for the struggles for political liberty had always been in the name of 'Rights', and in this conflict, 'the other side of the civic relation naturally fell out of sight'. By this Bryce meant that 'Duty' had been forgotten, whereas it was actually 'the correlative of Right'.[101] Since the late eighteenth century, there had developed the 'perfectionist doctrine' which claimed that 'government of the people by the people' was most appropriate, but according to Bryce, this had now been shown to be wrong. It had become 'painfully evident' that the majority of people did not possess the merits of 'Capable Citizens . . . In no European country is the average citizen what the citizen in a democracy ought to be.'[102] Ordinary people, he said, fell far short of the 'proper standard of duty' because they suffered from 'indolence . . . self-interest . . . [and] party spirit'.[103] The solution was for the 'wild stock' of the average man to be amended by the grafting on of 'the better conscience'.[104] And how could this best be achieved? 'The most obvious way to begin is through the education of those who are to be citizens.'[105]

The view that duties were being swamped by particular interests, each wallowing in an orgy of rights, was common

---

[99] E. J. Urwick, *A Philosophy of Social Progress* (1912; 1920 edn.), 150, 152.
[100] J. Bryce, *The Hindrances to Good Citizenship* (1909), 7.
[101] Ibid., 8–9.
[102] Bryce, *Hindrances*, pp. 11, 16.
[103] Ibid., 19.
[104] Ibid., 121.
[105] Ibid., 122.

among the Idealists, as it was among the New Liberals.[106] In place of rights, the intention was to emphasize the notion of 'service' on behalf of all interests in the community. John MacCunn, Professor of Philosophy at Liverpool University and author of several standard texts on citizenship and character, was keen to impress upon his readers that rights alone did not make the citizen; what mattered was the way in which they were used: democracy itself was only a beginning, not an end.[107] The importance of citizenship lay in the individual 'giving' to his city, rather than taking from it.[108] The same exhortation came from Henry Jones, another Professor of Idealist Philosophy, active in Welsh education matters, friend of Lloyd George and author of *The Principles of Citizenship*. Jones wrote in terms of 'Social Responsibilities' between 'Man and Society', arguing that it was 'Mutual Service and Mutual Obligations of State and Citizen' which kept the community alive and well; only 'the continued well-doing of its citizens' could sustain the State.[109] When he asked rhetorically, what 'services' can we render? the real answer, he said, lies 'in your own circumstances, your vocation and your character'; adding, significantly: 'Duty only binds those who discover it and impose it upon themselves.'[110]

Jones is expressing three central and fundamentally related features of Idealist ethics: the idea of service; the acceptance of one's position in society and a willingness to perform allotted tasks to the best of one's ability; and the belief that morality cannot be imposed by external forces, but that it must come from within the individual personality. The unspoken assumption which sustains these features is that they are easily defined and non-controversial, since all disputes were subject to Green's gospel of duty, with its moral and being the classless

---

[106] See, e.g., Freeden, *New Liberalism*, passim; Gordon and White, *Philosophers as Educational Reformers*, passim; Vincent and Plant, *British Idealists*, passim.

[107] J. MacCunn, *Ethics of Citizenship* (1894), 69–70, 81, and his *The Making of Character* (1900), 102–5.

[108] J. MacCunn, *The Ethics of Social Work* (1911).

[109] H. Jones, *The Principles of Citizenship* (1919), 86–111, and his *Working Faith of a Social Reformer* (1910), 296.

[110] Jones, *Faith of a Social Reformer*, p. 297. The importance of 'Duty' was made clear in school textbooks. See, e.g. F. R. Worts, *Citizenship* (1919), 210–78.

'common good'.[111] And though the notion of the 'common good' went through several transformations at the hands of the New Liberals, it continued, in Hobhouse's words, to require 'a readiness to forgo personal advantage for the general gain, a recognition of mutual dependence'.[112] But, of course, this was a conscious attempt by liberal theorists to settle political issues by reference to what T. H. Marshall has called ' social citizenship', thereby evading those more difficult questions of economic inequality which so concerned late Victorian and Edwardian commentators.[113]

The promotion of 'service', mediated via citizenship, was a constant theme throughout the debate on part-time day continuation schools because more than any other single aspect it emphasized the moral value of working conscientiously in a given occupation in order to contribute to the welfare of the community; hence the importance of creating the 'adaptable' worker. All those who were familiar with the works of Kerschensteiner knew that the task of the schools was to educate their pupils to serve their fellow citizens; they were to be taught the value of joy in work as service.[114] The end of all education, he said, was not merely the technically efficient workman, but one who 'not only seeks to advance his own welfare through his work, but also consciously places his work in the service of the community.[115] The *Report of the Consultative Committee on Continuation Schools* (no doubt under the influence of Sadler) quoted him approvingly when he wrote that apprentices should learn 'the truth of the maxim that the meaning of life is not to rule but to render service to one's neighbour, service to one's calling, service to one's native country, service to truth and to justice'.[116] Such an exhortation

[111] Freeden, *New Liberalism*, pp. 18, 27. For a note on the continuing influence in this context of youth workers such as Paterson see Bailey's comments on his role and objectives in the origins of the Borstal idea: V. Bailey, *Delinquency and Citizenship* (1987), 217.

[112] L. T. Hobhouse, *The Labour Movement* (1893), 5. For an example of a popular religious textbook, stressing 'service' see S. E. Keeble (ed.), *The Citizen of To-Morrow* (1906), Pt. III.

[113] T. H. Marshall, *Citizenship and Social Class* (1950), *passim*.

[114] Kerschensteiner, *Education for Citizenship*, p. 56.

[115] Kerschensteiner, Introduction to Best and Ogden, *Problem of the Day Continuation School*, p. xiv; see also his *Schools and the Nation*, pp. 144, 153.

[116] *Consultative Committee on Continuation Schools*, p. 153.

was meant to encourage adolescents to accept what was in
effect an ideological belief, namely, that 'any service for which
payment is accepted, however humble it may be, is to be
regarded as a service to the community and to be conscientiously performed.'[117] Writing in 1918, but with a little more
subtlety, J. Dover Wilson advised that the War had transformed
work from being 'a meaningless drudgery' into something
meaningful, because it brought about 'a common purpose',
which needed to be continued by encouraging workers to
regard 'production' not as 'forced labour', but as 'a social
service'.[118] Education was necessary in cultivating this belief,
for though it could not abolish the monotony of labour, 'it can
add value, meaning and even pride to the vocation of the
worker if it helps him to understand his relations with his
fellows, the importance of his contribution to the national
task.'[119]

This understanding of 'service' was crucial to the political
practicality of citizenship which always depended upon being
able to offer a reconciliation between 'personal rights' and,
despite the vacillating liberal reinterpretations, 'the community'.[120] 'Service, if consciously and freely given, seemed to
be the most appropriate way of achieving this end. But the
immediate significance of imbuing adolescents with such a
'civic idealism' lay, as Dover Wilson said, in transcending the
ordinariness of labour, in its transformation through ethical
principles into a moral act. If labouring was to be perceived as a
'moral' activity, then young workers had to be persuaded to see
'meaning' in wage-earning. Of course, this was both a political
and a disciplinary measure. Reformers were seeking to inte-
grate working-class adolescents into the 'common good' by
means of an educational programme which it was hoped would
lead them to internalize the community perspective and,
therefore, use it as the criterion for evaluating their own
wishes and responses. Labour, and its consequences, was not
the only factor involved but it was crucial in relation to the

---

[117] Best and Ogden, *Problem of the Day Continuation School*, p. 23.
[118] J. Dover Wilson, *Humanism*, p. 32.
[119] Ibid., 33. On contentment at work, see also *TES*, 15 Aug. 1918, p. 350.
[120] Freeden, *New Liberalism, passim*.

social problem, economic efficiency, industrial relations, and to sectional interests. Moreover, in the simplest of terms, it was correctly felt that occupational satisfaction, which a sense of 'service' could create, was a prerequisite of a stable political culture.

The call for education to buttress democracy by inculcating into young people the principles of citizenship became increasingly exaggerated and, in some senses, melodramatic. Henry Dyer, the Scottish educationalist, warned of the 'vast forces' which needed to be 'guided by an intelligent democracy' which itself could only be ensured by 'an adequate system of education', otherwise, everything 'will end in chaos and despotism'.[121] One of the most urgent pleas came from Haldane, who regarded the education of the working class as 'the new problem of the twentieth century'.[122] In his introduction to the English edition of Kerschensteiner's *The Schools and the Nation*, he wrote

Democracy is becoming a reality, the possessors of new and increasing political power are finding their feet, not less abroad than in this country. As their education and knowledge increase they are pressing more and more each year for better social conditions and for a larger share in the fruits of industry. The movement is one to be welcomed if it proceeds along the right lines, the lines along which it may develop and not hamper national life. But no compulsion can secure that it will proceed along those lines . . . it can only be supplied with the knowledge and training which may guide it to seek its own solution in the better state with higher ideals.[123]

For Fisher, speaking on his Education Bill in 1917, the 'governing conception' of the proposals was to ensure 'the production of good citizens', which was now a matter of some urgency since the extension of the franchise had put 'a greater demand than ever before upon the civic spirit'.[124] He was more

[121] Dyer, *National Life*, p. 103.
[122] Quoted in Vincent and Plant, *British Idealists*, p. 155.
[123] Kerschensteiner, *Schools and the Nation*, p. 109.
[124] *Hansard*, 97, 909 (10 Aug. 1917) and Board of Education, *Annual Report, 1917*, quoted in Waterfall, *Day Continuation School*, p. 52: 'We cannot doubt that the future will make new and increased demands—especially in a democratic community—on the health, character and intelligence of every citizen.'

explicit in his meeting with a deputation from the Federation of British Industries at which he said that the 'secret' of controlling young workers was to 'fill their minds with something like humane letters, or elements of science', then 'you get a humane outlook throughout the country and you get industrial relations more intelligently discussed'.[125] In general, Fisher was keen to stress the 'healing' qualities of education, telling a Newcastle audience how it 'dispels the hideous clouds of class suspicion and softens the asperities of faction'.[126] A. L. Smith, chairman of the Adult Education Committee at the Ministry of Reconstruction, also warned: 'If industrial harmony is to take the place of social unrest, education, on the moral and social side must be taken up in a way that had hardly been experimented upon as yet . . . Unless we educated our democracy there would be the greatest social and political trouble as the outcome of the war'.[127] The message was bluntly stated by the *Times Educational Supplement*: 'In these columns we have repeatedly declared that the new franchise and the new education are supplementary things. Without education, Bolshevism, or Syndicalism run mad, indicates the unconscious goal.'[128]

The compulsory part-time day continuation school for boys was meant to provide physical, vocational and 'humanistic' education with the intention of producing individuals who were disciplined, moral, contented, and possessed of a civic conscience. At one end of the spectrum of aims and aspirations stood the need to turn out adaptable workers, suitable for a developing labour-market; while at the other end there was the desire to educate young people for their role as adults in the evolving mass democracy. And in between were ranged a number of additional hopes and objectives all of which were intended to contribute toward the creation of the ideal citizen.

---

[125] Quoted in Sherington, *English Education*, p. 107.

[126] *TES*, 7 June 1917, p. 217, and Fisher's Preface to *Educational Reform* (Oxford 1918), vii–xvi.

[127] *TES*, 4 Jan. 1917, also quoted in Simon, p. 344.

[128] *TES*, 28 Feb. 1918, also quoted in Simon, p. 344. Similarly, after the war, Freeman and Hayward wrote: 'The workers are now seizing political and industrial power, and they are not equipped to use it wisely—because during childhood and adolescence they were not educated'. A. Freeman and F. H. Hayward, *The Spiritual Foundations of Reconstruction* (1919), 210.

In his diary for August, 1915, Sadler wrote 'Better education is vital in England'; it was necessary for trade competition, efficient use of resources, and for class co-operation.[129] Years earlier, in 1903, he had told a British Academy audience that 'Implicit in educational theory . . . is a theory of social order.' The 'fundamental difficulty at the present time', he continued, 'seems to be the impossibility of forecasting with confidence the future lines of social organization.'[130] Lodged in between these two dates were a number of factors which gave the issue a pressing urgency. First, 'boy labour' came to be defined as a problem which, together with the 'discovery' of adolescence, meant that working-class youth attained a hitherto unknown pre-eminence among social theorists and reformers. Second, the trade-union movement continued to grow while the Labour Party established itself (if only as an adjunct of Liberalism), and as both institutions were significant expressions of sectional interests, they created apprehension among the political authorities. Third, there was the severe deterioration of industrial relations in the few years prior to 1914 which brought with it violent strikes and syndicalism. Thus by the outbreak of war a number of questions and problems had forced themselves onto the agendas of middle-class society, and by the end of the war all these factors were resolved into one major consideration: the nature and control of 'industrial democracy'. The proposed continuation schools were seen as a means whereby the newly-discovered young workers would be given a 'liberal' education, involving a version of civic ethics which emphasized both occupational adaptability and community service. The intentions were to give the adolescents a 'character training'; to produce more efficient workers; and to educate youth in the duties of citizenship.

If, however, the schools offered the prospect of serving such obvious needs why, then, did the experiment collapse? Given that occupational 'adaptability', for instance, was such a prominent objective, why did the Federation of British Industries and employers in general oppose compulsory part-time day (though not evening) continuation classes? [131] In

---

[129] *Sadler Papers*, Diary, Typed notes. 23 Aug. 1915, C. 542, p. 1.
[130] *Proceedings of the British Academy* (1903), 12.
[131] For a survey of employer attitudes, see M. E. Sadler and M. S. Beard,

some respects, reformers found themselves isolated: working-class 'clients' on one side, uninterested middle-class business-men on the other. The answer lies in part in the social position of the reformers who belonged to the professional rather than the employing middle class: they were social workers, teachers, social scientists, philosophers, clerics, doctors, and psychologists, the majority of whom were distanced from the realities of the labour-market. Moreover, the distance was exaggerated by the educational character of their proposal, which employers recognized would restrict their freedom to use juvenile labour at their own discretion; and, given employers' traditional suspicion of further education, they regarded the whole idea as unnecessary, potentially expensive and disruptive of production schedules.[132] Nor were the moral and ethical themes of the reformers helpful in making the schools appear relevant: discipline, character, conscience, service, and so on. None of these had much significance for the hard-pressed businessman, struggling against his competitors at home and abroad, fighting off trade-union influence and coping with a growing volume of government-inspired social and industrial legislation. True, the reformers promised an 'adaptable' worker, but adaptability lay in the eyes of the beholder and, anyway, in the short term it was more relevant to the supply of, than the demand for, labour and, therefore, of little immediate interest to employers. However, the single most important factor militating against employers' co-operation was that they never regarded the 'problems' high-lighted by reformers—indiscipline, excessive occupational mobility, absence of vocational guidance, lack of systematic

'English Employers and the Education of their Workpeople', in Sadler (ed), *Continuation Schools*, pp. 265–317; see also p. 724. For the official employers' view, see Federation of British Industries, *Memorandum on Education* (Jan. 1918).

[132] The Consultative Committee noted that 'the great majority of employers are still indifferent to the educational needs of the young persons in their employment', *Report*, p. 96. This does not appear to have been so among certain groups of American business interests. See P. A. Sola, 'Vocational Guidance: Integrating School and Society in Chicago, 1912–16', *Vocational Aspect of Education* 28/71 (1976), 117–23, and his 'The Chicago Association of Commerce and Extra-Curricular Activities in the Chicago High Schools, 1914–25', *Vocational Aspect of Education*, 30/77 (1978), 119–27.

industrial training, and inadequate preparation for family responsibilities and exercise of the franchise—as problems for which they felt responsible; they had little interest in the search for solutions. While they might find 'delinquent' behaviour, in its many manifestations, irritating, as the role of juvenile labour in the production process was always either peripheral or auxilliary, the 'delinquency' was more than compensated for by the advantages of using young workers who were cheap, malleable, non-unionized, easy to recruit and just as easy to dismiss.[133]

Once again the spectre of the adolescent as worker and wage-earner returned to obstruct the aspirations of reformers who came into direct conflict with the priorities of market forces, including the evolving relationship between labour and technology, the urgency of the small firm for immediate profits, and the overwhelming influence of supply and demand. Such a reality had little sympathy for the training of character and the creation of citizens.

---

[133] These tend to be the characteristics of juvenile labour today, see Mark Casson, *Youth Unemployment* (1979), 28, 52–3. As Hay has shown, some employers were interested in the larger issues combining 'social control' and welfare, but these always excluded education. See J. R. Hay, 'Employers Attitudes to Social Policy and the Concept of Social Control, 1900–1920', in P. Thane (ed), *The Origins of British Social Policy* (1978), 107–25; 'Employers and Social Policy in Britain: The Evolution of Welfare Legislation, 1905–1914', *Social History* 2/4 (1977), 435–55; and 'The British Business Community, Social Insurance and the German Example', in W. J. Mommsen (ed.), *The Emergence of the Welfare State in Britain and Germany* (1981). See also review essay by K. Nield in *Bulletin of the Society for the Study of Labour History* 30 (Spring 1975), in which he argues that ' "the growth of collectivist sentiment" is but a poor metaphor for the political *will*, and the economic and ideological *necessity* to reorganise the State . . . through education and shrewd measures of social reform.': p. 67. In this respect, however, a major (collectivist) thrust in educational reform was successfully defeated by various political, economic and educational interest groups.

Conclusion

The shaping of adolescence by social and cultural forces
does not mean that there are no inherent biological and
hormonal changes during puberty. For adolescent behaviour
is determined by the interaction between cultural and
biological forces in a particular society at a particular
moment in history.[1]

Adolescence, like infancy, childhood, and old age, is real. What
matters is what is thought of it, how it is seen, what is done to
it, and what is expected from it. This study has been about
mainly the Edwardian moment. In the broadest terms, it has
been concerned with one aspect of youth history: how and
why, and with what consequences for age relations, middle-
class reformers put together a number of images of working-
class adolescents. These pages have described and examined
some of the ways in which groups of adults perceived young
workers, and how and why they sought to train, supervise, and
control them. However, they did not seek to achieve these
ends merely for reasons of age prejudice, though this was
always an important consideration; indeed, many of the other
reasons grew out of this prejudice. But of greater significance,
ultimately, was the attempt by youth workers, social scientists, educationalists, and politicians to solve a number of social
problems whose effects stretched well beyond young people
themselves, involving as they did the economy, labour, racial
hygiene, and political stability. In pursuit of their ends,
reformers and others were compelled to alter their perceptions
of (and attitudes toward) young people and, therefore, the
images which they used to order and define them. As the
images were changed so, too, were age relations, since the
former not only are always expressions of the latter, but also
clearly help to sustain them. But it can hardly be over-
emphasized that the new images were not constructed in any
artificial, mechanistic sense, separate, as it were, from atti-

[1] J. Springhall, *Coming of Age* (1986), 234.

tudes and real social relationships on the one hand and, on the other, the economic and political structures of society.

As the clarity of the perception of youth as a problem sharpened, so new images emerged. In some respects the period witnessed the birth of three principal sets of perceptions, involving changes in attitude, and associated in turn with 'boy labour', the psychology of 'adolescence', and the social critique of the young workers' personality. Each of these overlapped with the other; each depended on the other for either illustration, evidence, or knowledge, and each reinforced the other, providing both an individual and a collective logic and coherence.

The 'boy labour problem' was a feature of the larger social and political issues which dominated the Edwardian era, and obviously one that came to be taken seriously by contemporaries, in terms of the efficient functioning of the labour-market in general, and of specific problems deriving from the market, such as un- and underemployment, industrial training, casual and unskilled labour and, in the wider sphere, poverty and family morale. Once this had happened, attitudes toward, and images of, youth were profoundly altered (though, of course, the alteration was a process over time, not a dramatic moment) and a new pattern of age relations began to develop.

But there was another and ultimately more significant image under construction, especially during the Edwardian years, which involved the transformation of 'youth' into 'adolescence' as a 'stage of life'.[2] The process meant that adolescence ceased to be what an American scholar has called an 'idea' and became, in his words, a 'social fact'.[3] This study has illustrated the ways in which the social sciences created 'new knowledges' as they revolutionized themselves, and none more so than psychology which obtained its influential position by applying itself to a number of 'practices' involving problems of the 'abnormal functioning' of either individuals or institutions.[4]

[2] K. Keniston, 'Youth: A "New" Stage of Life', 39 *American Scholar* (1970), 631–2.
[3] D. Bakan, 'Adolescence in America: From Idea to Social fact', *Daedalus*, (Fall, 1971), 979–95.
[4] The idea of 'practices' is derived from N. Rose, *The Psychological Complex: Psychology, Politics and Society in England, 1869–1939* (1985), 3. and 5.

As a result of adolescence becoming a 'social fact', a specificity was bestowed on boy labour which gave the whole subject of juvenile employment an enhanced status in part derived from its scientific description, and in part from its social relevance. Of even greater importance, however, the concept united and ordered so many different facets in observable behaviour of the young and claimed to provide such insight and understanding of their physiology and psychology, in particular the significance of 'instincts', 'emotions', and 'habits', that everything about them, including their wage-earning capacity, could be made knowable and manageable. This explains why reformers were fundamentally optimistic about their ability to make youth more dependent and subservient and, therefore, less threatening.

The prominence of instincts and emotions in the social identification of boy workers as adolescents was emphasized not only by the nature of Edwardian social observation, but also by the social psychology of the crowd. In many respects the urban working class appeared to share some of the characteristics of young people: they were indisciplined, disordered, volatile, emotional, and liable to be subverted through undesirable influences, not least of which was their own collective personality. It seemed that while both the crowd and adolescents had within them potential for good, they also had a destructive or anarchic potential; in each there was a conflict, what Urwick had likened to Jekyll and Hyde. This theme is one which forcefully impressed itself upon Edwardian social politics, and thereafter. It explains how 'adolescence' as a concept could almost appear as a metaphor for human nature: dangerous if left untutored and 'natural', but capable of ennobling the race if the 'natural' was educated by, to quote Urwick again, 'the skilled hand'.[5] As an age-group, a stage of life, adolescents stood, clearly visible, defined and itemized, the embodiment of so many of the tensions and contradictions peculiar to the period, without which they would never have been 'discovered'.

We have also seen the complex procedures whereby under the influence of their stage of life, the economics of boy labour was thought to affect adolescents' social behaviour, which was usually defined in terms of their personality. This meant that

---

[5] See above, ch. 3.

an older social critique, whose pedigree went back hundreds of years, was expanded to take account of juvenile employment in such a manner as to make the critique more subtle, at least in the sense that some reformers began to suggest that the combination of juvenile psychology, conditions of labour and industrial training was influential far beyond the workplace and on a scale previously unrecognized. After all, one of the most important lessons of the sociological inquiries was to teach that demoralization was organic; it could not be confined and, therefore, all groups within the working class were at risk. Hitherto, youth, unlike children, had been largely ignored but the events and trends that so characterized the decades *circa* 1880 and 1920 brought young workers firmly within the investigative framework of the social sciences as report after report vividly illustrated their significance in most areas of society. In effect, the new images, emanating from sociology, economics, eugenics and psychology, projected adolescents as active participants in the social order, with a political identity, and capable of consequential behaviour.

Given the close relationship between the occupational behaviour of working-class adolescents and their 'personality', reformers faced certain difficulties: how to imbue them with approved ethical principles; how to turn them into efficient workers; how effectively to reorganize the labour-market for social and economic ends. One means was actually to take control of the youth's entry into full-time wage-earning, in order to control the transition from school to work and, by offering vocational guidance and encouraging attendance at continuation schools together with an after-care system, to set initial standards with regard to attitudes and behaviour. Leaving aside the question as to whether the State and reformers were successful in affecting young people, the process itself was instrumental in creating a new image for youth, one which in common with so many of its other images, emphasized incapacity while seeking to deepen its dependence on the appropriate agencies. A great deal of its significance in influencing 'attitudinal changes' derives from the power of the State to legitimize and enshrine new perceptions of young people. Something of the sort had been attempted by the late Victorian youth organizations, but these had been unable to reach the mass teen-age population; and had also failed to agree on a coherent programme attractive to the different reforming interests. Even so their contribution to the mechanisms whereby the new images were translated from theory to practice needs to be recognized. We know that they and other voluntary bodies, such as the ASEA, provided much of the procedural methodology, including the focus on individualism, and the personnel to staff the new committee structures.

Young workers, then, had come to be regarded as integral to the efficient functioning of the social and economic system and, moreover, to the development of 'character' throughout the working class. In particular, Edwardian reformers believed that labour conditions for adolescents were influential on their social behaviour in both the short and the long run, or, put another way, and taking into account the wider implications of 'personality', that labour conditions influenced the form of their social being. What happened, with reference to adolescents, was that the notion of 'character' underwent a kind of transformation and emerged in the company of, perhaps as, citizenship.[6] If character was the watchword of moral philanthropy as personified by, for example, the COS, so citizenship was the criterion by which it could be judged. But the COS had refused to acknowledge the role of economic forces with respect to character, justifying J. A. Hobson's jibe that their philosophy could be summed up in the phrase 'character is the condition of conditions'.[7] The debate on boy labour provided further evidence to undermine this view as economic life, argued reformers, could not be divorced from conditions.[8] The concept of citizenship allowed for this wider interpretation; it was sufficiently flexible (or vague) to be able to accommodate a variety of desirable qualities, which in recognizing the importance of labouring (in whatever capacity) as a service to the community, connected the economic to the social.[9]

[6] See discussion in M. Freeden, *The New Liberalism: An Ideology of Social Reform* (1978), pp. 170–8, and S. Collini, *Liberalism and Sociology*: L. T. Hobhouse and Political Argument in England, 1880–1914 (1970), 28–32.
[7] Quoted in A. Vincent and R. Plant, *Philosophy, Politics and Citizenship: The Life and Thought of the British Idealists* (1984), 102. See also Freeden, *New Liberalism*, 3, 176.
[8] But see ibid. 172, 174–5, and R. A. Bray, *Boy Labour and Apprenticeship*,
[9] This refers to Green's 'self-realisation' argument, see Vincent and Plant,

Citizenship as a subject of discussion was not peculiar to the early twentieth century, but it occupied a special place in the strategy of the boy labour group, and other reformers, in solving the problems posed by working-class adolescence. It is worth bearing in mind that reformers chose compulsory part-time day continuation schools as the principal means through which to preach the effectiveness of the doctrine. In terms of the practical implications for employers, this was a controversial proposal from the earliest days and it is clear that its implementation met with strenuous and effective opposition from different interests. This indicates a profound division of opinion between different sections of the middle class over methods and objectives. It should also serve as a warning against using the concept of social class in a crude explanatory manner. Either way, it tends to confirm the view that collectivist reforms were doomed unless industry and commerce gave their consent.[10] The failure of the continuation school movement shows that the *class* position of the prospective pupils, rather than any *age* relationship, determined that the significance of their labour power was more important than their further education, however that may have been defined.

But were the images of youth, as Gillis suggests, wedged between 'Conformity and Delinquency'?[11] Surely not. The argument herein has been to point to a range of images, which focused not so much on sociological types (conformist and delinquent behaviour), but on those pertaining to occupations, education, and the psychological state of 'personality'. Gillis gives the impression that reformers and other observers had only two perceptions of youth, whereas in reality there were several. Conformity was required only in the most general of senses. (It hardly fitted in with the Idealist conception of the

Philosophy, Politics and Citizenship, p. 104. However, even such sympathetic writers have trouble with the concepts of character and independence, see p. 105.

[10] See, e.g. J. R. Hay, 'The British Business Community, Social Insurance and the German Example', in W. J. Mommsen (ed.), *The Emergence of the Welfare State in Britain and Germany* (1981), and Hay 'Employers and Social Policy in Britain: The Evolution of Welfare Legislation, 1905–1914', *Social History* 2/4 (1977), 435–55.

[11] J. R. Gillis, *Youth and History* (1974), ch. 4.

active citizen). We have shown that the objectives of the youth movement, the juvenile labour exchanges and the proposed continuation schools were not so much the creation of conformist youth as of the adaptable, efficient citizen, motivated by service, mediated by humanism, and morally conscious. The alternative was not delinquent youth, but the ordinary boy whose vices and virtues resembled those of his parents: on the one hand, cheerful, plucky, generous; on the other, unstable, careless, superficial, noisy, thriftless, and so on. Thus we return to the inseparability of age and class.

The realities which provided the raw material for the new images were not confined to youth, but were issues of social class, race, poverty, work, democracy, and political harmony. And each of these continued to be important throughout at least the inter-war period. The images of youth arose from a society in which the middle class was reviving its claim to political and cultural leadership at the very time when it was being challenged by the new class politics. The problems, however, were not insoluble. There was little doubt among those concerned that through education youth could be made to exhibit the appropriate values. This optimism was borne out of a confidence in the ability of the social sciences to provide the basis for social policies; in the State to administer those policies; in the superiority of middle-class culture; and in psycho-medicine to understand and explain individual behaviour. The psychology of adolescence was crucial to the enterprise because it offered the possibility, indeed, the likelihood of change; it was grist to the mill of those whom Peter Clarke has termed 'moral' as opposed to 'mechanist' reformers.[12] The former believed that it was possible to regenerate people (this applied emphatically to the young) and, therefore, progress could be assumed.[13] The image of youth associated with regeneration (to be accomplished by Urwick's 'skilled hand') did much to categorize adolescents as 'pupils',

---

[12] P. Clarke, *Liberals and Social Democrats* (1978), 5. This refers to the optimistic view of human nature, in which a 'moral change, a change of heart, a new consciousness, will be the agent and sanction of transformation within society'.
[13] This view informed the work of Russell, Paterson, *et al.*, see V. Bailey, *Delinquency and Citizenship* (1987), *passim*.

and was used to compel those who refused to accept their new status.

The success of the image of youth as an age-group corralled by 'storm and stress' was noted long ago by Frank Musgrove in his pioneering study of adolescents. 'The position of youth in contemporary society', he wrote, 'is only intelligible in terms of the rise since the eighteenth century of a psychology of adolescence which has helped to create what it describes.'[14] And the disabling function of this image has remained visible throughout wide range of current psychological and socio-logical literature.[15] However, as John Springhall has recently argued, there is little evidence that teenagers suffer anything like an 'identity crisis' during their adolescent years.[16]

None the less, Springhall is unwilling to conclude that young people were repressed by adults. He asks rhetorically if there has been 'a deliberate conspiracy . . . to keep adoles-cents . . . in an inferior social and economic position'. In answering he correctly reminds us that young people are often of necessity in a subservient position as a result of their dependence on parents for food, clothing, and shelter; teachers for schooling; employers for employment; skilled workers for instruction in apprenticed trades; and on youth workers for leisure activities. On this basis he maintains that these adults should not be seen 'as agents of social control repressing the young—as reductionist social history might suggest—but as agents of socialization preparing them for their future roles as citizens in a society to which most adolescents gave unthink-ing and willing allegiance'.[17]

No one disputes that agents of socialization were hard at work on working-class adolescents. The important questions, and those which suggest exploitation and repression, are those which ask, who gave these agents their authority? What was meant by socialization? For what ends? And by what means? All socializing processes are political, just as they involve struggle between competing interests. Did the pursuit of citizenship, obedience, and rational recreation, to take but

[14] F. Musgrove, *Youth and the Social Order* (1964), 2.
[15] These are cited in Springhall, *Coming of Age*, pp. 225–7.
[16] Ibid., 227–31.
[17] Ibid., 231–2.

three examples, have nothing to do with class power, with stabilizing industrial relations, with inculcating notions of thrift and respectability, and with an implicit acceptance of one's place in society? And were not all of these contested values and beliefs? Were not adolescents being courted, persuaded and, where possible, forced to adopt modes of behaviour acceptable to established political and cultural authorities (which were often in conflict with those of their parents) ? When Springhall writes that adolescents gave their allegiance to 'society', this is at best a half-truth. The question is, whose society? That of youth workers, Philosophical Idealists, imperialists, eugenists, *et al*? Or that of their families, their communities, and their friends? If young people posed no threat in terms of allegiance, there would have been little need of so many reform programmes. Moreover, the complacent acceptance of socialization as a justification for adult authority denies adolescents the right to mount their own critiques, just as reformers never allowed the possibility of a reasoned and intelligent adolescent point of view. Psychology had sanctified the charge that youthful rebellion was evidence of the 'natural' condition of adolescence. We do not have to subscribe to a version of history which sees it simply in terms of a struggle between virtue and vice, nor do we have to believe that all adolescents were intelligent and admirable, in order to argue for the repression of young people, if only in terms of debilitating images.[18]

To conclude, the claim made in the introduction merits reiteration:' Age relations (including youth) are part of economic relations and the political and ideological structures in which they take place. It is not the relations between ages which explain change or stability in societies, but change in societies which explains relations between different ages.'[19] It

[18] Ibid., pp. 232–3. He admonishes me for being 'present-minded' in my wish to see young people given both a social and a political identity. I see nothing inherently wrong with such a commitment. It certainly does not necessarily imply that the historian must write in terms of vice and virtue, heroes and villians. In fact, it is worth pointing out that when Springhall cites Peter Burke's warning against this kind of history, he is paraphrasing what I have written elsewhere. See my 'The History of Childhood and Youth: A Guide to the Literature', Faculty of Modern Studies, Occasional Papers No. 1 Oxford Polytechnic (1981), 8, 10–11.

[19] S. Allen, 'Some Theoretical Problems in the Study of Youth', *Sociological Review* 16 (1968), 325–6.

has been a fundamental aim of this study to argue that the images of working-class youth, and their means of construction were inextricably bound up with the political, economic, social, and cultural issues of the time. What happened during the years between *circa* 1880 and 1920, was the beginning of a process whereby young workers were admitted to the public domain: their newly-defined significance meant that they required a new role, but one which had to be carefully circumscribed. The intention was to consolidate their power-lessness.[20] From the perspective of reformers and administrati, if collectivism was to participate in the restructuring of society by making provision for its efficient management, then working-class boys could no longer be ignored. These adolescents began to be designated as apprentices to a certain kind of maturity, suitable for an industrial and democratic age; and, with metaphorical binding written indentures, they were to be kept confined, while time-serving in the ante-room of respectable adulthood.

[20] P. Abrams, 'Rites de Passage. The Conflict of Generations in Industrial Society', *Journal of Contemporary History* 5/2 (1970), 175–90.

Appendix
Tables[1] for Chapter 2

TABLE 1. Age group 14–19 as % of total population aged 10 and upwards

Year	Total population	14–19 population	% 14–19	+/−
1901	25 323 844	3 913 916	15.4	
1911	28 519 313	4 023 876	14.1	1.3

Source: Census Papers, England and Wales, 1901, Cd. 1523, lxxxiv, summary tables 35, 36, and Census Papers, England and Wales 1911, Cd. 7929, lxxxi, summary tables 50, 54.

TABLE 2A. Occupied persons aged 14–19 as % total occupied population

Year	Total population	%+	14–19 population	%+	14–19	(10–19)	+/−
1901	14 328 727		2 913 551		20.3	(21.8)	
1911	16 284 072	14	3 030 887	4	18.6	(19.5)	−1.7

Source: Census Papers. England and Wales, 1901, Cd. 1523, lxxiv, summary tables 35; and Census Papers, England and Wales, 1911, Cd. 7929, lxxvi, summary table 54.

TABLE 2B. Occupied persons aged 14–19 as % of all occupied males and females

Year	All Males	All Females	Males 14–19	Females 14–19	Males %	Females %
1901	10 156 976	4 171 751	1 703 062	1 210 489	16.8	29.0
1911	11 453 665	4 830 407	1 740 819	1 290 068	15.2	26.7

Source: Census Papers. England and Wales, 1901, Cd. 1523, lxxxiv, Summary table 35; and Census Papers. England and Wales, 1911, Cd. 7929, lxxxi, Summary table 54.

[1] All tables refer to England and Wales for the period 1901–11.

TABLE 3. *Numbers and % of young persons aged 10–19 in each census order* [a]

Order	Nos. 1901	%	Nos. 1911	%
Domestic offices or services	(1 994 917) 557 042	27.9	(2 121 717) 532 585	25.1
Textile fabrics	(1 155 397) 374 126	32.4	(1 317 565) 403 094	31.0
Dress	(1 125 598) 294 588	26.2	(1 195 079) 312 093	26.2
Conveyance of men, goods, and messages	(1 267 825) 279 509	22.0	(1 423 868) 286,784	20.1
Metals, machines, implements, and cons	(1 237 196) 252 572	20.4	(1 578 147) 286,183	18.1
Agriculture	(1 128 604) 214 822	19.0	(1 235 237) 233 117	18.1
Food, tobacco, drink, and lodging	(1 073 809) 187 491	17.5	(1 388 248) 223 788	16.1
In and about and working and dealing in products of mines and quarries	(801 185) 153 751	19.1	(1 044 594) 190 454	18.2
Building and works of construction	(1 043 566) 147 963	14.2	(946 707) 70 837	7.5
Commercial	(590 629) 119 681	20.3	(790 163) 154 665	19.6
Other, general and undefined workers	(742 519) 108 277	14.6	(687 402) 89 245	13.0
Professional occupations and their subordinate	(606 260) 85 402	14.1	(714 621) 57 785	8.1
Papers, prints, books, and stationery	(278 957) 84 191	30.2	(340 960) 93 104	27.3
Wood, furniture, fittings, and decor	(257 592) 50 174	19.5	(283 986) 43 981	15.5
Bricks, cement, pottery, and glass	(175 513) 47 179	26.9	(173 838) 42 175	24.3
Defence	(168 328) 42 016	25.0	(205 817) 41 969	20.4
Precious metals, jewels, watches, instruments, and games	(149 438) 33 461	22.4	(125 394) 25 109	20.3

Table 3 *contd.*

Order	Nos. 1901	%	Nos. 1911	%
General and local government	(198 187) 30 649	15.5	(299 599) 33 550	11.2
Chemicals, oil, grease, soap, resin, etc	(128 640) 30 366	23.6	(171 983) 35 925	20.9
Skins, leather, hair, and feathers	(105 341) 22 481	21.3	(113 680) 23 478	21.3
Gas, water, electricity, and sanitary services	(71 425) 3 469	4.9	(102 355) 4 351	20.7
Fishing	(23 891) 2 733	11.4	(25 239) 2 227	8.8

^a Total work-force shown in brackets.

Source: *1901, summary table XXXV and 1911, Summary tables 50, 54, 48, and 14a*

TABLE 4. Number and % of young persons aged 10–19 in principal occupations

Occupations	1901	%	1911	%
Civil service messengers	20 300	34.0	—	—
Civil service officers and clerks	8 526	15.0	—	—
Other post-office officers and clerks	—	—	5 641	11.2
Post-office messengers	—	—	12 733	75.8
Soldiers	28 751	28.9	26 807	25.8
Navy and Marines	12 082	23.9	13 903	17.9
Law clerks	9 838	28.9	8 809	25.9
Teaching	56 813	24.7	21 737	8.7
Other domestic indoor servants	466 942	35.0	410 907	31.2
Domestic indoor servants in hotels, lodging- and eating-houses	19 101	30.9	21 581	28.5
Domestic coachmen, grooms	12 062	16.0	7 203	10.8
Domestic gardeners	12 683	14.4	18 059	15.2
Hospital, institutions (not poor law), and benevolent society services	—	—	7 696	13.0
Day girls, day servants	—	—	17 161	71.5
Laundry service and washing	32 181	15.7	31 631	17.7
Others engaged in service	—	—	9 297	28.2
Commercial or business clerks	107 113	29.4	136 343	28.5
Life, house, ship, etc., insurance officials, clerks, etc.	—	—	8 151	17.8

Occupations	1901	%	1911	%
Messengers, porters, watchmen (not government or railway)	133 551	72.0	171 448	74.0
Carmen, carriers, carters, waggoners (not farm)	46 346	17.0	20 109	7.2
Railway officials, clerks	15 484	22.8	12 079	14.2
Railway porters and servants	16 231	19.9	15 000	6.4
Railway-engine drivers, stokers, cleaners	10 411	15.8	7 329	10.5
Coachmen, grooms (not domestic) cabmen	15 507	5.7	—	—
Horsekeepers, grooms, stablemen (not domestic)	—	—	5 749	12.7
Van etc., guards, boys	—	—	16 211	96.2
Merchant service, seamen, bargemen, etc.	9 004	9.2	7 868	11.8
Telegraph, telephone service	7 753	34.0	—	—
Farmers', graziers' sons, daughters and other relatives assisting	39 725	36.9	52 361	34.3
Labourers in charge of horses and cattle	70 300	29.3	48 400	24.0
Agricultural labourers, farm servants, not otherwise distinguished	80 113	22.4	97 965	22.7
Gardeners (not domestic), nurserymen, seedsmen, florists	18 854	14.8	—	—
Other gardeners (not domestic)	—	—	8 223	10.7
Coal and shale mines, hewers	43 222	10.5	51 219	10.2
Coal and shale mines, other workers below ground	75 955	42.4	97 535	35.0
Coal and shale mines, workers above ground	16 483	29.9	26 592	28.0
Stone-quarriers, cutters, dressers	7 062	12.6	—	—
Erectors, fitters, turners	33 794	21.2	28 403	18.4
Ironfounders	20 573	20.5	17 186	16.9
Blacksmiths, strikers	22 595	16.5	15 552	12.4
Other or undefined engine-machine-makers	19 196	19.2	21 686	19.9
Boiler-makers	8 481	18.2	6 735	13.9
Puddling furnaces (iron and steel)	7 524	17.8	7 215	13.3
Other electrical apparatus makers	11 990	24.2	11 367	20.9

Table 4 *contd.*

Occupations	1901	%	1911	%
Electricians (undefined)	—	—	6 026	21.5
Bolt-, nut-, metal-, screw-, staple-makers	—	—	6 509	36.4
Tinplate-goods-makers	8 215	29.9	9 915	33.5
Other metal-workers	12 808	27.5	6 328	24.8
Other iron-goods-makers	—	—	8 756	23.2
Ship-platers, rivetters, etc.	—	—	6 170	19.0
Cycle-makers	—	—	9 889	28.0
Motor-car chassis-makers, mechanics	—	—	10 146	23.7
Cycle and motor manufacture	9 253	29.4	—	—
Goldsmiths, silversmiths, jewellers	—	—	7 006	26.0
Labourers (builders, carpenters, bricklayers, masons, plasterers)	24 672	12.0	10 609	6.5
Carpenters, joiners	50 061	18.4	18 604	8.9
Painters, decorators, glaziers	19 158	12.0	14 801	8.1
Plumbers	16 322	25.1	11 634	17.9
Cabinet-makers	11 092	21.3	7 224	14.4
French-polishers	5 964	28.4	—	—
Upholsterers	6 179	23.6	—	—
Sawyers, wood-cutting machinists	5 706	17.7	7 073	17.5
Brick-, plain tile-, terra-cotta-makers	16 104	25.1	10 529	20.2
Earthenware, china, porcelain manufacturers	19 352	31.0	20 391	29.1
Curriers, leather-goods-makers	6 688	22.8	—	—
Saddlers, harness, whip-makers	6 427	21.0	—	—
Leather-goods-, portmanteau-, bag-, strap-makers	—	—	5 640	31.0
Chemists, druggists	—	—	6 144	19.0
Paper manufacture	7 581	31.3	6 153	24.0
Printers	29 650	28.0	36 057	26.1
Bookbinders	11 717	36.8	10 304	32.9
Cotton-spinning processes	43 522	44.0	51 270	36.8
Cotton-weaving processes	84 671	35.0	86 122	31.5
Cotton-winding, warping, etc. processes	23 937	28.9	19 946	25.0

Occupations	1901	%	1911	%
Cotton card-blowing processes	20 906	35.0	—	—
Cotton-workers in other processes or undefined	14 289	31.0	8 169	34.7
Cotton-workers undefined	—	—	7 794	41.1
Wool and worsted spinning processes	34 809	63.3	39 564	56.0
Wool and worsted weaving processes	20 719	23.4	21 914	23.9
Wool and worsted workers in other processes or undefined	11 610	24.4	8 674	22.7
Hosiery manufacture	16 600	34.3	18 999	33.7
Fancy goods (textiles) small ware, etc. manufacture	7 333	35.5	—	—
Lace manufacture	10 133	27.9	9 941	24.1
Drapers, linen drapers, mercers	36 643	27.0	37 130	24.5
Milliners	19 607	40.2	28 634	43.0
Tailors	57 319	24.1	59 311	23.8
Dress-makers	102 780	31.9	102 256	30.0
Clothiers, outfitters, dealers	—	—	7 478	20.4
Shirtmakers, seamstresses	23 442	26.8	20 944	24.5
Boot-, shoe-makers	46 158	21.1	41 446	20.4
Wig-makers, hairdressers	8 016	23.7	12 314	25.1
Milksellers, dairymen	8 172	23.1	9 785	17.1
Butchers, meat-salesmen	21 500	20.4	27 447	22.4
Bread-, biscuits-, cake-, etc.-makers	21 251	27.7	21 372	24.1
Grocers, tea, coffee, chocolate dealers	40 041	20.7	41 119	18.8
Greengrocers, fruiterers	7 856	15.0	10 389	14.3
Tobacco manufacture	13 603	49.4	9 943	36.5
Barmen	15 785	28.0	—	—
Waiters (not domestic)	—	—	9 664	19,1
Others in inn, hotel, eating-house service	9 602	24.0	10 974	33.5
Costermongers, hawkers, street sellers	9 872	15.3	—	—
Newsboys, vendors	—	—	13 249	82.0
General labourers	50 810	12.3	23 559	8.0

Table 4 *contd.*

Occupations	1901	%	1911	%
General shopkeepers, dealers	9 505	18.4	14 087	16.3
Factory labourers, undefined	10 538	32.1	—	—
Engine-drivers, stokers, firemen (not railway, marine or agriculture)	—	—	7 787	7.0

Source: Calculated from *Census Papers. England and Wales, 1901,* Cd. 1523, summary table 35; and *Census Papers. England and Wales, 1911,* table 50.

TABLE 5. *Numbers of males and females aged 10–19 in each census order*

Order	Males 1901	Males 1911	Females 1901	Females 1911
General or local government	26 839	27 369	3 800	6 181
Defence	42 016	41 969	—	—
Professional occupations and their subordinate services	30 362	31 017	54 730	26 768
Domestic offices	53 875	57 838	503 167	474 748
Commercial occupations	98 606	111 531	21 075	43 129
Conveyance of men, goods, and messages	270 364	274 448	9 145	12 336
Agriculture	204 618	200 973	10 204	22 114
Fishing	2 703	2 188	30	39
In, about and dealing in products of mines and quarries	151 788	188 689	1 963	1 765
Metals, machines, implements, and conveys	224 281	242 711	28 291	43 242
Precious metals, jewels, watches, instruments, and games	24 825	16 044	8 636	9 245
Building and works of construction	147 944	70 833	18	16
Wood, furniture, fittings, and decorators	41 678	35 343	8 496	8 638
Brick, cement, pottery, and glass	33 304	27 077	13 781	15 098
Chemicals, oil, grease, soap, resin, etc.	16 900	19 821	13 445	16 104
Skin, leather, hair, and feathers	12 534	12 005	9 815	11 473
Paper, prints, books, and stationery	42 142	44 227	42 049	48 877
Textile fabrics	124 222	142 453	249 894	260 641
Dress	67 636	73 008	226 962	239 895
Food, tobacco, drink and lodging	128 515	144 505	59 976	79 283

Order	Males 1901	1911	Females 1901	1911
Gas, water, electricity	3 433	4 427	36	24
Other general	92 287	69 765	15 990	19 480

Sources: Census Papers. England and Wales, 1901, Cd. 1525, lxxiv, summary table 35; and *Census Papers, England and Wales, 1911,* Cd. 7929, lxxxi, summary tables 3, 50, 54.

TABLE 6. *Occupation index number: 1881–1911* [a]

	1881	1891	1911
General or local government	69	83	130
Commerce	70	81	119
Food, tobacco, drink, lodging	87	98	115
Gas, water, electricity	48	69	113
Defence	83	86	109
Professional and subordinate	91	96	105
Conveyance	82	91	101
Mines and quarries	86	93	115
metals, machines, etc.	87	89	106
Textiles	124	117	101
Agriculture	148	123	96

[a] 1901 = 100.
Source: D. Read, *England, 1868–1914* (1979), 386.

TABLE 7 *Number of male apprentices, all ages in industries (1906)*

Engineering	94 100
Shipbuilding	18 100
Railway carriage and wagon	4 500
Iron and Steel	5 000
Other Metal	20 000
Wire-drawing etc.	1 200
Gold, silver, electro-plate	2 000
Electrical and telegraph	2 300
Building	100 200
Printing, lithography, paper, stationery	16 300
Book-binding	2 100
Various textile	4 100
Tailoring	4 100
Shoemaking	3 300
Hatting	700
Utilities	700
Railway Work	1 200

Table 7 *contd.*

Pottery	3 300
Glass	2 000
Baking and confectionery	6 300
Leather-makers, saddlers and harness-makers	3 800
Cabinet-making	16 600
Sawmilling	3 600
Coach-building, carriage-bodymaking	4 100
Wheelwrights	2 100
Coopers	1 400
Brushmakers	800
Basket-weavers	800
Other artisan (shoemakers, tailors)	8 500
Misc. maintenance workers	10 000
	343 200
Distributive and mercantile	52 500
TOTAL	395 700

Source: C. More, *Skill and the English Working Class, 1870–1914* (1980), 99–100, 103.

TABLE 8. *% of male trainees returned (1909)*

Industry	Indentured apprentices	Apprentices under agreement	Learners
Engineering	29.0	35.0	36.0
Shipbuilding	51.3	22.1	26.6
Precious Metals	70.9	11.6	17.5
Pottery	4.6	28.8	66.6
Glass	55.8	44.2	—
Building	37.0	63.0	—
Furniture	33.0	26.1	40.9
Sawmilling	31.5	20.1	48.4
Wooden vehicle building	26.3	40.3	33.4
Printing	64.5	30.2	5.3
Wool Textile	30.6	32.4	37.0
Boot and Shoe	25.0	26.0	49.0
Clothing	33.5	24.1	42.4
Leather and Goods	35.8	26.0	38.2
Baking	19.1	39.9	41.0
Electricity supply	16.1	83.9	—
All above industries	36.2	37.7	26.1

Source: Enquiry into Apprenticeship and Training in 1925–6, 7 vols. *General Report,* (HMSO. 1927–8), 34.

TABLE 9. *Occupation on leaving school*

Occupation	On leaving school	at 16
Country workers	7	4
Seamen	4	5
Apprentices of learners	8	20
Message- boys and milk-boys	55	13
Van-boys	17	6
Vanmen	—	9
Boys of labourers in factories or works	40	49
General labourers	9	30
Miscellaneous (offices, workrooms)	10	14

Source: R. H. Tawney, 'The Economics of Boy Labour', *Economic Journal* 19 (Dec. 1909), 525.

TABLE 10. *Length of apprenticeship (1909) (%)*

	3yrs.	4 yrs.	5 yrs.	5–7 yrs.[a]	6 yrs.	7 yrs.
Engineering	0.1	0.9	53.5	10.0	8.0	27.5
Shipbuilding	0.2	—	53.0	0.6	18.0	28.2
Building	0.7	5.1	33.8	12.1	21.4	26.9
Furniture	2.3	15.2	39.9	15.7	16.9	10.0
Printing	—	—	4.2	6.6	4.8	84.4

[a] Depending on whether or not 14, 15, or 16 was the starting age.
Source: Enquiry into Apprenticeship and Training in 1925–6, Report, vii. 179.

TABLE 11. *Reasons for occupational mobility (%)*

No. of jobs	No. of boys	Apprenticeship Promotion	Wages	Dislike of job	Other reasons	Dismissal
1–2	483	71.2	8.7	5.8	9.5	4.8
3–4	123	29.2	16.3	38.2	11.3	5.0
5 +	61	10.0	11.4	44.2	26.2	8.2

Source: T. Ferguson and J. Cunnison, *The Young Wage Earner: A Study of Glasgow Boys* (*1951*), 91, table 30.

Select Bibliography

ARCHIVE MATERIALS

1. Public Record Office
Board of Education papers: Ed. 24/246, 248, 249 and 46/15A.
Cabinet Papers: CAB 37/19/17.
2. Bodleian Library
C. V. Butler Papers (at the time of search these were divided between the Bodleian and Oxford City Local History Library).
R. D. Denman Papers.
Arthur Greenwood Papers.
Michael E. Sadler Papers.
3. Liverpool University
British Psychological Society, 'Child Study Minutes'.
4. County of Avon Central Library
'Bristol People's Oral History Project'.
Essex University (Sociology Department)
'Family and Work Experience Archive'.
5. London Federation of Boys' Clubs
Annual Reports, 1918–23.
6. Local Authority Reports and Minutes
Birmingham Education Committee, *Report of the Special Sub-Committee on the Institution of a Juvenile Employment Bureau and Care Committee in Birmingham* (1910).
Birmingham Central Care Committee, *Reports*, 1912–15. (Birmingham Central Reference Library).
Birmingham Juvenile Employment Committee, Reports on Birmingham Trades (1913–16).
City of Oxford Education Committee, Juvenile Employment Committee, *Reports*, 1913–15.
City of Oxford Education Committee, Minute Book No. 2, 1909–15 (City of Oxford Local History Library).

OFFICIAL PUBLICATIONS

Annual Reports of the Board of Education, 1909–18.
Annual Abstract of Statistics, 1912–14.
Census Papers. England and Wales, 1901 Summary tables, 1903, Cd. 1523, lxxiv.
General Report (1904), Cd. 2174, iii.

Census Papers. England and Wales, 1911 Summary tables, 1914–16. Cd. 7929, lxxxi.

Occupations and Industries, 1913, Cd. 7018–19, lxxviii and lxxix.

General Report, 1917–18. Cd. 8491, xxxv.

Guide to the Census Reports, 1801–1966, HMSO, 1977.

Children's Employment Commission, 1863–7, Cd. 3170, 3414-I, 3548, 3678, 3796, xviii, xxii, xx, xxiv, xvi.

Royal Commission on Technical Instruction, Reports 1884, C. 3981, xxix; C. 3981, I, xxx; C. 3981, II, xxxi; C. 3981, III, xxxi (1).

*Royal Commission on the Depression of Trade and Industry, 1886, Second Report,*C. 4715, xxi, and *Final Report,* C. 4893, xxiii.

Education: Elementary Schools (Children Working for Wages), Pt. 2, 1899, lxxv.

Royal Commission on Labour, 1892–94., C. 6795, III, (1892), ii; C. 6894, VII, (1893), iii; C. 6894, x, iii; C. 6795, IV, (1892), xxxvi, Pt. 1.

Board of Trade: Agencies and Methods for Dealing with the Unemployed, C. 7182 (1893–4), lxxxii.

Interdepartmental Committee on the Employment of School Children, Report Cd. 849 (1902), xxv.

House of Lords Select Committee on Betting. Report and *Evidence,* v, (389) (1902).

Board of Education. Special Reports on Educational Subjects, C. 8447, 8988, 835, 836, 3860, (1897, 1898, 1902, 1908).

Report of Inspector-General of Recruiting for 1901, Cd. 1501 (1903), xxxviii.

Department Committee on the Employment of Children Act, 1903, Report, Cd. 5229 (1910), xxviii.

Interdepartmental Committee on Physical Deterioration. Report and Evidence, Cd. 2175 and 2120 (1904), xxxii.

House of Lords Select Committee on Juvenile Smoking Bill, IX (1906).

Interdepartmental Committee on Partial Exemption from School Attendance; Report, Cd. 4791 (1909), xvii.

Royal Commission on the Poor Laws and Relief of Distress; Report, Cd.44999 (1909), xxxvii; Appendix vol. VIII, *Unemployment,* Cd. 5066 (1910), xlviii; Appendix vol. IX, *Unemployment,* Cd. 5068 (1910), xlix; Appendix vol. XIX, *Report on the Effects of Employment or Assistance given to the Unemployed since 1886 as a Means of Relieving Distress outside the Poor Law,* Cd. 4795 (1909), xlix; Appendix vol. xx, *Report on Boy Labour in London and Certain other Towns,* Cd. 4632 (1909), xliv.

Board of Education: Consultative Committee on Attendance, Compulsory or Otherwise, at Continuation Schools. Report and Summaries of Evidence, Cd.4757–8 (1909), xvii.

Departmental Committee on Hours and Conditions of Employment

of Vanboys and Warehouse Boys: Report, Cd. 6886–7 (1913), xxxiii.
Standing Committee on Boy Labour in the Post Office: Reports. Cd. 5504, 5575, 6959, 7556 (1909, 1911, 1913, 1914), xxxix, xxxviii, xlix.
Board of Trade: Enquiry into the Conditions of Apprenticeship and Industrial Training, 'Report' (1915) (Printed but not published. Copy in British Library of Political and Economic Science).
Departmental Committee on Juvenile Education in relation to Employment after the War, Final Report, Cd. 8512 (1917–18), xi.
Enquiry into Apprenticeship and Training in 1925–6, 7 vols. HMSO (1927–8).
Board of Education: Report of the Consultative Committee on the Education of the Adolescent, HMSO (1927).
Ministry of Labour and National Service, Report of the Committee on the Juvenile Employment Service, HMSO (1945).
Hansard, 1910–18.
Board of Trade, *Labour Gazette* (1910, 1914–15).

REPORTS, ETC.

Pamphlets on Personal Morals. (Bod. 26521. f. 24.)
Young Men's Magazine, Sheffield YMCA publications (1893).
Report of the Committee on Youth of Methodism (1898).
YMCA, Occasional Papers (Dec. 1899).
Eighth Annual Report, 1899–1900 Church Lad's Brigade (1900).
Sadler, M. E., 'National Ideals in Education', An Inaugural Lecture at University College of Wales, Aberystwth, 1903.
The Apprenticeship Question, London County Council (1906).
Twentieth Anniversary Souvenir of the Church Lads' Brigade, 1891–1911 (1911).
Report and Proceedings of the National Conference on the Prevention of Destitution (1911, 1912).
The Boys' Brigade Manual (1913).
The Church Lads' Brigade and the Church Scout Patrols . . . and . . . Our Young Men of a Few Years Hence, Church Lads' Brigade (1912).
The Cinema. Its Present Position and Future Possibilities: Report and Evidence of the Cinema Commission of Inquiry, National Council of Public Morals (1917).
Report of National Conference on Educational Reconstruction, Workers' Education Association (1917).
Memorandum on Education, Federation of British Industries, (January 1918).
Trades for London Boys and How to Enter Them, Apprenticeship and Skilled Employment Association (1908).
Education Reconstruction, Education Reform Council (1917).

Education Policy, The Incorporated Association of Head Masters (1917).

NEWSPAPERS AND PERIODICALS

Charity Organisation Review
Child
Child Study
Contemporary Review
Economic Journal
Eugenics review
School Child
School Government Chronicle
Sociological Review
Times Educational Supplement
Toynbee Record

PRIMARY SOURCE BOOKS.

Place of publication is London, unless otherwise stated.
ANON., *Boys Life Brigade* (1900).
ANON., *The Church Lads' Brigade; Some Account of Its Objects, Its Work, Its Needs* (1908).
BADEN-POWELL, R., *Scouting for Boys: A Handbook for Instruction in Good Citizenship* (1908; 1910 edn.).
BARNETT, H., *Canon Barnett: His Life, Work and Friends* (1918; 1919 edn.).
BARON, B., *The Growing Generation: A Study of Working Boys and Girls in Our Cities* (1911).
BARRY, W., 'Unclean Fiction', in J. Marchant (ed.), *The Cleansing of a City* (1908).
BELL, LADY FLORENCE, *At the Works: A Study of a Manufacturing Town, Middlesbrough* (1907).
BEST, R. H. and OGDEN, C. K., *The Problem of the Continuation School and Its Successful Solution in Germany: A Consecutive Policy* (1914).
BEVERIDGE, W. H., *Unemployment: A Problem of Industry* (1909; 1917 edn.).
BOOTH, C., *Life and Labour of the People of London* (1897; 1902, 1903 edns.).
BOSANQUET, B. (ed.), *Aspects of the Social Problem* (1895).
—— *The Education of the Young in the Republic of Plato* (Translation and Introduction), (Cambridge, 1917).
BOSANQUET, H., *Rich and Poor* (1896; 1908 edn.).

BOSANQUET, H., *The Standard of Life* (1898; 1906 edn.).
—— *The Strength of the People* (1902).
—— *The Family* (1906).
—— *Social Work in London, 1869–1912* (1914; 1970 edn.).
BOWLEY, A. L., and BURNETT-HURST, A. R., *Livelihood and Poverty* (1915).
BRAITHWAITE, W. J., 'Boys' Clubs', in E. J. Urwick, (ed.), *Studies of Boy Life in Our Cities* (1904).
BRAY, R. A., 'The Boy in the Family', in E. J. Urwick, E. J. (ed.), *Studies of Boy Life in Our Cities* (1904).
—— *The Town Child* (1907).
—— *Boy Labour and Apprenticeship* (1911).
BRITTEN, J., *Catholic Clubs* (1891).
BROOKE HUNT, V., *Clubs for Boys and Young Men* (1897).
BRYCE, J., *The Hindrances to Good Citizenship* (1909).
BUTLER, C. V., *Social Conditions in Oxford* (1912).
CADBURY, E., MATHESON, M. C., and SWANN, G., *Women's Work and Wages* (1906).
CLOUSTON, SIR T., *The Hygiene of Mind* (1906).
—— *Unsoundness of Mind* (1911).
—— *Morals and Brain* (1912).
—— 'The Psychology of Youth' in T. N. Kelynack, (ed.), *Youth* (1913).
DAVIES, M, F., *School Care Committees: A Guide to their Work* (1909).
DEARLE, N. B., *Industrial Training* (1914).
DENDY, H., 'The Children of Working London', in B. Bosanquet (ed.) *Aspects of the Social Problem* (1895).
DOVER WILSON, J., *Humanism in the Continuation School* (1921).
DUNLOP, J. O., and DENMAN, R. D., *English Apprenticeship and Child Labour* (1912).
DYER, H., *Education and National Life* (1912).
—— *Education and Industrial Training of Boys and Girls* (1913).
FINDLAY, J. J., *The School: An Introduction to the Study of Education* (1911).
—— (ed.), *The Young Wage-Earner and the Problem of his Education* (1918).
FITZGERALD, REVD W. B., *Wesley Guild Manual* (1896).
FREEMAN, A., *Boy Life and Labour: The Manufacture of Inefficiency* (1914).
—— and HAYWARD, F. H., *The Spiritual Foundations of Reconstruction* (1919).
FREEMAN, F., *Religious and Social Work Among Girls* (1901).
FRERE, M., *Children's Care Committees* (1909).

GIBB, REVD S. J., *Boy Work and Unemployment* (1903).
—— *The Problem of Boy Work* (1906).
—— *The Boy and his Work* (1911).
GORST, J., *The Children of the Nation* (1906).
GREENWOOD, A., *Juvenile Labour Exchanges and After-Care* (1911).
GRIFFITHS, D., (ed.), *What is Socialism: A Symposium* (1924).
HALDANE, R. B., *Education and Empire* (1902).
HAWKINS, C. B., *Norwich. A Social Study* (1910).
HAYWARD, F. H., *Day and Evening Schools with Special Reference to the Problems of Adolescent Education* (1914).
KEELING, F., *The Labour Exchanges in Relation to Boy and Girl Labour* (1910).
—— *Child Labour in the United Kingdom* (1914).
KELYNACK, T. N. (ed.), *Youth* (1913).
KENT, N. B. (ed.), *Cambridge in South London: The Work of the College Missions, 1883–1914* (Cambridge, 1914).
KERSCHENSTEINER, G., *Education for Citizenship* (Eng. trans. 1912).
—— *The Schools and the Nation* (1914).
KEYNES, M. N., *The Problem of Boy Labour in Cambridge* (1911).
KNOWLES, G. W., *Junior Labour Exchanges: A Plea for Closer Co-operation between Labour Exchanges and Education Authorities* (Manchester 1910).
LE BON, G., *The Crowd* (Eng. edn. 1895).
—— *The Psychology of Revolution* (Eng. edn. 1913).
LEWIS, L., *The Children of the Unskilled.: An Economic and Social Study* (1924).
LEWIS, M. A., *A Club for Boys: Why Not Open One?* (1905).
LOANE, M., *The Next Street But One* (1907).
—— *Neighbours and Friends* (1910).
LOCH, C. S. (ed.), *Methods of Social Advance* (1904).
MACCUNN, J., *The Ethics of Citizenship* (Glasgow, 1894).
—— *The Making of Character* (Cambridge, 1900).
—— *The Ethics of Social Work* (1911).
MCDOUGALL, W., *An Introduction to Social Psychology* (1908).
MAGNUS, C. (ed.), *National Education: A Symposium* (1901).
MARCHANT, J. (ed.), *The Cleansing of a City* (1906).
—— *J. B. Paton, MA, DD: Educational and Social Pioneer* (1909).
MARSHALL, A., *Principles of Economics* (1890; 1961 edn.).
MASTERMAN, C. F. G. (edn), *The Heart of the Empire: Discussions of Problems of Modern City Life in England* (1901).
—— *The Condition of England* (1909).
MAYHEW, H., *London Labour and the London Poor* (1861).
MILLIS, C. T., 'Trade Schools for Boys and Girls', in M. E. Sadler (ed.),

Continuation Schools in England and Elsewhere (Manchester, 1907).

MONEY, L. G. CHIOZZA, *Riches and Poverty* (1905).

—— *Things that Matter* (1912).

MONTAGU, L., 'The Girl in the Background' in E. J. Urwick, (ed.), *Studies of Boy Life in Our Cities* (1904).

MURSTERBERG, H., *Psychology and Industrial Efficiency* (1913).

NEUMAN, P., *The Boys' Club* (1900).

NEWMAN, G., *Infant Mortality: A Social Problem* (1906).

PATERSON, A., *Across the Bridges* (1911).

PATON, J. L., *Cleansing the City* (1908).

—— *John Brown Paton: A Biography* (1914).

PATON, REVD J. P., 'The Moral Training of our Youth', in Marchant, (ed.), *The Cleansing of a City* (1906).

PELHAM, REVD H. S., *The Training of the Working Boy* (1908).

PELHAM, T. H. W., *Boys' Clubs* (1890).

PEPLER, D., *The Care Committee, the Child and the Parent* (1914).

PIGOU, A. C., *Unemployment* (1913).

PILKINGTON, E. M. S., *An Eton Playing Field* (1896).

REASON, W., *Poverty* (1909).

REEVES, M. P., *Round About a Pound a Week* (1913).

ROGERS, REVD E., *The Making of a Man in the CLB* (1919).

ROWNTREE, S., *Poverty: A Study of Town Life* (1901).

—— and LASKER, B., *Unemployment: A Social Study* (1911).

RUSSELL, C. E.B., *Manchester Boys* (1905).

RUSSELL, C. E. B., and RIGBY, L. M., *Working Lads' Clubs* (1908 and 1932).

—— *Social Problems of the North* (1913).

—— *The Problem of Juvenile Crime* (Oxford, 1917).

SADLER, M. E. (ed.), *Continuation Schools in England and Elsewhere* (Manchester, 1907).

SALEEBY, C. W., *Parenthood and Race Culture* (1909).

—— *The Methods of Race Regeneration* (1911).

—— *Woman and Womanhood* (1912).

—— *The Progress of Eugenics* (1914).

SHAND, A. F., *The Foundation of Character* (1914).

SMITH, F. (ed.), *The Band of Hope Jubilee Volume* (1987).

SMITH, W. A., *The Story of the Boys' Brigade* (Glasgow, 1888).

SOLLY, H., *Working Men's Social Clubs and Educational Institutes* (1867).

STANLEY, M., *Clubs for Working Girls* (1904).

STEVENS, K., 'Child Study', in F. Watson (edn.), *Encyclopaedia and Dictionary of Education* (1921).

STOCKTON, C. E., 'The Continuation Schools of Munich', in M. E. Sadler (ed.), *Continuation Schools in England and Elsewhere* (1907).

KING ALFRED'S COLLEGE LIBRARY

SULLY, J., *Outlines of Psychology* (1884).
—— *The Teacher's Handbook of Psychology* (1886).
TAWNEY, R. H., *Education for All* (1922).
URWICK, E. J. (ed.), *Studies of Boy Life in Our Cities* (1904).
WATERFALL, E., *The Day Continuation School in England* (1924).
WEBB, S. and B., *Industrial Democracy* (1897; 1920 edn.)
WHITEHOUSE, J. H. (ed.), *Problems of Boy Life* (1912).
WILLIAMS, A., *Life in a Railway Factory* (1915).
WILLS, F., *Church Polytechnics for Young Men and Lads* (1886).
WRAY, W. J., and FERGUSON, R. W., *A Day Continuation School at Work* (1920; 1926 edn.).
YEAXLEE, B., *Working Out the Fisher Act* (1921).

PRIMARY SOURCE ARTICLES

ANON., 'The Boy in Industry', *Toynbee Record* (June 1905), 151–61.
ANON., 'Work on a Skilled Employment Committee', *The Oxford House Magazine* 11/8, (Oct. 1910), 32–7.
BAGGALLAY, F. W., 'Child Labour in Factories and Workshops', *Economic Review* (July 15, 1909), 292–308.
BARRETT, R, M., 'The Treatment of Juvenile Offenders', *Journal of the Royal Statistical Society* (June 1900).
BESANT, W., 'From Thirteen to Seventeen', *Contemporary Review* 49 (March 1886), 413–25.
BEVERIDGE, W. H., 'The problem of the Unemployed', *Sociological Papers* 3 (1906), 323–41.
—— 'Labour Bureaux', *Economic Journal*, 16/63 (Sept. 1906), 436–9.
—— 'Labour Exchanges and the Unemployed', *Economics Journal* 17/65 (Mar. 1907), 66–81.
BLACK, R., 'City Life for Working Lads', *Parents Review* (Aug. 1907), 619.
BOSANQUET, H., 'The Industrial Residuum', *Economic Journal* (1893), 600–16.
BOURDILLION, H., 'Apprenticeship Work and How to Carry It On', *Charity Organisation Review* 17 NS. 100 (April 1905), 207–10.
BRAY, R. A., 'The Apprenticeship Question', *Economic Journal* (Sept. 1909), 404–15.
—— 'Apprenticeship: Old and New', *Local Government Review* (Jan. 1910), 117–19.
CHAMBERLAIN, N., 'Labour Exchanges and Boy Labour', *Economic Review* (Oct. 1909), 400–9.
CHURCHILL, W., 'The Untrodden Field in Politics', *The Nation* (Mar. 1908).

CHAPMAN, S. J., and ABBOTT, W., 'The Tendency of Children to Enter their Fathers' Trades', *Journal of the Royal Statistical Society* (May 1913), 599–604.

CLOUSTON, SIR T., 'Adolescence', *Child Study* 5/1 (Apr. 1912), 1–7.

—— 'Adolescence', *Child Study* 5/2 (July 1912), 90–6.

CUNNINGHAM, B., 'Apprenticeship', *Charity Organisation Review* (July 1905), 39–51.

D'AETH, F. G., 'An Enquiry into the Methods of Obtaining Employment in Liverpool', *Transactions of Liverpool Economic and Statistical Society* (1907), 28–60.

DAVISON, R. C., 'The Voluntary Social Worker and the State', *Economic Review* 22/3 (July 1912), 264–71.

DEARLE, N. B., 'The Organisation of Boy Labour', *Clare Market Review* (June 1910), 102–6.

GIBB, REVD S. J., 'The Choice of Employment for Boys', *Economic Review* (Oct. 1904), 436–48.

GORDON, MRS OGILVIE, 'Juvenile Employment Bureaux', *Contemporary Review*, 546 (June 1911), 723–32.

GREENWOOD, A., 'The Organisation of the Juvenile Labour Market', *Progress* (Apr. 1911), 97–105.

—— 'Juvenile Labour Problems', *The Child* (Oct. 1911), 25–34.

—— 'Blind-Alley Labour', *Economic Journal*, 22 (June 1912), 309–14.

—— and KETTLEWELL, E., 'Some Statistics of Juvenile Employment and Unemployment', *Journal of the Royal Statistical Society* 75 (June 1912), 744–53.

JACKSON, C., 'Apprenticeship and the Training of the Workman', *Edinburgh Review* (Oct. 1912), 411–27.

JEVONS, H. W., 'Industrial Prospects for Boys and Girls', *Charity Organisation Review* 20/117 (Sept. 1906), 125–39.

JONES, T., 'Unemployment, Boy Labour and Continued Education', *Socialist Review* (July 1909), 857–70.

KITTERMASTER D. B., 'Unemployment and Boy Labour', *Saint George* 10/37 (Jan. 1907), 1–10.

LESSER, E., 'Boy Labour and Unemployment', *The Toynbee Record* (March 1909), 98–9.

LIGHTBODY, W. M., 'The Problem of Unskilled Labour', *Economic Review* (Oct. 1909), 423–31.

LONGMAN, M., 'Children's Care Committees', *Contemporary Review* (Dec. 1910), 733–42.

McDOUGALL, W., 'The Will of the People', *Sociological Review* 5/2 (April 1912), 89–104.

MACKENZIE, W. L., 'The Family and the City: Their Functional Relations', *Sociological Review* 1/2 (Apr. 1908), 118–38.

MARSHALL, M. E., 'Labour Exchanges and Juvenile Employment', *Women's Industrial News*, NS, 55 (July 1911), 91.

MEDLEY, K. I. M., 'Van-Boy Labour', *Economic Review* (1911), 57–62.

'MILES', 'Where to get the Men', *Contemporary Review* (Jan. 1902), 78–86.

MYERS, J., 'The Juvenile Side of the National Labour Exchange', *School Child* (May 1910), 9–12.

—— 'The Juvenile Side of Labour Exchanges', *School Child* (Sept. 1910), 5–8.

—— 'The Juvenile Side of the Labour Exchange', *School Child* (Oct. 1910), 5–9.

PARSONS, J., 'The Work of a Skilled Employment and Apprenticeship Committee', *Toynbee Record* (Mar. 1907), 74–82.

—— 'The Work of an Apprenticeship and Skilled Employment Committee', *Toynbee Record* (Apr. 1907), 88–92.

—— Work of an Apprenticeship and Skilled Employment Committee, *Toynbee Record* (May 1907), 102–5.

— 'Skilled Employment Committees', *Charity Organisation Review* xxii 22/127 (July 1907), 19–40.

RUSSELL, C. E. B., 'City Lads', *Child* (Apr. 1911), 587–93.

—— 'Adolescence', *Converging Views of Social Reform* (1913), 44–56.

SADLER, M. E., 'The Ferment in Education on the Continent and in America', *Proceedings of the British Academy* (1903), 81–94.

—— 'The School in Some of its Relations to Social Organization and to National Life', Paper read before Sociological Society, LSE (13 Dec. 1904).

—— 'The Fading Influence of Laissez-Faire', *Journal of Education* (Jan. 1904), 80–2.

SCHARLIEB, M., 'Adolescent Girlhood under Modern Conditions with special reference to Motherhood', *Eugenics Review* 1/3 (Oct. 1909).

—— 'The Recreational Activities of Girls during Adolescence', *Child* 1/7 (Apr. 1911), 571–86.

—— 'Adolescent Girls from the View-Point of the Physician', *Child* 1/12 (Sept. 1911), 1013–31.

SHANN, G., 'The Effect of the Non-Living Wage upon the Individual, the Family and the State', *Industrial Unrest and the Living Wage* 2 (1913), 81–105.

S. M., 'Young Adolescents (Male)', *Toynbee Record* (Apr. 1911), 102–5.

TAYLOR, D. M., 'The Child Study Conference of 1911. Some Problems of Adolescence', *Child* 1/12 (Sept. 1911), 1044.

TAWNEY, R. H., 'The Economics of Boy Labour', *Economic Journal* 19 (Dec. 1909), 517–37.

TAWNEY, R. H., ' "Blind Alley" Occupations and the Way Out', *Women's Industrial News* 52 (Oct. 1910), 1–10.

—— 'The Halving of Boy and Girl Labour', *Crusade* (June 1911), 108–11.

TROTTER, W., 'Herd Instinct and its Bearing on the Psychology of Civilized Man', *Sociological Review* 1/3 (July 1908), 227–48.

URWICK, E. J., 'Apprenticeship and Skilled Employment: A Criticism', *Toynbee Record* (May 1907), 102–5.

—— 'Apprenticeship and Skilled Employment: A Criticism', *Toynbee Record* (June 1907), 117–19.

SECONDARY SOURCE BOOKS

Place of publication is London unless otherwise stated.

ABRAMS, P., *The Origins of British Sociology, 1834–1914* (Chicago, 1968).

ARGLES, M., *South Kensington to Robbins* (1964).

ASHBY, E., and ANDERSON, M., *Portrait of Haldane at Work on Education* 1974.

ASHTON, D. N., and FIELD, D., *Young Workers* (1976).

ATLEE, C. R., *As it Happened* (1954).

BAILEY, P., *Leisure and Class in Victorian England: Rational Recreation and the Contest for Control, 1830–1885* (1978).

BAILEY, V., *Delinquency and Citizenship: Reclaiming the Young Offender, 1914–1948* (Oxford 1987).

BARKER, R., *Education and Politics: A Study of the Labour Party* (Oxford, 1982).

BENTLEY, M., *Politics without Democracy* (Oxford 1985).

—— *The Climax of Liberal Politics* (1987).

BINFIELD, C., *George Williams and the YMCA* (1973).

BIRCH, A. E., *The Story of the Boys' Brigade* (1959).

BLANCH, M., 'Imperialism, Nationalism and Organized Youth', in J. Clarke, C. Crichter, and R. Johnson (eds.), *Working Class Culture: Studies in History and Theory* (1979).

BOYD, W., *Emile for Today. The Emile of Jean-Jacques Rousseau* (1956).

BRANNEN, P. (ed.), *Entering the World of Work: Some Sociological Perspectives* (1975).

BRENNAN, E. J. T., *Education for National Efficiency: The Contribution of Sidney and Beatrice Webb* (1975).

BRIGGS, A., *Social Thought and Social Action: A Study of the Work of Seebohm Rowntree, 1871–1954* (1961).

BRISTOW, E. J., *Vice and Vigilance: Purity Movements in Britain since 1799* (1977).

BUNT, S., *Jewish Youth Work in Britain* (1975).

BURGESS, K., *The Challenge of Labour* (1980).

CAMERON, C., LUSH, A., and MEARA, G., *Disinherited Youth* (1943).

CARTER, M. P., *Home, School and Work: A Study of Education and Employment of Young People in Britain* (1962).

—— *Into Work* (Harmondsworth, 1966).

CASSON, M., *Youth Unemployment* (1979).

CLARKE, P., *Liberals and Social Democrats* (Cambridge, 1978; 1981 (edn.).

CLEGG, H. A., FOX, A., and THOMPSON, A. F., *A History of British Trade Unions since 1889* i (Oxford, 1964).

COLEMAN, B. I. (ed.), *The Idea of the City in Twentieth-Century Britain* (1973).

COLLINI, S., *Liberalism and Sociology: L. T. Hobhouse and Political Argument in England, 1880–1914* (Cambridge, 1979).

COLLIS, H., HURLL, F., and HAZLEWOOD, R., *B-P's Scouts: An Official History of the Boy Scouts Association* (1961).

CORINA, J., *Labour Market Economics* (1972).

COTGROVE, S. F., *Technical Education and Social Change* (1958).

CROSSICK, F., *An Artisan Elite in Victorian Society* (1978).

DAWES, F., *A Cry from the Streets. The Boys' Club Movement in Britain from the 1850s to the Present Day* (Hove, 1975).

DENT, H. C., *Part-Time Education in Great Britain* (1949).

DENT, K. S. (ed.), *Informal Agencies of Education* (1979).

DOERINGER, P. B., and PIORE, M. J., *Internal Labour Markets and Manpower Analysis* (Lexington, 1971).

DOVER WILSON, J., *Milestones on the Dover Road* (1969).

DYHOUSE, C., *Girls Growing up in Late Victorian and Edwardian England* (1981).

EAGAR, M. McG., *Making Men: The History of Boys' Clubs and Related Movements in Great Britain* (1953).

FERGUSON, T., and CUNNISON, J., *The Young Wage Earner: A Study of Glasgow Boys* (1951).

FIDO, J., 'The Charity Organisation Society and Social Casework in London, 1869–1900', in A. P. Donajgrodzki, (ed.), *Social Control in Nineteenth Century Britain* (1977).

FISHER, H. A. L., *An Unfinished Autobiography* (1940).

FLUGEL, J. C., *A Hundred Years of Psychology* (1933, 1951 edn.).

FORD, P., *Social Theory and Social Practice: An Exploration of Experience* (Shannon, 1968).

FOX, A., *A History of the National Union of Boot and Shoe Workers* (1958).

FREEDEN, M., *The New Liberalism: An Ideology of Social Reform* (1978).

GIBBON, F. P., *William A. Smith of the Boys' Brigade* (1934).

GILBERT, B. B., *The Evolution of National Insurance in Great Britain* (1966).

GILLIS, J. R., *Youth and History: Tradition and Change in European Age Relations, 1770–Present* (1974).

GINZBERG, E., *et al.*, *Occupational Choice* (New York, 1951).

GOLLAN, J. *Youth in British Industry* (1937).

GORDON, P., and WHITE, J., *Philosophers as Educational Reformers: The Influence of Idealism on British Educational Thought and Practice* (1979).

GRAVES, J. J., *Policy and Progress in Secondary Education, 1902–1942* (1943).

GRIER, L., *Achievement in Education* (1952).

HARCOURT, WILLIAM, with OLAVE, LADY BADEN-POWELL, *Baden-Powell: Two Lives of a Hero* (1964).

HARRIS, J., *Unemployment and Politics: A Study in English Social Policy, 1886–1914* (Oxford, 1971).

—— *William Beveridge: A Biography* (Oxford, 1977).

HAY, J. R., 'The British Business Community, Social Insurance and the German Example', in W. J. Mommsen (ed.), *The Emergence of the Welfare State in Britain and Germany* (1981).

HEARNSHAW, L. S., *A Short History of British Psychology, 1840–1940* (1964).

—— *Cyril Burt, Psychologist* (1979).

HEASMAN, K., *Evangelicals in Action: An Appraisal of their Work in the Victorian Era* (1962).

HEGINBOTHAM, H., *The Youth Employment Service* (1951).

HINTON, J., *The First Shop Stewards' Movement* (1973).

HOBSBAWM, E. J., *Industry and Empire* (1969).

HUMPHRIES, S., *Hooligans or Rebels? An Oral History of Working-Class Childhood and Youth* (1981).

HUNT, E. H., *British Labour History, 1815–1914* (1981).

HUNTER, L. C., and MULVERY, C., *Economics of Wages and Labour* (1981).

INGLIS, K. S., *Churches and the Working Classes in Victorian England* (1963).

JEFFRYS, J. B., *The Story of the Engineers* (1946).

JEWKES, J. and S., *The Juvenile Labour Market* (1938).

KENT, W., *The Testament of a Victorian Youth* (1938).

KETT, J. F., *Rites of Passage: Adolescence in America, 1790 to the Present* (New York, 1977).

KIERNAN, R. H., *Baden-Powell* (1939).

LEES, A., *Cities Perceived: Urban Society in European and American Thought, 1820–1940* (Manchester, 1985).

LEVINE, A. L., *Industrial Retardation in Britain, 1880–1914* (1967).

LIPMAN, V. D., *A Century of Social Service, 1859–1959: The Jewish Board of Guardians* (1959).

MACINTYRE, A., *A Short History of Ethics* (1966).

MCLEOD, H., *Class and Religion in the Late Victorian City* (1974).

MAIZELS, J., *Adolescent Needs and the Transition from School to Work* (1970).

MANGAN, J. A., *Athleticism in the Victorian and Edwardian Public School* (Cambridge, 1981).

MARSHALL, T. H., *Citizenship and Social Class* (Cambridge, 1950).

MARSON, D., *Children's Strikes in 1911*, Ruskin History Workshop Pamphlets, No. 9 (1973).

MEACHAM, S., *A Life Apart: The English Working Class, 1890–1914* (1977).

MELLER, H. E., *Leisure and the Changing City, 1870–1914* (1976).

—— *The Ideal City* (Leicester, 1979).

MILLER, C., and SWIFT, K., *Words and Women* (1976).

MONTAGU, L., *My Club and I* (1942).

MORE, C., *Skill and the English Working Class, 1870–1914* (1980).

MORGAN, A. E., *The Needs of Youth* (1939).

MOSCOVICI, S., *The Age of the Crowd* (Cambridge and Paris, 1981, 1985).

MOWAT, C. L., *The Charity Organization Society, 1869–1913. Its Ideas and Work* (1961).

MURPHY, G., *Historical Introduction to Modern Psychology* (1929).

MUSGRAVE, P. W. (ed.), *Sociology, History and Education* (1970).

MUSGROVE, F., *Youth and the Social Order* (1964).

NEWCOMBE, W. L., *Army Cadet Force* (1949).

NEWSOME, D., *Godliness and Good Learning* (1961).

OGG, D., *Herbert Fisher, 1865–1940: A Short Biography* (1947).

ORR, K., 'Moral Training in the Boy Scout Movement', in S. Murray-Smith (ed.), *Melbourne Studies in Education* (Melbourne 1963).

ORWELL, G., 'Politics and the English Language' in *Selected Essays* (1957).

PEACOCK, R. S., *Pioneer of Boyhood: The Story of Sir William Smith, Founder of the Boys' Brigade* (1954).

PEARSON, G., *Hooligan. A History of Respectable Fears* (1983).

PERCIVAL, A., *Youth Will Be Led* (1951).

PHELPS BROWN, E. H., *The Growth of British Industrial Relations: A Study from the Standpoint of 1906–1914* (1959).

PIMLOTT, J. R., *Toynbee Hall: Fifty Years of Social Progress, 1834–1934* (1935).

PINCHBECK, I., and HEWIT, M., *Children in English Society*, 2 vols. (1969, 1973).

PLATT, A. M., *The Child Savers. The Invention of Delinquency* (Chicago, 1969, 1977 edn.).

PROCHASKA, F. K., *Women and Philanthropy in 19th Century England* (Oxford, 1980).

READ, D., *Edwardian England* (1972).

—— *England, 1868–1914* (1979).

REEDER, D. A., 'Predicaments of City Children: Late Victorian and Edwardian Perspectives on Education and Urban Society', in his *Urban Education in the 19th Century* (1977).

REYNOLDS, E. E., *Baden-Powell* (1949).

RICHTER, M., *The Politics of Conscience: T.H. Green and his Age* (1964).

ROBERTS, E., *A Woman's Place: An Oral History of Working-Class Women, 1890–1940* (Oxford, 1984).

ROOFF, M., *A Hundred Years of Family Welfare* (1972).

ROSE, N., *The Psychological Complex: Psychology, Politics and Society in England, 1869–1939* (1985).

ROSENTHRAL, M., *Baden Powell and the Boy Scouts: A Character Training Factory* (1986).

ROSS, D., *G. Stanley Hall; The Psychologist as Prophet* (Chicago, 1972).

ROUTH, G., *Occupation and Pay in Great Britain, 1906–1979* (1968; 1980 edn.).

ROWE, J. W. F., *Wages in Practice and Theory* (1928).

RULE, J., *The Experience of Labour in Eighteenth-Century Industry* (1981).

SEARLE, G. R., *The Quest for National Efficiency* (Oxford, 1971).

—— *Eugenics and Politics in Britain, 1900–1914* (Leydon, 1976).

SELLECK, R. J. W., *The New Education, 1870–1914* (1968).

SEMMEL, B., *Imperialism and Social Reform* (1960).

SHERINGTON, G., *English Education: Social Change and War, 1911–1920* (Manchester, 1981).

SIMEY, T. S. and M. B., *Charles Booth: Social Scientist* (Oxford, 1960).

SIMON, B., *Education and the Labour Movement, 1870–1920* (1965).

—— and BRADLEY, I. (eds.), *The Victorian Public School* (1975).

SIMONS, D., *Georg Kerschensteiner: His Thought and Its Relevance Today* (1966).

Soffer, R. N., *Ethics and Society in England: The Revolution in the Social Sciences, 1870–1914* (1978).

Springhall, J., *Youth, Empire and Society: British Youth Movements, 1883–1940* (1977).

—— *Coming of Age: Adolescence in Britain, 1860–1960* (Dublin, 1986).

—— Fraser, B., and Hoare, M., *Sure and Stedfast: A History of the Boys' Brigade, 1883–1983* (1983).

Stedman Jones, G., *Outcast London* (Oxford, 1971).

Summerfield, P., 'The Effingham Arms and Empire: Deliberate Selection in the Evolution of the Music Hall in London', in E. and S. Yeo (eds.)., *Popular Culture and Class Conflict, 1590–1914* (Sussex, 1981).

Summers, A., 'A Home from Home. Women's Philanthropic Work in the Nineteenth Century', in Burman, S. (ed.), *Fit Work for Women* (1979).

Tallents, S., *Man and Boy*, (1943).

Terrill, R., *R. H. Tawney and his Times* (1974).

Thompson, P., *The Edwardians* (1977).

Treble, J. H., 'The Market for Unskilled Male Labour in Glasgow, 1891–1914', in I. MacDougall (ed.), *Essays in Scottish Labour History* (Edinburgh, 1978).

Troen, S. K., 'The Discovery of the Adolescent by American Educational Reformers, 1900–1920: An Economic Perspective', in L. Stone (ed.), *Schooling and Society* (1976).

Veness, T., *School Leavers: Their Aspirations and Expectations* (1962).

Vincent, A., and Plant, R., *Philosophy, Politics and Citizenship: The Life and Thought of the British Idealists* (Oxford, 1984).

Wagner, G., *Barnado* (1979).

Walton, R. G., *Women in Social Work* (1975).

Walvin, J., *Leisure and Society, 1830–1950* (1978).

Willis, P., *Learning to Labour: How Working-Class Kids Get Working-Class Jobs* (Farnborough, 1977).

Woodroofe, K., *From Charity to Social Work in England and the United States* (1962).

Young, A. F., and Ashton, E. T., *British Social Work in the Nineteenth Century* (1956).

Young, R. M., *Mind, Brain and Adaptation in the Nineteenth Century* (Oxford, 1970).

SECONDARY SOURCE ARTICLES

Abrams, P., 'Rites de Passage. The Conflict of Generations in

Industrial Society', *Journal of Contemporary History* 5/2 (1970), 175–90.

ALLEN, S., 'Some Theoretical Problems in the Study of Youth', *Sociological Review* 16 (1968), 319–31.

BAKAN, D., 'Adolescence in America: From Idea to Social Fact', *Daedalus* (Fall, 1971), 979–95.

BEN-DAVID, J., and COLLINS, R., 'Social Factors in the Origins of a New Science: The Case of Psychology', *American Sociological Review* 31/4 (Aug. 1966), 451–65.

BOSANQUET, N., and DOERINGER, P. B., 'Is there a Dual Labour Market in Great Britain?', *Economic Journal*, 83 (June 1973), 421–35.

BRADBURY, D. E., 'The Contribution of the Child Study Movement to Child Psychology', *The Psychological Bulletin* 34/1 (Jan. 1937), 249–72.

BRIGDEN, S., 'Youth and the English Reformation', *Past and Present* 95 (1982), 37–67.

COLLINI, S., 'Political Theory and the "Science of Society"', in Victorian Britain', *Historical Journal* 23/1 (Mar. 1980), 223–6.

—— 'The Idea of "Character" in Victorian Political Thought', *Transactions of the Royal Historical Society* (1986), 29–50.

CAWS, A. G., 'Child Study Fifty Years Ago', *Quarterly Bulletin of British Psychological Society* 1/3 (Jan. 1949), 104–9.

DAVIN, A., 'Imperialism and Motherhood', *History Workshop* 5 (Spring, 1978), 9–65.

DEMOS, J. and V., 'Adolescence in Historical Perspective', *Journal of Marriage and Family* 31 (Nov. 1969), 632–38.

DENNIS, W., 'Historical Beginnings of Child Psychology', *Psychological Bulletin* 46/2 (Mar. 1949), 224–35.

DOHERTY, B., 'Compulsory Day Continuation Education: An Examination of the 1918 Experiment', *Vocational Aspect* 18/39 (Spring 1966), 41–56.

DYHOUSE, C., 'Social Darwinistic Ideas and the Development of Women's Education in England, 1880–1920', *History of Education* 51/1 (1976), 41–58.

FOX, V. C., 'Is Adolescence a Phenomenon of Modern Times?', *Journal of Psychohistory* 5/2 (Fall 1977), 271–90.

GILLIS, J. R., 'The Evolution of Juvenile Delinquency in England, 1880–1914', *Past and Present* 67 (1975), 96–126.

GORHAM, D., 'The "Maiden Tribute to Modern Babylon": Child Prostitution and the Idea of Childhood in Late-Victorian England', *Victorian Studies* 21/3 (Spring 1978), 353–81.

GRINDER, R. E., 'The Concept of Adolescence in the Genetic Psychology of G. Stanley Hall', *Child Development* 40/2 (June 1969), 355–69.

GRINDER, E. E., and STRICKLAND, C. E., 'G. Stanley Hall and the Social Significance of Adolescence', *Teachers' College Record* 64 (Feb. 1963), 390–9.

HALLIDAY, R. J., 'The Sociological Movement: The Sociological Society and the Genesis of Academic Sociology in Britain', *Sociological Review* 16/3 (Nov. 1968), 377–98.

—— 'Social Darwinism: A Definition', *Victorian Studies* (June 1971), 389–405.

HARRISON, B., 'For Church, Queen and Family: The Girls' Friendly Society, 1874–1920', *Past and Present* 61 (1973), 107–38.

HAY, J. R., 'Employers and Social Policy in Britain: The Evolution of Welfare Legislation, 1905–1914', *Social History* 2/4 (1977), 435–55.

HENDRICK, H., 'The Leeds Gas Strike, 1890', *Thoresby Society Miscellany* 16, pt 2 (1974), 78–98.

——'"A Race of Intelligent Unskilled Labourers": The Adolescent Worker and The Debate on Compulsory Part-Time Day Continuation Schools, 1900–1922', *History of Education* 4/2 (1980), 159–73.

—— 'The History of Childhood and Youth: A Guide to the Literature', *Faculty of Modern Studies, Occasional papers, No. 1* (Oxford Polytechnic) (1981), 1–56.

—— 'Personality and Psychology: Defining Edwardian Boys', *Youth and Policy* 18 (1986), 33–43.

—— Review of Springhall and Gillis in *Social History* 3/2 (1978), 249–52.

JOHNSON, R., 'Educational Policy and Social Control in Early Victorian England', *Past and Present* 49 (1970), 96–119.

KENISTON, K., 'Youth: A "New" Stage of Life', *American Scholar*, 39 (1970), 631–54.

MACKENZIE, D., 'Eugenics in Britain', *Social Studies of Science* 6 (1976), 499–532.

MACLEOD, D. I., 'Act Your Age: Boyhood, Adolescence and the Rise of the Boy Scouts in America', *Journal of Social History* 16/2 (Winter 1982), 3–20.

MCKIBBON, R. I., 'Social Class and Social Observation in Edwardian England', *Transactions of the Royal Historical Society* 28 (1978) 175–99.

—— 'Working-Class Gambling in Britain 1880–1929', *Past and Present* 82 (1979), 148.

MOORE, M. J., 'Social Work and Social Welfare. The Organization of Philanthropic Resources in Britain, 1990–1914', *Journal of British Studies* (Spring 1977), 85–104.

POPE, R., 'Adjustment to Peace: Educational Provision for Unemployed Juveniles in Britain, 1918–19', *British Journal of Educational Studies* 27/1 (1979), 69–80.

SCHLOSSMAN, S. L., 'G. Stanley Hall and the Boys' Club: Conservative Applications of Recapitulation Theory', *Journal of the History of the Behavioural Sciences*, 9 (1973), 140–7.

SHIMAN, L.L., 'The Band of Hope Movement: Respectable Recreation for Working-Class Children', *Victorian Studies* 17/1 (1973), 49–74.

SOFFER, R. N., 'The New Elitism: Social Psychology in Pre-War England', *Journal of British Studies* 8 (1969), 111–40.

SOLA, P. A., 'Vocational Guidance: Integrating School and Society in Chicago, 1912–16', *Vocational Aspect of Education*, 38/71 (1976), 117–23.

—— 'The Chicago Association of Commerce and Extra-Curricular Activities in the Chicago High Schools, 1914–25', *Vocational Aspect of Education*, 30/77 (1978), 119–27.

SPRINGHALL, J., 'The Boy Scouts, Class and Militarism in relation to British Youth Movements, 1908–1930', *International Review of Social History* 16/2 (1971), 125–58.

STONE, L., 'Family History in the 1980s: Past Achievements and Future Trends', *Journal of Interdisciplinary History* 12/1 (Summer 1981), 51–87.

THOMAS, K., 'Age and Authority in Early Modern England', *Proceedings of the British Academy* 62 (1976), 205–48.

THOMS, D., 'The Emergence and Failure of the Day Continuation School Experiment', *History of Education* 4/1 (1975), 36–50.

WARREN, A., 'Sir Robert Baden-Powell, the Scout Movement and Citizen Training in Great Britain, 1900–1920', *English Historical Review* (Apr. 1986), 376–98.

WILKINSON, P., 'English Youth Movement, 1908–1930', *Journal of Contemporary History* 4/2 (1969), 1–23.

YARBOROUGH, A., 'Apprentices as Adolescents in Sixteenth Century Bristol', *Journal of Social History* (Fall, 1979), 69–81.

UNPUBLISHED THESES

BLANCH, M., 'National, Empire and the Birmingham Working Class, 1899–1914', Birmingham University Ph.D. thesis (1975).

BROOKS, I., 'The London Day Continuation Schools', London University MA thesis (1923).

BROWN, J. C., 'Ideas concerning Social Policy and their Influence on Legislation in Great Britain, 1902–1911', London University Ph.D. thesis (1964).

DEDMAN, M. J., 'Economic and Social Factors affecting Development of Youth Organizations for Urban Boys in Britain, 1880–1914', LSE Ph.D. thesis (1985).

FLEET, L., 'Some Margins of Continued Education. Some Limitations of the Concept of Universal Compulsion with special regard to the School Leaving Age and Educational Minority', Bristol University Ph.D. thesis (1976).

FRASER, B., 'The Origins and History of the Boys' Brigade from 1883 to 1914', Strathclyde University Ph.D. thesis (1981).

HENDRICK, H. J., 'The "Boy Labour Problem" in Edwardian England: A Study in the Relationship between Middle-Class Reformers and Working-Class Adolescents', Sheffield University Ph.D. thesis (1985).

KNOX, W. W., 'British Apprenticeship, 1880–1914', Edinburgh University Ph.D. thesis (1981).

LEVINE, A. L., 'Industrial Change and its Effects upon Labour, 1900–1914', London University Ph.D. thesis (1954).

SANDLER, C., 'Working-Class Adolescents in Birmingham: A Study in Social Reform, 1900–1914', Oxford University D. Phil. thesis (1987).

SPRINGHALL, J., 'Youth and Empire. Studies in the Propagation of Imperialism to the Young in Edwardian Britain', Sussex University Ph.D thesis (1968).

WOOLDRIDGE, A., 'Child Study and Educational Psychology in England, c.1880–1950', Oxford University D.Phil. thesis (1985).

Index

294 *Index*

Youth organization (*cont.*)
discipline in 160
and friendship 161
inadequacy of 177–80
main features of 158

organized religion
uniformed groups 159–67
personnel of 57, 179
youth work practice 158

KING ALFRED'S COLLEGE
LIBRARY